The Open University

D1331993

A207 FROM ENLIGHTENMENT
TO ROMANTICISM, *c*.1780–1830

Block 3
Religion, Exploration and Slavery

This publication forms part of an Open University course A207 *From Enlightenment to Romanticism, c.1780–1830*. Details of this and other Open University courses can be obtained from the Course Information and Advice Centre, PO Box 724, The Open University, Milton Keynes MK7 6ZS, United Kingdom: tel. +44 (0)1908 653231, e-mail general-enquiries@open.ac.uk

Alternatively, you may visit the Open University website at http://www.open.ac.uk where you can learn more about the wide range of courses and packs offered at all levels by The Open University.

To purchase a selection of Open University course materials visit the webshop at www.ouw.co.uk, or contact Open University Worldwide, Michael Young Building, Walton Hall, Milton Keynes MK7 6AA, United Kingdom for a brochure. tel. +44 (0)1908 858785; fax +44 (0)1908 858787; e-mail ouwenq@open.ac.uk

The Open University
Walton Hall, Milton Keynes
MK7 6AA

First published 2004. Reprinted 2005

Edited, designed and typeset by The Open University.

Printed and bound in Malta by Gutenberg Press.

ISBN 0 7492 8597 4

1.4

The paper used for this book is FSC-certified and totally chlorine-free. FSC (the Forest Stewardship Council) is an international network to promote responsible management of the world's forests.

Contents

Introduction to Block 3

Prepared for the course team by David Johnson

The concerns of the Enlightenment and Romanticism marked the lives and thoughts of many people besides the great composers, philosophers and political leaders of the period 1780–1830. In this block, we turn from the achievements of famous figures such as Mozart, Hume and Napoleon, and consider how the ideas of the Enlightenment and Romanticism were expressed in the popular writings of British religious thinkers, travel writers and emancipated slaves.

In Units 10–11, John Wolffe introduces the major developments in Evangelical Christianity in Britain in the late eighteenth and early nineteenth centuries by focusing in Unit 10 on the *Olney Hymns* (1779) written by John Newton and William Cowper, and in Unit 11 on the writings of William Wilberforce, particularly *A Practical View of the Prevailing Religious System of Professed Christians* (1797) and his two major publications on slavery, which appeared in 1807 and 1823. In Units 12–13, Bernard Waites introduces travel writing in his discussion of *Travels in the Interior Districts of Africa* (1799) by Mungo Park. In Units 14–15, David Johnson introduces slave writings by discussing first *Thoughts and Sentiments on the Evil of Slavery* (1787) by Quobna Ottobah Cugoano, and then in Unit 15 *The Horrors of Slavery* (1824) by Robert Wedderburn and *The History of Mary Prince* (1831) recounted by Prince herself.

Specific objectives are stated at the beginning of each unit, but it is helpful at the outset of the block to highlight some concerns that run through the material. First and foremost, there is the critical analysis of set texts. Second, there is an account of the religious climate of late eighteenth- and early nineteenth-century Britain, with particular reference to the Evangelical movement. Third, there is description of the institutional and intellectual context of travel writing in the late eighteenth century, with detailed attention to scientific and religious ideas. Fourth, there is discussion of the economic and political contexts of slavery, with emphasis on the arguments for and against abolition. Finally, we examine how these writers on religion, travel and slavery give expression to important varieties of Enlightenment and Romantic thought.

We have already encountered religious issues in earlier units in the writings of Enlightenment thinkers such as Hume, who rejected the traditional teachings of the Church. In Units 10–11, however, we develop a complementary viewpoint through the eyes of writers who remained firmly committed to Christianity, while seeking to interpret and communicate its beliefs in fresh ways that were responsive to the cultural and social climate of the day. These writers showed how the Enlightenment could develop religious as well as non-religious manifestations, and they made important contributions to the advance of Romanticism. The first two units of the block are specifically concerned with religion, introducing you to some key religious ideas by means of the *Olney Hymns*, and exploring their impact through study of William Wilberforce's career and writings. As we move on to read Mungo Park's *Travels*, religion remains a key dimension of the text being studied, evident through the formative effect of Park's own Christian convictions, and through his accounts of Islam and of African indigenous religion. In the final two units of the block, we note how ideas drawn from Christianity were used on both sides of the argument about slavery, and how slaves themselves were strongly influenced by Christianity.

In Units 12–13 the central focus shifts to exploration, as we examine one of the most celebrated travel narratives of the period, Mungo Park's *Travels*. The editors of a recent eight-volume collection of travel writing declare that 'the period 1770–1835 was the age of the exploration narrative' (Fulford and Kitson, 2001, p.xiii), as the expanding reading public in Britain consumed vast numbers of travellers' tales, vicariously sharing the adventures of travellers. Travel writings describing distant parts of the globe influenced the perceptions of not only the general reading public, but also policy-makers and imaginative writers. The appetite for travel narratives was met in part by the republication of many earlier tales of exploration, but contemporaneous accounts like that of Park were much more popular. What makes Park especially interesting for our purposes is that his commitments to scientific inquiry, Christian faith and exploration exemplify important strands in Enlightenment thought. Furthermore, his writings provide an instructive contrast with the ideas of both the Evangelical writers of Units 10–11 and the slave writers of Units 14–15.

Controversy regarding slavery runs through this block and attracted the passionate interest of all the writers studied here. As a political issue, slavery was second only to the wars with France in dominating public debate in Britain during the years 1780–1830, and each of these writers made a distinctive contribution to these debates. Newton's status as a reformed slave-trader lent great authority to his Evangelical message; Cowper's poem 'The Negro's complaint' gave vivid and popular expression to the abolitionist cause; Wilberforce's fame rested upon his successful political campaigns first to end the slave trade, and then to emancipate all slaves; one of the principal aims of Park's journey in West Africa was to observe the African dimension of the slave trade; and the three slave writers – Cugoano, Wedderburn and Prince – brought all the rhetorical skill they could muster to make the case against slavery.

Our focus here is exclusively on British slavery, but it is important to register that slavery had long played a central role in *all* European societies, and that in the period 1780–1830 Britain was but one of several European nations deeply dependent upon profits from it. The **chattel slavery** of the ancient world had persisted after the fall of the Roman empire, but from the eighth to the fifteenth centuries underwent an interrupted and uneven decline in Europe, as serfdom gradually became the dominant form of labour. Atlantic slavery resembled chattel slavery in giving masters absolute property rights over their slaves. It was, nevertheless, historically distinctive in the way it combined slave labour with agricultural industries – principally growing and processing cane sugar – and a system of commercial exchange linking three continents. In the fifteenth century, Atlantic slavery emerged as an alternative source of labour, as the Portuguese started to acquire African slaves. Portuguese traders initially tapped into the long-established trans-Sahara slave trade, and diverted West African slaves from the Muslim-controlled routes to the East to European markets in Lisbon and Seville. Later, they provided slaves for the new sugar plantations in the Atlantic islands of Madeira, the Canaries and the Azores, and soon afterwards set up the transporting of slaves to the Caribbean and the Americas. The Spanish conquests and the European diseases that accompanied them devastated indigenous populations in the Americas – the population of the Americas plummeted from 50 million in 1500 to barely eight million in 1600 (Blackburn, 1997, p.132) – and the severe labour shortage was met by transporting increasing numbers of slaves across the Atlantic. In 1516, only 24 years after Christopher Columbus had landed in the Americas, the first sugar grown by African slaves in the Caribbean was taken back to Spain. The Spanish trade in slaves and sugar peaked in the late sixteenth century, and the Spanish were superseded briefly once again by the Portuguese, who were then themselves replaced by the British as the principal European power in the cultivation and trade of sugar.

Following the Spanish and Portuguese, John Hawkins (1532–95), the first successful English slave-trader, joined the triangular trade in European manufactured goods, slaves and Caribbean produce that was to expand in the next two centuries into such a spectacularly lucrative enterprise (see map on p.8). With royal approval and the financial backing of London merchants, Hawkins sailed in 1562 to the west coast of Africa with three ships and 100 men, and captured 300 Africans. He then transported the 300 enslaved Africans to the Caribbean, where he traded them for tropical goods, including sugar and tobacco. On returning to England – thus completing what came to be known as the **slave triangle** – Hawkins sold the tropical produce 'with prosperous successe and much gaine to himself and the aforesayde adventurers' (Walvin, 1992, p.25). Consumer demand in Europe for tropical products such as sugar, chocolate, tobacco and cotton ensured that the triangular trade expanded dramatically in the next two centuries, with sugar by some distance the most important product from the Americas. Annual sugar consumption in England, for example, increased from four pounds per person in 1700–9 to 18 pounds per person in 1800–9, and the quantity of tobacco exported annually from Virginia to Britain increased from 65,000 pounds in 1620 to 220 million pounds in 1775. By 1800, the European use of tropical goods produced by slave labour, particularly in Britain,

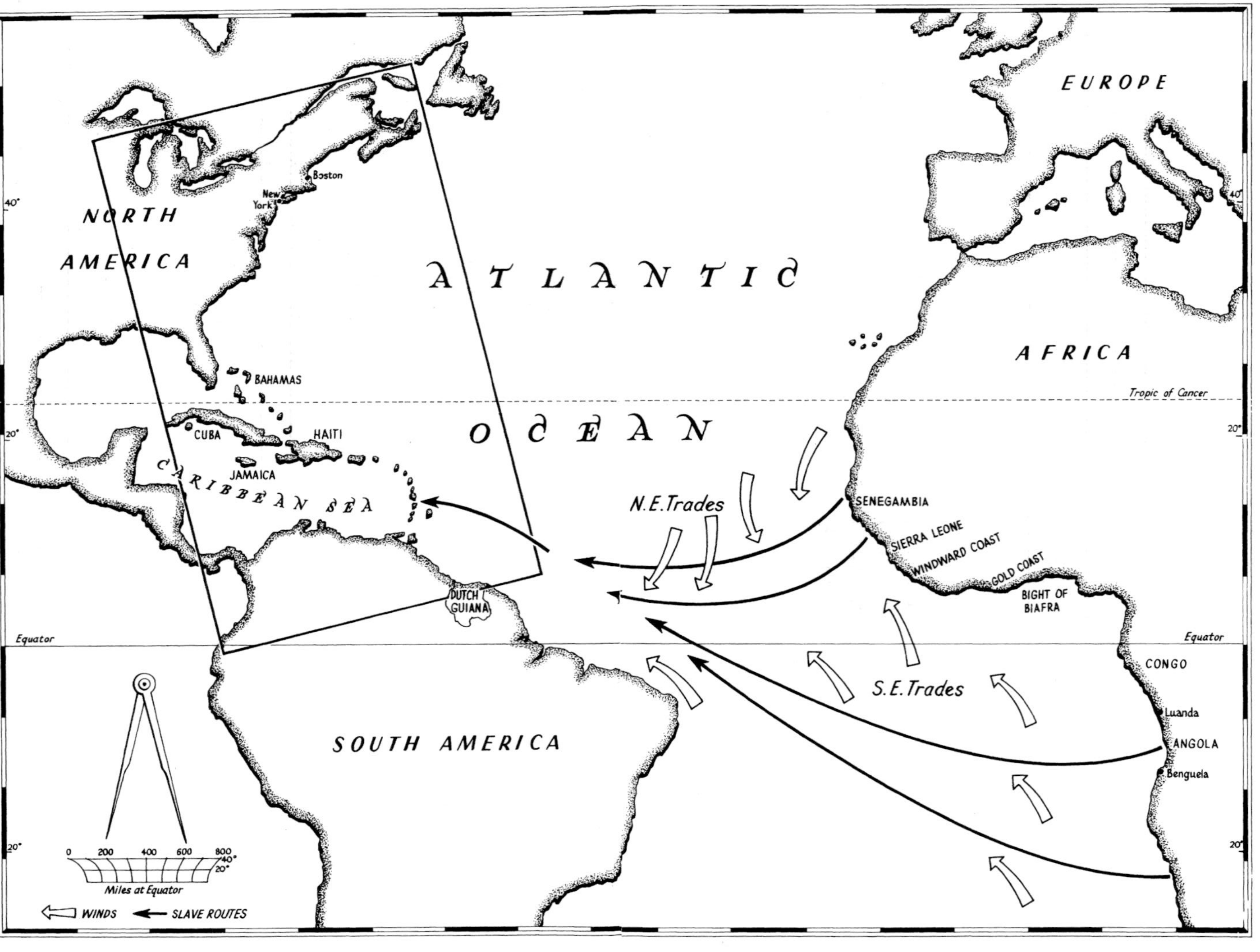

Map of West Africa and the Caribbean, from James Walvin, Black Ivory: A History of British Slavery, *1992, HarperCollins Publishers, London.*

had become so widespread that they were regarded less as luxuries than as taken-for-granted everyday pleasures.

The period 1780–1830 is critical in the history of Atlantic slavery, as it saw both the zenith of the Atlantic slave system and also its precipitous collapse in the British colonies. The number of slaves transported from Africa to the Americas peaked at 100,000 slaves per year in 1800, and vast numbers of slaves worked the plantations: in 1770 there were 2,340,000 slaves in the Americas, and by 1800 the figure had reached three million (Blackburn, 1988, p.543). All the western European powers had colonies with large slave labour forces: in 1790 there were 650,000 slaves in the French Antilles and 450,000 in the British West Indies; and in 1810 there were one million slaves in the Portuguese colony of Brazil, 225,000 in the Spanish colonies of South America, and 200,000 in Cuba (Blackburn, 1988, pp.163, 334, 383). These are intimidating statistics, and in 1780 the sponsors and agents of the slave economies in Europe, Africa and the Americas were justifiably confident that their profits would continue to escalate for many years to come.

However, by the 1830s the slave-owning class in Britain had been dealt devastating blows, with the slave trade abolished in 1807, and legislation for the emancipation of all slaves in British dependencies to follow in 1833. Although slavery persisted for several more decades – until the 1860s in the southern USA and until the 1880s in Brazil – the example set by Britain in abolishing slavery contributed to the combination of economic, political and moral pressures that ultimately led to the end of slavery in the Americas. The reasons for the rapid end of Atlantic slavery in British colonies in the period 1780–1834 have long divided historians, but there is at least scholarly consensus that the large-scale campaigns first for the abolition of the slave trade and later for the emancipation of slaves played a major role. The scale of abolitionist campaigning fluctuated through the period, but at its peaks attracted enormous public support: in 1790, anti-slavery petitions to Parliament far outnumbered those for all other causes, and again in the early 1830s petitioning, pamphleteering and public meetings dominated British politics.

In addition to exploring the themes of slavery, religion and travel, the course authors have tried to provide the following:

- First, we have sketched the context of each writer in some detail, setting out not only personal biographical details, but also a sense of their respective intellectual climates. In the case of Newton, Cowper and Wilberforce, this involves careful consideration of the doctrinal subtleties in Christian thought, and particularly its Evangelical variations. In the case of Park, this involves a thorough examination of the Enlightenment scientific aspirations that so powerfully motivated him, and that were effectively mobilized on his behalf by Sir Joseph Banks through the Royal Society and the African Association. In the case of the slave writers, this involves introducing in more detail the different strands within abolitionist politics, from the cautious and respectable to the subversive and radical.

- Second, we have attended closely to the language used by these different writers in giving expression to their ideas and arguments. This involves not only analysing the language of the texts themselves, but also identifying how their particular use of language intersects with actual language usage in the society more generally. The term we use to describe this actual language usage in society is **discourse**. We can define 'discourse' more precisely as 'language in actual use within its social and ideological context' (Baldick, 1990, p.59), though the term is perhaps best explained by examples. In Units 10–11, we might refer to 'religious discourse', which means the vocabulary, terminology, idioms and linguistic conventions people actually use when they discuss religion. In Units 12–13, we might refer to 'scientific discourse', which means the vocabulary, terminology, idioms and linguistic conventions people actually employ when they discuss scientific matters. Attention to discourse enables us to go beyond the individual texts selected and to reflect upon their social dimension, so that, for example, we might consider how the texts we study might have reproduced or indeed challenged the discourse of slavery in the years 1780–1830.
- Third, we have related the particular ideas in these selected texts to the major preoccupations of the Enlightenment and Romanticism. In the *Olney Hymns*, for example, we note 'a shift from reason to sentiment and passion' (Unit 10, p.43), a shift at the heart of the complex transition from Enlightenment to Romanticism. In Park's *Travels*, we note both the influence of Enlightenment conceptions of scientific reason on Park and 'the notion of travel as enlightenment' (Units 12–13, p.136). In Unit 14, we identify nine occasions in Cugoano's *Thoughts and Sentiments* where 'reason' or 'enlightenment' are invoked as authorities in support of Cugoano's abolitionist arguments.

Before you start the block, a word of caution. Do not expect consistency from the writers of the texts you are about to encounter, either individually or collectively. The debates of the day were controversial and furiously contested, and our selected writers disagreed with each other (not always consciously) in quite fundamental ways about many important issues. The course authors have done no more than provide a sympathetic paraphrase and analysis of each of them in turn. It is for you to read the texts carefully, to come to grips with their respective ideas, and finally – if you so wish – to make judgements about which of them provides the most convincing diagnosis of their society.

References

Baldick, C. (1990) *Oxford Concise Dictionary of Literary Terms*, Oxford, Oxford University Press.

Blackburn, R. (1988) *The Overthrow of Colonial Slavery 1776–1848*, London, Verso.

Blackburn, R. (1997) *The Making of New World Slavery: From the Baroque to the Modern 1492–1800*, London, Verso.

Fulford, T. and Kitson, P.J. (eds) (2001) *Travels, Explorations and Empires: Writings from the Era of Imperial Expansion 1770–1835*, vol. 1, London, Pickering and Chatto.

Walvin, J. (1992) *Black Ivory: A History of British Slavery*, London, HarperCollins.

Unit 10
Olney Hymns

Prepared for the course team by John Wolffe

Contents

Study components

Weeks of study	*Supplementary material*	*Audio-visual*	*Anthologies and set books*
1	AV Notes	Audio 4 Video 2	Anthology I

Objectives

When you have completed your work on Unit 10 you should have developed:

- a general understanding of the religious climate of later eighteenth-century England, with particular reference to the Evangelical movement and its beliefs;
- a knowledge of the specific context and content of *Olney Hymns* in relation to the lives of its authors;
- an appreciation of the significance of hymns as religious texts and as indicators of cultural trends.

1 Introduction

A few years before the dying David Hume coolly faced up to his own mortality, John Newton (1725–1807), the local clergyman in the small north Buckinghamshire town of Olney, composed a hymn to accompany his sermons for New Year's Day 1773. These lines were to become an enduringly popular expression of confidence in the reality of the afterlife:

Amazing grace! (how sweet the sound)
That sav'd a wretch like me!
I once was lost, but now am found,
Was blind, but now I see ...

Yes, when this flesh and heart shall fail,
And mortal life shall cease;
I shall possess, within the vail [veil],
A life of joy and peace.

(*Olney Hymns*, Book 1: no.41)

It will be argued in this unit that 'Amazing grace' was in its way quite as much a product of the Enlightenment as Hume's 'Of the immortality of the soul'. It is the best known of the *Olney Hymns*, published in 1779, and the joint work of Newton and his parishioner and friend, William Cowper (1731–1800). Newton had had a colourful past as a slave ship captain, but was now a leading figure in the Evangelical movement that sought to reform and revive British Protestant Christianity. Cowper was a brilliant yet anguished writer, prone to periods of prolonged depression, but one of the greatest poets of the age, whom Evangelicalism also powerfully influenced. Their work illustrates important strands in late eighteenth-century culture that contrast strongly with the scepticism of writers such as Diderot, Hume and Voltaire.

In Newton and Cowper's Olney we are in a very different world from the high political and military drama of Napoleon's meteoric career, which you have been studying in the previous block. The cultural currents flowing in Olney were, however, in their way, equally profound. The *Olney Hymns* were an early and eloquent expression of a revitalized form of Christianity that was to have a major impact on the lives and values of ordinary people in late eighteenth- and early nineteenth-century Britain and America. Evangelical beliefs were a potent ideological force in many communities, particularly in the face of the dislocation of traditional structures of society in the context of rapid industrialization and migration. As we shall see in the next unit, they also provided inspiration for social and political change, and played an important role in reshaping British attitudes to the non-European world, particularly in relation to the campaign against slavery. In the later units of this block, as we move beyond Evangelicals themselves, we shall still detect their impact in Mungo Park's responses to the religions and cultures of West Africa, and in the beliefs and experiences of the slaves themselves. The horizon of the *Olney Hymns* might at first sight appear limited by the low hills of rural Buckinghamshire, but in reality they provide key insights into much wider networks and processes.

In order to gain some initial orientation regarding Evangelicalism and its impact, you should now view Video 2, band 3 (*Evangelicalism, Slavery and Urban Community*). The first section provides context that is immediately relevant to the *Olney Hymns*, while the second and third sections explore some aspects of the development of the movement in other parts of Britain, and over the rest of the period covered by the course. Look also at the AV Notes and bear in mind as you watch what is said there about things to look out for on a first viewing. Then return to the unit.

2 Evangelicals and eighteenth-century religion

In order to appreciate the significance of religion in the eighteenth century, try to stand back from your twenty-first-century perception of organized religion, and think what life would be like if you and most of your family, friends and neighbours regularly attended religious worship. You may think at once, 'But I (and/or they) don't believe ...', but that response is rooted in our contemporary western view of religion as primarily the preoccupation of a committed minority who participate because of a strong sense of personal identification with its teachings. Remember too that people then had very few of the social and leisure options available to us today: imagine a world without television, telephone, easy transport or any of the community support structures we take for granted. In such a world, even if you did not think of yourself as a believer, you might well have found it worth your while to go to church. This would partly be because you had little else of interest to do on a Sunday, but also because it would be a valuable opportunity for social interaction and maintaining relationships – both with your neighbours and your local superiors – that could well prove useful to you in hard times. The sense of the Church as an expression of social community and hierarchy was confirmed by the box-pew internal church furnishings characteristic of the period (see Figure 10.1). Possession of a large or central pew signified high status in the community, whereas a pew in a corner or, worse still, a mere bench was a sign of inferiority. Except for those with a clear-cut atheist outlook (very much in a minority in the eighteenth century) there was likely also to be a feeling that it was worthwhile keeping on good terms with God. Christian teaching offered some hope of comfort and security beyond the uncertainties of present existence in a world where sudden and unforeseen death, even for

Figure 10.1 St Mary's, Avington, Hampshire. Photo: reproduced by kind permission of Allan Soedring.

An eighteenth-century Church of England interior, such as this one, was characterized by a prominent pulpit and box pews.

young people, was much more widespread than it is today. Such religion did not normally generate intensive commitment or activity, but it was an integral part of the fabric of life for most people.

The focus of this unit is on England, but it is worth taking a moment to survey the broader pattern of religion in western Europe. This presented a complex and variegated picture, but very broadly speaking the divisions and religious wars of the sixteenth and seventeenth centuries left Roman Catholicism predominant in the south, as well as in France and Ireland, and Protestant state churches in control of northern countries, including the British Isles. Roman Catholicism maintains that God reveals himself primarily through the teachings and traditions of the institutional Church, whereas Protestants defer rather to the Bible as the ultimate source of religious authority. In England, Wales and Ireland the Anglican State (or 'Established') Church took something of a hybrid form, being headed by bishops, a form of leadership shared with Roman Catholicism. In Scotland, however, the State Church was Presbyterian, without bishops, and, in general, the Church of Scotland had been more strongly influenced by more radical developments of Protestant thought than its English counterpart. Outside the state churches there were Protestant **Dissenters** (as they were called) who had refused to conform to the Church of England after the Restoration of Charles II in 1660. This was because they perceived it either as insufficiently Protestant or as disastrously compromised by its connection with the state. Their numbers were small during much of the eighteenth century, but increased rapidly during the period covered by this course. There were also Roman Catholics, a small minority at this time in England, Scotland and Wales, but the majority of the population in Ireland, which made the privileged establishment status of the (Anglican) Church of Ireland a matter of ongoing controversy. Jews were an even smaller minority in Britain, but a growing and increasingly influential one, especially in the business world.

For sceptics such as Hume and Sade, and even for a deist like Rousseau, the fundamental problem with the eighteenth-century Church was that it believed too much, preaching a creed that was at best a pious delusion maintained by self-interested and indolent clergy, and at worst a vehicle for cultural and social oppression. This was especially worrying for them precisely because the majority of people conformed to it. Evangelicals may be characterized as those at the opposite pole of religious thought. They felt that the religious ethos of the age was lukewarm, and needed to be revived by renewed experience of the reality and power of God and by the confident assertion of life-changing beliefs. Nevertheless, it is also important to emphasize the broad common ground that they shared with sceptical philosophers in terms of a perception of contemporary mainstream Christianity as compromised by hypocrisy, mixed motives and association with secular power structures. Moreover, Evangelicals too were men and women of the Enlightenment to the extent that they perceived themselves as advocates of a coherent alternative religious system, requiring personal commitment founded on tested experience and an integrated view of the world. They also saw their beliefs and spiritual experience very much as light shining in darkness. Their perception of religion as founded in clear-cut belief pointed towards that prevalent today. Also, as we shall see, they both stimulated and reflected the growth of cultural attitudes that came to be identified with Romanticism.

The Evangelical view of what William Wilberforce (1759–1833), whom we shall encounter in the next unit, was to call in 1797 'the prevailing religious system of professed Christians', was a caricature that pointed up its key deficiencies. Like all effective caricatures, however, it was one whose power came from the fact that it contained far more than a grain of truth. Whereas the seventeenth century, in England as elsewhere, had been a period of intense religious argument, experimentation and consequent conflict, by the mid-eighteenth century the dominant mood appeared more spiritually easy-going. Bishop Joseph Butler (1692–1752) was representative of the Anglican leadership of his own and immediately following generations when he said to the Methodist leader

John Wesley (1703–91) that 'the pretending to extraordinary revelations and gifts of the Holy Ghost is a horrid thing, a very horrid thing!' (quoted in Curnock, 1909–16, vol. 2, p.257). For Butler and those others who set the tone of the Church of England in the mid-eighteenth century, the danger of over-intense religion was that it led to political conflict and even insurrection (as in the English Civil War in the 1640s) and divided local communities. A widespread eighteenth-century conception of religion was of an undemanding Christianity that could provide a basis for national political consensus, local social cohesion, and individual comfort and support, centred around the parish church. The weakness of such an aspiration was that it provided an easy cloak for corrupt use of church appointments for political purposes. It also encouraged parish clergy to see themselves merely as relatively high-minded members of the leisured gentry classes, who served their purpose simply by being there, and did not feel obliged to pursue their spiritual responsibilities with any energy.

There were though some indications of a more positive religious vitality. It is important to appreciate that the scepticism of the French *philosophes* and of David Hume was but one strand in Enlightenment thought and culture. Even in France, there were churchmen who were influenced by the Enlightenment as well as those who rejected it. In general in England and Scotland, as in Germany, the Enlightenment was a religious quite as much as a secular movement, which 'throve ... within piety' (Porter and Teich, 1981, p.6). Bishop Butler was himself the author of a thoughtful and widely read defence of orthodox Christianity against both scepticism and deism, the *Analogy of Religion, Natural and Revealed, to the Constitution and Course of Nature*, published in 1736. David Hume's contemporary William Robertson, Principal of Edinburgh University, was an influential historian in the Enlightenment school who led a notable intellectual revival among the ministers of the Church of Scotland. During the late eighteenth century there were numerous published responses to the attacks on Christianity made by Hume (Rivers, 2001). A sense of deeper spiritual commitment was cultivated by voluntary societies such as the Society for the Promotion of Christian Knowledge and the Society for the Propagation of the Gospel. There were also small informal groups cultivating the devotional lives of their members. These included the 'Holy Club' at Oxford in the 1720s and 1730s, centred around the brothers John and Charles Wesley and forming an important part of the prehistory of the Evangelical movement. Among Protestant Dissenters from the Church of England there was a continuing strong current of piety that provided a living link back to the **Puritanism** (radical Protestantism) of the seventeenth century: as we shall see, the Dissenting influence was strong in Olney in Cowper and Newton's time.

In order to illustrate some features of earlier eighteenth-century Christian piety and to set the context for our study of the *Olney Hymns*, I should now like you to look at the first two hymns in Anthology I (pp.229–31), those by Joseph Addison ('The spacious firmament on high') and Isaac

Watts ('When I survey the won'drous Cross')[1]. Both men were highly educated and responsive to the intellectual and cultural trends of the time. Addison (1672–1719) can be seen as representative of restrained establishment Anglicanism; Watts (1674–1748) was a Dissenter who had affinities with the Puritans as well as being very much a man of his time.

EXERCISE

1 Try to summarize in your own words the broad conceptions of God and of the reasons for having religious belief as presented in these hymns.

2 In what ways are these hymns consistent with your understanding of Enlightenment culture?

DISCUSSION

1 Do not worry if you found it difficult to think of exact phrases and sentences. I hope though that you have at least got a sense of the contrasts. On the one hand, there is Addison's sense of God as the sublime creator of the universe, the beauty and order of which testify to his reality and power. To Addison, Christian belief is founded in the empirical evidence of the unchangeable stability of nature. On the other hand, there is Watts's much more personal and human view of Jesus as the divine Son of God dying on the Cross, whose 'love so amazing' inspires belief and commitment. (Note that here Watts anticipates a central strand of Evangelical belief, the conviction of the centrality of Jesus' self-sacrifice on the Cross in God's scheme for the salvation of humankind.)

2 Addison's verses, with their emphasis on order and reason, are very obviously an Enlightenment work and serve to remind us that such modes of thinking by no means always led to sceptical conclusions. Although Addison himself was an orthodox Anglican, his 'argument from design' – that the sheer orderliness of the universe means that there must be a controlling divine force – would also have been supported by deists. Watts is harder to categorize: the intense religious emotion that he expresses might tempt us to feel that he really 'belongs' in an earlier or later age. Such an approach though would distort historical reality, and we cannot tidily categorize changes in religion in this way. Note, moreover, that Watts, like Addison, has an underlying positive view of nature – it is not evil or hostile, but rather inherently good, only paling before the supreme goodness and love of Jesus Christ himself. It is also static and potentially controllable: a 'present', however magnificent, that can in

[1] The texts of the hymns in Anthology I and also the quotations from Cowper's verse in this unit are given in the form in which they were originally published. Some punctuation and spelling may therefore seem a little strange, but the meaning should still be clear. It is important in studying these texts to be aware that in later editions there have been subtle (and sometimes not so subtle) changes to what the authors originally wrote.

imagination be packaged up and handed back to God. In this respect Watts shares in an orderly Enlightenment view of the world around him. (Bear in mind that there is no space here to do more than indicate such suggestive straws in the wind and that it is important not to generalize too much from these texts.)

The beginnings of Evangelicalism are conventionally dated to the late 1730s, with the 'conversion' of John Wesley, the founder of Methodism, often seen as a symbolic defining moment. As already suggested, however, early Evangelicals drew strongly on existing religious currents, not only within the British Isles but also from continental Europe. In particular the **Pietist movement** in later seventeenth-century Germany, with its emphasis on renewed personal experience of God and individual and corporate study of the Bible, anticipated many of the features that were later to be seen as characteristic of Evangelicals in the Anglo-American world. A specific link between the German Pietists and England was provided by the communities of so-called Moravians, centred on the estate of their leader Count Nikolaus von Zinzendorf (1700–60) at Herrnhut in Saxony. Moravians travelled widely, established a presence in England, and had a profound influence on John Wesley.

There is also a more general sense in which it is appropriate to emphasize continuity in the origins of Evangelicalism. The word 'Evangelical' is derived from the Greek for Gospel (meaning 'good tidings'), and literally means simply someone who adheres to the basic truths of Christianity, with an implied emphasis on the authoritative status of the Bible. (You should not be confused by current theologically imprecise use of the term to denote zealous adherence to any belief system, and the word is used in these units with a capital E to make its specific application clear.) The word was therefore already a widespread part of the self-image and characterization of Protestant Christians, particularly in Germany and Scandinavia but also in the British Isles.

Nevertheless, something demonstrably new did happen in the 1730s. Evangelicalism was a movement that spanned the Atlantic, with developments centred on the ministry of Jonathan Edwards at Northampton, Massachusetts (at that time still a British colony) in 1734–5 slightly predating those in Britain. The preaching of Edwards together with that of British counterparts, including George Whitefield and (in Wales) Howel Harris as well as John Wesley, was the catalyst for collective intense spiritual experiences, known as **revivals**. A distinctive feature of early Evangelicalism was that preaching very often occurred in the open air (see Figure 10.2) as the use of churches and other buildings was refused. In the countryside they used fields or any available open space; in London Whitefield preached among the street traders and sideshows at Moorfields, then on the outskirts of the city.

Figure 10.2 John Griffiths, Enthusiasm Displayed, *engraving on paper, Corporation of London Libraries and Guildhall Art Gallery, London. Photo: © Corporation of London.*

George Whitefield is shown here preaching in Old Street, London, not far from his usual location in Moorfields. Note the informality of the setting and the potential in a public place to draw in passers-by, some of whom appear interested but others indifferent.

Evangelicals themselves perceived revivals, of which one of the most spectacular was stirred by Whitefield's preaching at Cambuslang in central Scotland in 1742, as demonstrations of the work of the Holy Spirit of God in human beings. They were characterized by intense collective responses to the exhortations of the preacher. Many hundreds – and eventually thousands – of people believed themselves to have had an authentic experience of God, exactly the kind of direct encounter with the supernatural that Bishop Butler thought to be fraudulent and hence greatly disliked.[2] This could lead to strong emotional and even physical reactions, such as weeping, shaking and falling to the ground (as in the

[2] The question of whether such phenomena have a material or supernatural/divine origin is essentially a theological debate that falls outside the remit of a historical study such as that on which we are currently engaged. Modern writers who share Butler's scepticism would be likely to 'explain' the phenomenon in terms of processes such as mass hysteria, adolescent sexual tension, unresolved guilt and wish-fulfilment, but the passionate conviction of early Evangelicals that they were experiencing an authentic encounter with God needs to be taken very seriously.

biblical model of Saul of Tarsus in Acts 9:4). Such experiences were seen as conversions in which individuals decisively turned their backs on a previous sinful or 'worldly' existence, and committed themselves to following Jesus Christ. The sense of decisive movement from darkness to light in conversion reflects a broader Enlightenment state of mind. Many recalled the precise date, or even hour of their conversion, believing it to be a moment when life was changed fundamentally to the extent that they felt themselves 'reborn'. Thus John Wesley noted that his conversion occurred on 24 May 1738 at a quarter to nine in the evening. He wrote that:

> I felt my heart strangely warmed, I felt I did trust in Christ, Christ alone, for salvation, and an assurance was given me that He had taken away my sins, even mine, and saved me from the law of sin and death.
>
> (Quoted in Curnock, 1909–16, vol.1, pp.475–6)

Central to this trust in Christ was the belief that his self-sacrifice on the Cross (as so movingly described by Watts) had satisfied the need of a just God to punish the sins of humanity, a doctrine known as **atonement**. Evangelical religion was further characterized by an activist zeal to spread the blessings of the Christian faith to others, and by deference to the Bible – rather than Church tradition or abstract reason – as the ultimate source of truth in religious matters.

In order to gain further insight into the Evangelical experience of conversion and central emphasis on the sacrificial death of Jesus Christ on the Cross, look now at the next hymn in Anthology I, Charles Wesley's 'And can it be ...?' (pp.231–2). See how Wesley makes quite explicit links between Jesus' death and the salvation of the believer who has 'an interest in the Saviour's blood'. The word 'interest' is used here not in the sense of mere curiosity, but means having a share of ownership, by analogy with having an interest in financial capital, land or a commercial company. Such complete identification with Jesus' suffering is the means by which believers secure release from their own sinful and earthbound nature. Wesley has elements of an enquiring Enlightenment mind insofar as he starts by seeking to understand the divine 'design', but ultimately he perceives it as a mystery beyond comprehension. The convert moves from the darkness of imprisonment 'in sin and nature's night' to the self-assurance that comes from his sense of being united to Christ. Think too about the impact of this hymn on the consciousness of those who sang it in the later eighteenth century: they would not have shared Wesley's eloquence, but his language gave them a framework in which to express, confirm and articulate their own experience.

The Evangelical world-view stood in an ambivalent relationship to the Enlightenment. On the one hand, its emotionalism and sense of direct spiritual inspiration seemed at odds with the predominant cultural climate of the age and closer to a Romantic sensibility. On the other hand, though, many Evangelicals were fascinated by science and nature, and believed their convictions to be systematically verifiable both by the divinely ordered state of the natural world and the testimony of the Bible. In this period, before there had been significant critical scholarly study of the biblical text, as far as the Evangelicals were concerned the rationality of trust in the reliability of Scripture was not at issue. You will recall moreover that even David Hume rarely ventured explicitly to question it, although he made his views clear to those who read between the lines. John Wesley himself was a man of considerable learning, an Oxford college fellow before his conversion, and a serious student of Enlightenment philosophy who presented his arguments in a rational and orderly fashion. For him Christian conviction was supremely rational, and was supported by empirical and verifiable experience of encounters with God. In response to Bishop Butler he *denied* pretending to any 'extraordinary revelations or gifts of the Holy Ghost' (quoted in Curnock, 1909–16, vol.2, p.257). One leading scholar asserts that 'increasingly, Wesley is being recognized as an Enlightenment thinker in his own right' (Bebbington, 1993, p.52). This view is founded not only on his empirical, logical cast of mind, but also on his support for Enlightenment causes such as religious tolerance and anti-slavery.[3]

One distinctive manifestation of Evangelicalism was **Methodism**, which began life as a society *within* the Church of England intended to renew the devotional life of its adherents and to broaden the popular appeal of the Church. Converts formed local societies and eventually chapels. These were subdivided into class meetings, which provided a basis for mutual spiritual and social support. Full-time preachers itinerated tirelessly around the country, while part-time local preachers similarly served the societies in their own immediate vicinity. Critics, amused by this systematic and methodical approach to religion, initially coined the tag 'Methodist', but it stuck and was accepted by the movement itself. It was further testimony to its rational and Enlightenment dimensions. The initial euphoria of revivals could not be sustained, but Methodism held a growing appeal to relatively humble people for whom conversion had given meaning and purpose to their lives. Membership in England reached 22,410 in 1767 and had more than doubled to 56,605 by the time of John Wesley's death in 1791 (Gilbert, 1976, p.31). By this time the institutional dynamic of Methodism had set it on an inexorable course to development as a separate family of denominations. A central reason for separation was the refusal of Anglican bishops to ordain Wesley's preachers, who were liable to be perceived as irregular and potentially subversive of due order in Church and society.

At the same time, though, Evangelicalism was also having a significant impact on existing denominations: while initially at least it would be true

[3] This view of Wesley is, however, a matter of ongoing scholarly debate. For a recent alternative perspective see Kent, 2002.

to say that all Methodists were Evangelicals, there were always Evangelicals who were not Methodists. Evangelicalism led to a recovery of momentum in the Dissenting groups that had left the Church of England in the seventeenth century. In Wales it stirred a great upsurge in religious Dissent. It inspired a vigorous Evangelical movement within the Church of Scotland, but also stimulated secessions from it. In the Church of England, a number of clergy became converts, but chose to remain in their existing parish ministries rather than follow Wesley and Whitefield into independent itinerant preaching. In doing so they developed significant local centres of Evangelical influence. Men of this kind included William Grimshaw and Henry Venn in Yorkshire, William Romaine in London, and Samuel Walker in Cornwall. Our specific concern in the rest of this unit is with another leading figure in this group of early Anglican Evangelicals, John Newton, and with his friend William Cowper, and their hymn writing at Olney.

Before turning to this more detailed case study, however, it is worth reflecting a little on the wider context of Evangelicalism. Although Wesley and others conceived their religion as grounded in the spiritual application of empiricism and rationality, it also conspicuously manifested elements of a more emotional, dramatic and less orderly world, characteristics that the Enlightenment elite tended to denigrate as 'enthusiasm'. This word was also applied by contemporaries to audacious and intense forms of expression in art. There is a further significant secular parallel in the fervour and expectation of the French revolutionaries for a radically changed world, later translated into the infatuated veneration accorded by his army to Napoleon. Like the statue of a dead man walking in from the darkness to shatter the superficial sophistication of Don Giovanni's dinner table, such challenges to rational order point up the cultural complexity of later eighteenth-century Europe. Moreover, in Evangelical enthusiasm and its secular counterparts we can discern a significant factor in the emergence of Romanticism.

3 Newton, Cowper and Olney

In 1764 John Newton (see Figure 10.3) was ordained in the Church of England and took charge of the parish of Olney. It marked a radical change of direction in his life. He was an only child, his father a merchant sea captain and his mother a Dissenter, who gave him a pious early upbringing and hoped that he would eventually enter the ministry. She died when John was only six. He received little formal education, and by the time he began a seafaring life in the early 1740s, he had turned his back on Christian practice and convictions, inventing blasphemies and joining in heavy drinking. One night in March 1748, however, while in fear of imminent death in a severe storm at sea, he experienced a sense of renewed awareness of God, prayed for mercy,

Figure 10.3 H. Robinson, after a drawing by W. Harvey, John Newton, *engraving, published 1836, Baldwin and Cradock, Paternoster Row, London. Photo: Mary Evans Picture Library.*

John Newton appears here in later life, probably after he left Olney for London in 1780.

reviewed his past life, and became convinced of the truth of the Christian Gospel. Like John Wesley, Newton recalled this moment of conversion with great precision and commemorated it annually for the rest of his life. For the moment though he continued to work as a merchant seaman, and progressed to be a captain, taking command of slave ships carrying human cargo from Africa to the West Indies, having at that time no scruples about the morality of the trade. Meanwhile, he increasingly cultivated his spiritual life and sought to educate himself, studying both Latin and religious works. Following a prolonged courtship he married Mary Catlett in 1750. In 1754 he suffered an epileptic fit which obliged him to give up working at sea, and after a period of uncertainty he secured a shore job as surveyor of tides at Liverpool. Now that he was permanently in England he was able to develop his friendships and contacts with other members of the Evangelical movement, both Anglicans and Dissenters. He began to seek ordination in the Church of England. He was initially rebuffed by several bishops, ostensibly because of his lack of the usual university degree, but more probably because his known Evangelicalism and contacts with Dissenters made them fear he would be a subversive influence. In 1764 he published his autobiography, under the title of *An Authentic Narrative of Some Remarkable and Interesting Particulars in the Life of ********* . This work, with its human excitement and spiritual drama, rapidly became popular and came to be seen as a classic account of an Evangelical darkness to light conversion. Meanwhile, Newton had come to the attention of the influential Earl of Dartmouth, who was able both to persuade the Bishop of Lincoln (in whose diocese Olney was then located) to ordain him and, as patron, to secure his appointment as curate-in-charge of the town, deputizing for the absentee vicar.

William Cowper (see Figure 10.4) also had a turbulent emotional and spiritual life, but in a very different context from Newton. He was the son of an Anglican clergyman, and his family background was a socially superior one, with links to the landed gentry. Like Newton, though, he lost his mother at the age of six, later describing himself as 'Wretch even then, Life's journey just begun' (quoted in Baird and Ryskamp, 1980–95, vol.3, p.56). The consequent emotional insecurities were very much apparent in his later life. He was educated at Westminster School and then sought to follow a legal career, being called to the Bar in 1754. Like Newton, he had a lengthy and intense youthful romance with his cousin Theodora, but for Cowper this concluded in 1756 not in marriage but in painful separation. He remained unmarried. This disappointment combined with the deaths both of his closest friend and of his father to trigger Cowper's first descent into the depression with which he was intermittently troubled for the rest of his life. He expressed his feelings in verse:

Figure 10.4 John Russell, William Cowper, *c.1763, pastel drawing, The Cowper and Newton Museum, Olney. Photo: © The Open University.*

This pastel drawing of William Cowper was made in about 1763 when he was in his early 30s, four years before he moved to Olney. His nervous manner contrasts strikingly with Newton's much more self-assured appearance.

> Doom'd, as I am, in solitude to waste
> The present moments, and regret the past;
> Depriv'd of every joy, I valued most
> My Friend torn from me, and my Mistress[4] lost; ...
>
> Why all, that soothes a heart, from anguish free,
> All that delights the happy – palls with me!
>
> (Quoted in Baird and Ryskamp, 1980–95, vol.1, pp.62–3)

In 1763 Cowper was offered a lucrative post as Clerk of Journals in the House of Lords, but the prospect of being publicly examined by the House as to his fitness precipitated a further acute mental crisis and a botched attempt at suicide. He was taken to an asylum where, under treatment that was humane and progressive by the standards of the period, he eventually made a good recovery. This process was catalysed and supported by a powerful conversion experience. A major factor contributing to Cowper's depression had been a conviction that he had committed unforgivable sin and would accordingly be damned to burn in hell when he died. He had been counselled by his cousin, Martin Madan, an Evangelical clergyman. Madan encouraged him to believe that he was no more or less sinful than the rest of the human race, and that the atoning death of Jesus on the Cross meant that he could still be forgiven by God. Cowper's account of the day of his conversion in June 1764 shows how this doctrine suddenly became a powerful spiritual reality for him. As you read the following passage do not worry too much about understanding all the technical theological language. Seek, however, to grasp the sense of tremendous excitement, happiness and new beginnings that Cowper, in common with other Evangelicals, experienced at the moment of conversion, and note the sense of light banishing darkness that represents intriguing common ground with the language of more secular Enlightenment writers.

> The happy period that was to strike off my fetters and to afford me a clear opening into the free mercy of the Blessed God in Jesus was now arrived. I flung myself into a chair near the window seat and, seeing a Bible there, ventured once more to apply to it for comfort and instruction. The first verse I saw was the twenty-fifth of the third chapter to the Romans[5] where Jesus is set forth as the propitiation for our sins. Immediately I received strength to believe it. Immediately the full beams of the sun of righteousness shone upon me. I saw the sufficiency of the atonement He had made, my pardon sealed in His blood, and all

[4] In Cowper's day (and earlier) this word did not have its modern sexual connotations.

[5] 'God presented him [Jesus] as a sacrifice of atonement (or as the one who would turn away his wrath, taking away sin), through faith in his blood. He did this to demonstrate his justice, because in his forbearance he had left the sins committed beforehand unpunished' (New International Version).

> the fullness and completeness of my justification. In a moment I believed and received the Gospel. Whatsoever my friend Madan has said to me so long before recurred to me with the clearest evidence of its truth, 'with demonstration of the Spirit and with power'. Unless the Almighty Arm had been under me I think I should have died with gratitude and joy. My eyes filled with tears and my voice was choked with transport. I could only look up to Heaven in silence, overwhelmed with love and wonder! But the work of the Holy Ghost is best described in His own words. It was 'joy unspeakable and full of glory'. Thus was my Heavenly Father in Christ Jesus pleased to give me the full assurance of faith at once, and out of a stony and unbelieving heart to raise up a child unto Abraham.
>
> (Quoted in Ella, 1993, pp.90–1)

In 1765 Cowper found himself mentally restored and a zealous new convert to Evangelicalism, but with limited financial means and without regular employment. He took lodgings at Huntingdon in order to be near to his brother in Cambridge. He shortly became friendly with the family of Morley Unwin, an Anglican clergyman, and moved in to share their home. Unwin was killed in a riding accident in June 1767, and Cowper continued to live with his widow, Mary, and their adult son and daughter. Gossips were to speculate about the nature of Cowper's relationship with Mrs Unwin, but it was almost certainly never more than close friendship, in which she may well have been a mother figure to him but not a lover. Cowper and the Unwins wanted to live in a place where they could share in a strong Evangelical ministry, and were recommended to Newton by a mutual friend. Accordingly they moved to Olney late in 1767, settling in a house on the market-place (see Figure 10.5), a short walk from Newton's newly extended vicarage.

In settling at Olney Cowper was decisively separating himself from the turmoil of life in London where he had spent his early adult years. In his verse he was to uphold the countryside as a 'purer' environment in which one could be closer to God and escape the corruptions and superficialities of the city, an outlook reminiscent of Rousseau's idealization of nature. Cowper later eloquently stated this outlook in part of his longest and most famous poem, *The Task*, published in 1785 and enormously popular at the end of the eighteenth century:

> God made the country, and man made the town.
> What wonder then, that health and virtue, gifts
> That can alone make sweet the bitter draught
> That life holds out to all, should most abound
> And least be threatened in the fields and groves?
> Possess ye therefore, ye who borne about
> In chariots and sedans, know no fatigue
> But that of idleness, and taste no scenes
> But such as art contrives, possess ye still

Figure 10.5 Cowper's house, Olney, photograph, Buckinghamshire County Museum collections.

Cowper's house in Olney market-place made up the right-hand half of the large building. It is shown here in an early photograph dating from sometime in the later nineteenth century. Note its size and appearance of importance relative to the cottages around it.

Your element; there only ye can shine,
There only minds like yours can do no harm.
Our groves were planted to console at noon
The pensive wand'rer in their shades. At eve
The moon-beam, sliding softly in between
The sleeping leaves, is all the light they wish,
Birds warbling all the music. We can spare
The splendor of your lamps, they but eclipse
Our softer satellite. Your songs confound
Our more harmonious notes. The thrush departs
Scared, and th'offended nightingale is mute.

(*The Task*, I.749–68, quoted in Baird and Ryskamp, vol.2, p.136)

Olney was a market town with a population of about 2,000, situated on the banks of the river Great Ouse, a landscape evoked by Cowper in *The Task*:

The Ouse, dividing the well-water'd land,
Now glitters in the sun, and now retires,
As bashful, yet impatient to be seen.

(*The Task*, I.323–5, quoted in Baird and Ryskamp, vol.2, p.125)

Its tall church spire, then as now, was the centrepiece of picturesque views across the water meadows from the south. The population was mostly of low economic status, once described by Cowper as 'the half-starved and ragged of the earth' (quoted in Hindmarsh, 1996, p.172). They were mostly tradesmen and artisans, with a large proportion of lacemakers who led a particularly hand-to-mouth existence, and were very vulnerable to fluctuations in the market for their product. Cowper's and Newton's were the only households in the town that could afford servants. Note therefore that while the predominant contemporary audience for many of the texts that you will study in this course was a cultural and social elite, the *Olney Hymns* were first written with poorer and less well-educated social groups very much in mind.

Olney's location on the borders of Buckinghamshire, Bedfordshire and Northamptonshire (see Figure 10.6) placed it in the centre of a region with a strong tradition of religious Dissent (see above, p.18). Notable figures were John Bunyan, the author of *Pilgrim's Progress*, at Bedford in the seventeenth century, and more recently Philip Doddridge (1702–51), another important pioneer hymn writer, at Northampton. Olney itself had had a substantial Puritan presence in the seventeenth century, and at the time of Newton and Cowper's arrival its legacy was still very much apparent in the existence of two Dissenting chapels. Olney had also been influenced by visits from George Whitefield in 1739 and from Moses Browne, Newton's immediate predecessor (and non-resident vicar throughout Newton's curacy), who was also an Evangelical.

Newton was very well suited to this religious environment. He was now an ordained clergyman of the Church of England, which gave him privilege and status, but his prior associations with Dissenters meant that it was easy for him to conciliate rather than confront his neighbours. He rapidly gained a reputation as a preacher worth hearing, and within a year of his arrival at Olney a gallery was added to the church in order to accommodate the increased congregation. As, with this addition, the already large church could now hold almost the entire population of the town, it seems that he drew a very substantial proportion of it to Sunday worship. That in itself, however, was insufficient for Newton, as he was all too well aware of the very mixed motives (see above, pp.16–17) that caused his contemporaries to attend church services. His aim was not primarily to see the church full, but rather to see nominal Christians experience Evangelical conversions that would make them whole-hearted and committed believers. His preaching was primarily directed to that end. It was supplemented by additional meetings for enquirers and believers – both adults and children – in which he sought to develop and

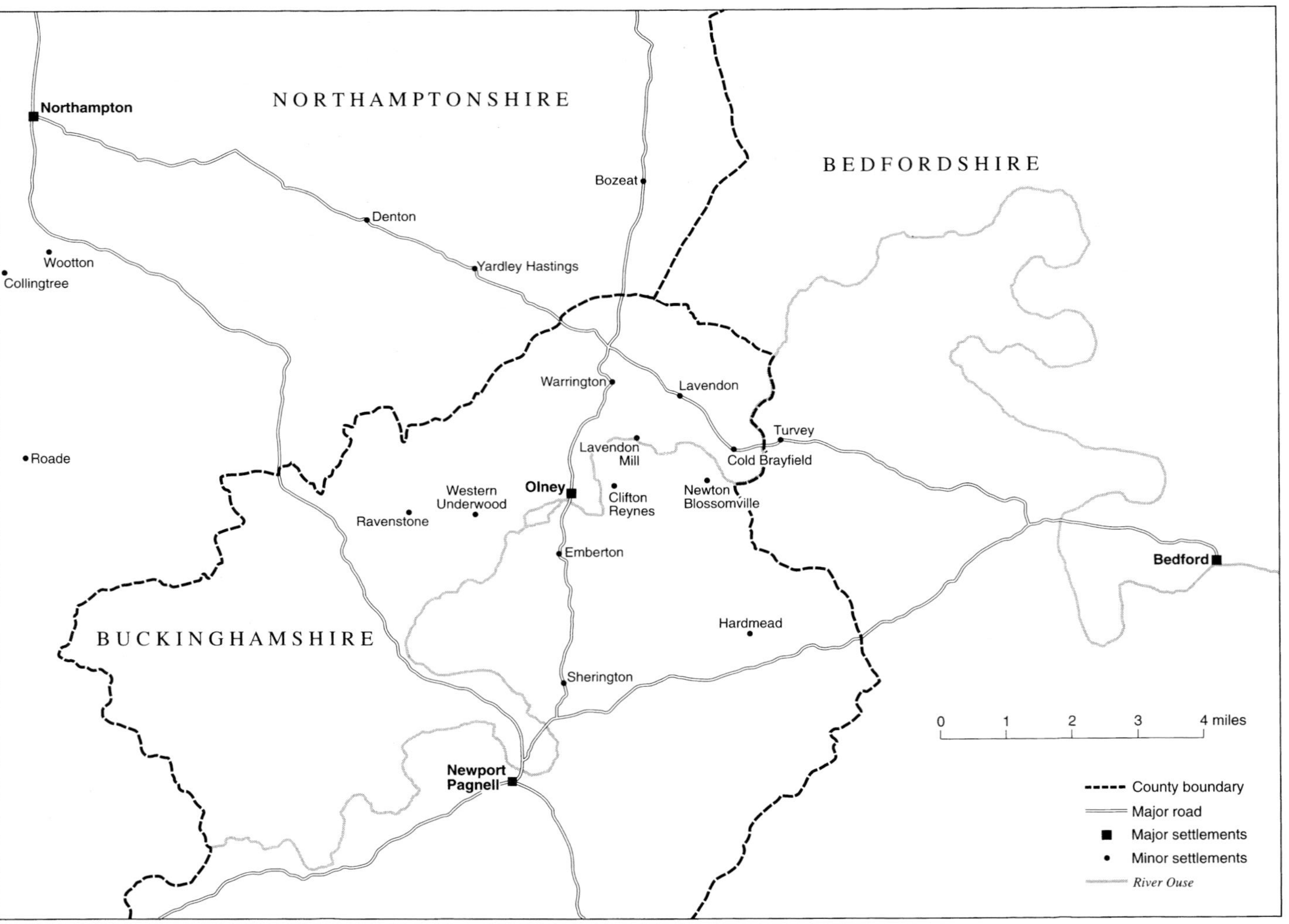

Figure 10.6 Map showing Olney in relation to nearby towns and county boundaries, from D. Bruce Hindmarsh, John Newton and the English Evangelical Tradition between the Conversions of Wesley and Wilberforce, *1996. Reprinted by permission of Oxford University Press, Oxford.*

consolidate spiritual interest. He was also assiduous in pastoral visiting of the parish, a task in which Cowper and the Unwins assisted him.

Cowper and Newton were both **Calvinists**, holding to the system of belief originally deriving from the leader of the sixteenth-century Reformation in Geneva, John Calvin. Calvin believed strongly in the omnipotence of God, and held that whether or not individuals found faith in Jesus Christ and hence salvation in the afterlife was due to God's preordaining (sometimes termed 'election') rather than to their own choice. People might feel they were making their own choices, but in reality they were following the spiritual path that the all-seeing God had prepared for them. More extreme Calvinists – sometimes called hyper-Calvinists – adopted a fatalistic position, believing that as God had predetermined everyone's eternal destiny, human efforts to make converts to Christianity were at best pointless and at worst impious. Newton and Cowper, however, were moderate Calvinists who believed that even though salvation was ultimately predetermined by God, human beings were themselves essential instruments of God's purposes in bringing others to saving faith. Newton himself was fond of analogies of cultivation and gardening in explaining the relationship between human agency and divine purpose. Human involvement was essential in digging the ground, planting seed and pruning trees, but successful growth and harvest depended on forces outside a person's control. In just the same way, Christians could make people aware of their spiritual need and preach the Gospel to them, but God alone determined whether or not this led to inner change in their lives. Similarly, gardeners find that not all the trees they carefully cultivate will bear fruit. (For examples of Newton's statement of this outlook look at *Olney Hymns,* 1:103 and 2:26 on pp.247–8 and 249–50 of Anthology I.) As men and women were working on God's behalf to achieve the divine intentions, they must not slacken in their appointed task. Calvinism is very much apparent in the *Olney Hymns*, in the sense of an all-seeing divine purpose and in the perception of humanity as divided between 'saved' and 'sinners'. (Other Evangelicals, including most importantly John Wesley, were not Calvinists but Arminians – from another Reformation theologian, the Dutchman Jakob Hermans, also known as Jacobus Arminius – who believed that salvation was potentially available to *all* human beings provided they responded personally to the Gospel.)

This was the context in which the *Olney Hymns* took shape. Although in part an expression of Cowper's and Newton's personal religious faith and experience, they were primarily intended for immediate use in Newton's ministry. They were sometimes sung, either in church or at the various other weekday and Sunday meetings, as an expression of collective worship. They could also though be used without music as a means of helping people to understand and remember Christian teaching, as a focus for a lecture by Newton. We shall be looking at the text itself more systematically in the next section of this unit. Before we do this, however, I should like you to read three of the hymns that give particular insights into the religious environment of Olney in the 1760s and 1770s, as perceived by Newton and Cowper, and of their response to it. Read now *Olney Hymns*, 2:26 (Newton: 'What contradictions meet', Anthology I, pp.249–50), 2:43 (Newton: 'O Lord, our languid souls inspire', pp.253–4) and 2:44 (Cowper: 'Jesus, wheree'er thy people meet', pp.254–5). The second and the third of these hymns were written for a specific occasion, the move in April 1769 of a weekly prayer meeting from the cramped quarters of the parlour of Newton's vicarage to a much larger room in the 'Great House', Lord Dartmouth's uninhabited mansion nearby.

EXERCISE Read the hymns once again, this time more closely, and consider the following questions:

1 What kind of religion do the hymns emphasize?

2 How would you contrast this with predominant eighteenth-century low-key attitudes to religion, as characterized in section 2 of this unit?

DISCUSSION 1 The three hymns convey a sense of a faith that is immensely powerful and precious to the writers. Newton is moved to great exertions to share his sense of 'The Saviour's dying love/The soul's amazing worth' (26, verse 3) and of the potential of his Lord to 'give the troubled conscience ease/The wounded spirit heal' (43, verse 4). Cowper writes of 'The sweetness of thy [Jesus'] saving name' (44, verse 3). The emphasis is on Jesus as personal loving Saviour rather than God as an almighty but distant creator (contrast Addison's hymn 'The spacious firmament on high'). Although there is much reference to 'sin' and 'sinners', in these hymns at least they are to be won over by the positive attractions of the Christian life, rather than by fear of judgement and punishment. Nevertheless, the overwhelming impression is of a 'them and us' situation, a Calvinist separation between the 'chosen few' (44, verse 3) and the 'many sinners round' (43, verse 7). Newton though strives to convert sinners in 26, and in 43, verse 7 he hopes they will be awakened 'to come and fill this place', while Cowper longs for Jesus to make a 'thousand hearts' his own (44, verse 6). You may well think verse 5 of hymn 44 one of Cowper's less successful stanzas and it was omitted from later hymn-books, but it is a revealing account of their immediate situation.

2 This sense of true Christianity as being the preserve of a committed and converted minority contrasts strongly with the more prevalent view of religion as a matter of undemanding consensus woven closely into the social fabric. Evangelical belief as promoted by Cowper and Newton implied division between 'saved' and 'unsaved' in society as a whole, even if among the converted there was 'holy peace/And love, and concord' (43, verse 4). It was this potential of Evangelicals, especially Calvinists, to divide communities that lay

behind much of the opposition to the movement from both ecclesiastical and secular authorities. This is one specific example of a tension between two conceptions of religion – social cohesion and personal salvation – that was very widespread in the period.

4 The text of *Olney Hymns*

In this section I shall be asking you to look at some more specific extracts from the *Olney Hymns* (see Figure 10.7). In doing so I want you not only to think about them as religious texts, but also to consider the ways in which they fit into the wider patterns of cultural change with which we are concerned in this course. The primary motive for their

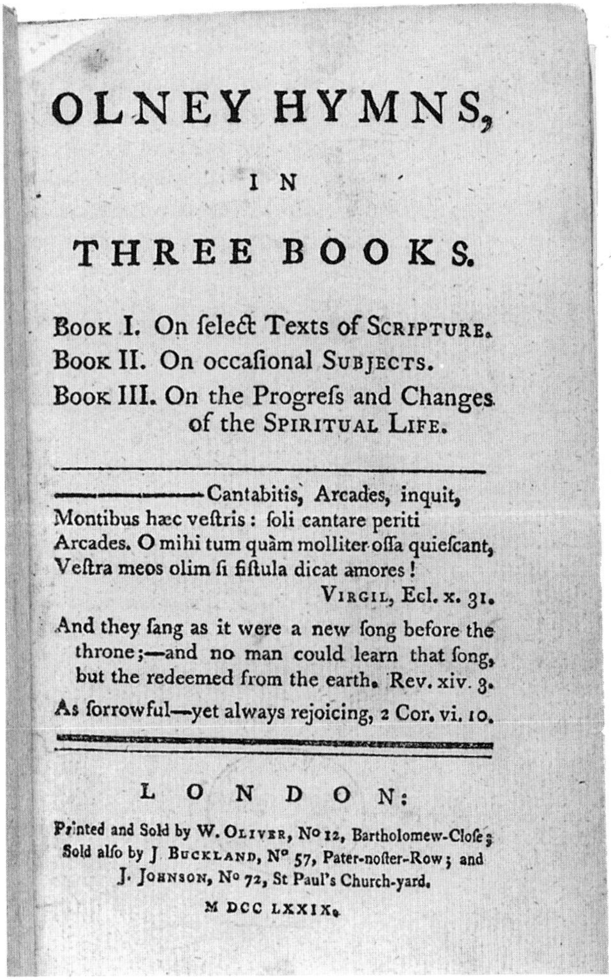

OLNEY HYMNS,

IN

THREE BOOKS.

BOOK I. On ſelect Texts of SCRIPTURE.
BOOK II. On occaſional SUBJECTS.
BOOK III. On the Progreſs and Changes of the SPIRITUAL LIFE.

————Cantabitis, Arcades, inquit,
Montibus hæc veſtris: ſoli cantare periti
Arcades. O mihi tum quàm molliter oſſa quieſcant,
Veſtra meos olim ſi fiſtula dicat amores!
VIRGIL, Ecl. x. 31.

And they ſang as it were a new ſong before the throne;—and no man could learn that ſong, but the redeemed from the earth. Rev. xiv. 3.
As ſorrowful—yet always rejoicing, 2 Cor. vi. 10.

LONDON:

Printed and Sold by W. OLIVER, No 12, Bartholomew-Cloſe; Sold alſo by J. BUCKLAND, N° 57, Pater-noſter-Row; and J. JOHNSON, No 72, St Paul's Church-yard.

M DCC LXXIX.

Figure 10.7 Title page from the first edition of Olney Hymns, *John Newton and William Cowper, 1779, British Library, London. Photo: by permission of the British Library, London (shelfmark 1220.d.19).*

The Latin quotation from Virgil's Eclogues *can be translated: 'He said, "You will sing, ye Arcadians, these things to your mountains; you are uniquely skilled in singing, Arcadians. Oh, how softly my bones would rest then if once your shepherd's pipes would speak of my loves!"'*

composition was, however, a religious one. It is therefore important, especially if you do not think of yourself as religious, to make a conscious effort to step into a mental world where the spiritual issues with which they are concerned were taken with great seriousness. Do not worry if you sometimes find it hard to grasp the particular theological ideas being advanced, but concentrate on getting a sense of the overall states of mind conveyed by the text.

By the 1760s hymns had established themselves as an important, though not uncontroversial, feature of the religious devotion of Evangelicals. The earliest English hymns were versifications of the biblical text of the psalms (known as metrical psalms) and began to be written soon after the Reformation, from the mid-sixteenth century onwards. Subsequent writers drew more widely on other biblical passages and also began to write hymns that were not directly based on the text of the Bible. Cowper and Newton would themselves have used books such as that compiled by Cowper's spiritual counsellor Martin Madan, *A Collection of Psalms and Hymns Extracted from Various Authors* (who included Isaac Watts, Charles Wesley and his fellow Methodist John Cennick), published in 1760. Hymn singing was a central feature of the Methodist movement, and was also well established among Evangelical Dissenters. Hymns other than metrical psalms were, however, of questionable legality in the public worship of the Church of England until the 1820s, because they were not explicitly sanctioned in the Book of Common Prayer. Their proponents were accordingly cautious, tending to sing them in meetings other than the main Sunday services and in private and household devotion. Even some Evangelical clergy, such as William Romaine, were opposed to singing anything other than the psalms in church, on the grounds that hymns were human creations rather than the word of God.

Although Cowper, at least, began to write hymns in the years immediately before 1767, it was the context of the two men's shared ministry at Olney between 1767 and 1773 that stirred the writing of many of the hymns. The specific requirements of Newton's ministry and the nature of his congregation were very much in mind. Initially there were no clear plans for publication, although some of the hymns found their way into print, in magazines and elsewhere, sometimes without the authors' knowledge and agreement. By the early 1770s Cowper and Newton were planning to publish a collection of their work, but in 1773 a recurrence of Cowper's depression incapacitated him from making further contributions. Newton, however, continued to write hymns, finding them a powerful means of expressing his own beliefs and communicating them to his parishioners. In February 1779 he eventually decided that he had enough material to go ahead with a compilation, although of the 384 hymns only 67 were Cowper's. You can read Newton's own account of the circumstances of the writing of *Olney Hymns* in the first paragraph of the Preface, reproduced in Anthology I (pp.232–3). Note his double motive for publication, his concern to promote 'the faith and comfort of sincere christians', but also his sense of the book as a permanent monument of his friendship with Cowper.

The *Olney Hymns* were subdivided into three books, from which a cross-section is reproduced in Anthology I. The titles of the books themselves are suggestive of key Evangelical preoccupations. Book One reflects the Evangelical sense of the Bible as the ultimate source of religious authority, and the importance of the believer acquiring a deep familiarity with its contents. The hymns are designed to serve that end through verse that would have been easier for semi-literate people to remember than the text of the King James Bible. The hymns though go beyond the actual Bible texts in pointing up their significance in relation to the wider Christian scheme of belief and experience: for example, in 1:28 (pp.237–8) Newton explicitly links David's fight with Goliath to the Christian's battle against Satan, understood in a very personal way. The 'Occasional Subjects' addressed in Book Two are ones that reflect the priorities of the Evangelical spiritual life. New Year is a moment for awareness of the passage of time, and hence of one's own mortality; the seasons and creation as a whole are presented as metaphors for the individual's spiritual state. There is a lack of hymns that relate directly to the various festivals of the Church's year, but rather more that relate to ongoing devotion in prayer and the taking of the sacrament of Holy Communion. A section on 'Providences' is indicative of the Evangelical sense of God's controlling hand being present in the events of personal and community life. It includes several funeral hymns together with 2:69 (pp.257–8), which sees God as speaking to sinners through a large fire in Olney in September 1777. Finally, in Book Three Newton organized the hymns to reflect what he believed to be the stages in the spiritual awakening and salvation of the individual. Sinners are solemnly made aware of their potential fate and need for repentance, and then moved to seek God. Inner conflict ensues which is ultimately resolved through conversion and divine comfort, which moves the new believer to self-dedication and surrender to Jesus Christ. There continue, however, to be potential pitfalls, notably hypocrisy and complacency, in the Christian life, but the true believer will come through these to rejoice in praising God.

EXERCISE Look now at the remainder of Newton's Preface to the *Olney Hymns* (Anthology I, pp.233–4). What do you think significant in what he says about his approach to hymn writing?

DISCUSSION This is quite an open-ended question, and even if the points that occur to you are different from mine, they may well still be worthwhile and interesting ones. I would like you though to note the following:

(a) Newton explicitly regards hymns as being in a middle position between the culture of the privileged and that of the people as a whole. Thus he aims to write hymns that are not high-flying 'odes', although he is also anxious not to offend 'readers of taste'. The primary aim though is to make them accessible to 'plain people'. Newton here reflects a general growth of awareness in this period that the less well-educated must be taken into account.

(b) He stresses the extent to which the hymns are a product of personal experience and views. (You may already have noticed how frequently the pronoun 'I' appears in Newton's hymns!) Here Evangelicalism both reflected and contributed to the increased preoccupation with the self and individual identity that was a characteristic feature of Romanticism. Newton's sphere of life might appear far removed from Napoleon's, but he shared a sense of asserting his own individuality and destiny in the turmoil of competing movements and ideas.

(c) Hymns are perceived not as an end in themselves, but as a valuable part of Newton's wider Christian ministry.

EXERCISE I would like you to focus your reading of the hymns around three themes: first, Newton's and Cowper's view of the life and fate of unbelievers; second, their experience of life as Christians; and third, their use of nature and natural imagery in the hymns. In order to illustrate my first theme, their view of the unconverted, now read 1:55 ('God gives his mercies to be spent', p.242), 2:3 ('See! another year is gone!', pp.248–9) and 3:1 ('No words can declare', pp.259–60). As you might expect, the picture conveyed is a gloomy one, but as you read try to stand back from your personal reactions and think how contemporaries, especially the people of Olney in the 1770s, might have reacted to these hymns. Form some impressions and ideas of your own before reading on.

In 1:55 Cowper portrays everyday human life as a matter of pointless endeavour. Wealth is accumulated but is of no value because it is not shared with others; superficial respect merely conceals underlying hatred; the fleeting pleasures of eating honey cannot be separated from the pain of being stung by the bees. Moreover, even the pleasures of life, such as they are, will come to an end, and for those who reject God the afterlife will be 'endless woe'. Hymn 2:3 powerfully conveys Newton's sense of the fragility of life. The years pass quickly, and, particularly when stirred to reflection on the unexpected deaths of the previous year, no one can be sure they will outlive the present year. According to Newton, we are always standing on the brink of 'vast eternity'. Most dramatically in 3:1 Newton presents his vision of hell, to him a place that is a very real prison and place of torment for sinners who ignore God's repeated warnings to them. Note that Newton is not preoccupied here with specific sins so much as describing a general state of mind and manner of life in which people are perceived to be in rebellion against God. Underlying all three hymns is a Calvinist sense of sharp black and white distinctions between vain human pleasures and God's 'everlasting arms', between fragile life in this world and the confidence of the 'saints' for eternity, between doomed sinners and those who turn to Jesus.

Cowper's and Newton's denunciations are of course strong indirect testimony to the prevalence in Olney of the unspiritual states of mind they so dislike! At the same time they help to explain the appeal of their religion for those who had a sense of disappointment and vulnerability in life, perhaps through poverty, bereavement or illness, experiences which were also widespread in the period. The unpredictable ravages of epidemic disease and the risks of childbirth for women meant that even younger people would be likely readily to identify with the sentiments of hymn 2:3. If enjoyment of material pleasures were at best transient and at worst a high road to hell, then one had little cause to regret one's lack of access to them. Moreover, in the late eighteenth century a consciousness of hell and judgement was by no means confined to Evangelicals (you will recall Don Giovanni's fate in Mozart's opera). Such insecurities and fears of what lay beyond death could provide fertile soil for religious preaching. In the 'Providences' section of the *Olney Hymns* Newton sought to stir spiritual responses to particular crises in personal, community and national life. Elsewhere, initial phases of Evangelical revival in particular communities can sometimes be linked to local disasters, such as a fatal mining accident or the loss of a fishing vessel at sea. The surge in Methodist numbers that was to occur in the 1790s can be linked to the widespread social stresses apparent in that turbulent decade.

I would now like you to look at a number of hymns that speak of the positive attractions of the Christian life. Despite the darker side of the *Olney Hymns* that we have just been exploring, such more appealing texts tend to predominate in the book, and include quite a few that have survived the test of time and feature in modern Christian hymn-books. Let us look first quite closely at two of the best known of the *Olney Hymns*: 1:3 (Cowper's 'Oh! for a closer walk with God', p.235) and 1:41 (Newton's 'Amazing grace', pp.238–9). Study these texts in conjunction with my analysis below.

Three central beliefs apparent in these hymns are: first, a sense of the active providence of God; second, an awareness of sin; and third, a consciousness of personal encounter and relationship between the believer and God. All these themes are very much evident in 1:3, one of Cowper's enduringly popular hymns. First, let us try to set this hymn in context by pinpointing Cowper's understanding of providence. His sense of a 'road' that leads him to the Lamb (Jesus)[6] is a vivid expression both

[6] The image of Jesus as a sacrificial lamb is extensively used in the New Testament, asserting continuity with the Jewish Passover ritual, which entails the sacrifice of a lamb by every family.

of an underlying Calvinist belief in preordained salvation, and of a conviction (not necessarily specifically Calvinist) that God has an overruling purpose and plan for each human life. Cowper's God is neither the watchmaker of the deists who creates the world and then leaves it to run on its own, nor an arbitrary tyrant who intervenes in unpredictable ways. In Cowper's mind God follows a middle course, actively concerned and interventionist in human affairs, while following patterns and purposes that are ultimately consistent and orderly. This was the widespread eighteenth-century religious conception of providence, in which the supernatural was viewed as part of a rationally ordered Enlightenment world rather than being at odds with it. Although Cowper's state of mind as he walks along the road of his life is volatile, there is a sense of direction and movement that does not falter. Second, though, Cowper is painfully conscious of sin, not only in the explicit reference (verse 4) to the 'sins that made thee mourn', but also in his sense of wandering from the peace he once enjoyed (verse 3) and in committing idolatry (verse 5). Third, God is Cowper's personal companion on the journey, albeit one who sometimes seems a little distant. God is invoked in the different aspects of the Christian Trinity, not only the Father but the Son, Jesus, who presents a 'soul-refreshing view' to the weary traveller, and the 'holy Dove', the Holy Spirit, presented as offering 'rest' and intimate companionship.

Look now at 1:41, 'Amazing grace', which has retained its appeal well outside conventionally religious circles. An underlying theme is again the stability and order brought by God's providence into the turbulence and ultimate transience of earthly existence. The first two stanzas express Newton's acute sense of his own past sinfulness, as a 'wretch' who was once 'lost' and 'blind', who needed to be rescued by the 'amazing' grace of God. Once converted, however, the writer enjoys a sense of continued close personal relationship with God, his 'shield and portion' (verse 4) while alive, who will be 'for ever mine' (verse 6) after death. In 'Amazing grace' as in 'Oh! for a closer walk with God' we see the attraction of the Enlightenment ideal of an ordered world, but to Cowper and Newton such order emphatically requires not the absence of the supernatural, but God's abiding presence to control human disorder. In this emphasis on encounter with the deity, we seem closer to the emerging Romantic cultural world, with a strong emphasis on personal experience and the sentimental, even passionate, sense of the writer's relationship to God. (For further illustration of this point, look at hymn 1:57 ('How sweet the name of Jesus sounds', p.243), one of Newton's most intense and moving expressions of his personal feelings for Jesus.)

EXERCISE In order further to develop your understanding of Evangelicalism, read through the following four hymns: 1:60 ('Glorious things of thee are spoken', pp.244–5), 1:79 ('There is a fountain fill'd with blood', p.246), 2:62 ('The Spirit breathes upon the word', pp.255–6) and 3:48

('Sometimes a light surprizes', p.262). Then reread them and list the features of Evangelical religious belief that are evident in these hymns.

DISCUSSION My list is below. Do not worry if you have not picked up all these points for yourself, but if you are struggling to see more than one or two of them, you might benefit from rereading pages 21–5 of this unit, in order to consolidate your understanding of Evangelicalism.

(a) A sense of God as the underlying source of order, for example through the eternity of the heavenly city (1:60) contrasting with the 'fading' of the world.

(b) Calvinism, for example in Newton's sense of confident self-identification with 'Zion's children', even in this life (1:60, verse 5).

(c) The conviction that the self-sacrificial death of Jesus on the Cross satisfied the need of a just God to find some means of punishing human sinfulness, and that through close identification with that death believers would experience divine forgiveness. To Cowper and Newton that identification is such an intense personal experience that they express it in terms of being washed in Jesus' blood (1:60, verse 4; 1:79).

(d) The divinely-inspired text of the Bible as the underlying source of light and consistency in human experience (2:62).

(e) God's providential care of the individual believer (3:48).

(f) Confidence in the reality of eternal life after death (1:60, verse 5; 1:79, verse 7).

A significant number of the *Olney Hymns* reflect on the natural world in some way, and are of particular interest in illustrating cultural transitions. These include 1:46 ('How tedious and tasteless the hours', pp.239–40), 1:52 ('Ere God had built the mountains', pp.240–1), 1:103 ('The church a garden is', pp.247–8), 2:85 ('The moon in silver glory shone', pp.258–9), 3:15 ('God moves in a mysterious way', pp.260–1) and 3:83 ('Winter has a joy for me', p.264).

EXERCISE Read through these hymns, and note down answers to the following questions:

1 What attitudes to nature are apparent in these hymns? How do Newton's and Cowper's approaches differ from each other?

2 How would you relate these attitudes to a process of transition between Enlightenment and Romantic cultural worlds? (It may help to think again about the hymns by Addison and Watts that you read earlier in the unit.)

DISCUSSION 1 Two views predominate:

(a) Nature is seen as symbolic of spiritual realities that lie behind it (1:103, 2:85; 3:15, 3:83). Newton (2:85, verse 3) self-consciously looks at nature in order to 'try/Instruction to obtain'. You may justly feel that there is a contrast to be drawn between the hymns by Newton, where the spiritual symbolism seems either contrived (1:103) or predictable (2:85), and those by Cowper, where the associations are much richer and more poetic. In Cowper's lines the link is clearly but subtly made between the different phases of nature (the changing weather in 3:15, changing seasons and times of day in 3:83) and the different manifestations of a mysterious but ultimately benevolent God. The image in 3:83, verse 5, is an especially striking one, where Cowper is inspired by the vivid reds of the sunrise to think of Christ's sacrificial death on the Cross. The shocking oxymoron (i.e. an apparently self-contradictory phrase) 'bleeding beauties' and the association between something (the sunrise) we agree is beautiful and something that seems extremely ugly (a brutal execution) give a powerful insight into the centrality of the Cross in the Evangelical belief system.

(b) For Newton, though not necessarily for Cowper, nature is regarded as ultimately ephemeral in relation to the goodness, power and reality of God. For Newton in 1:46 the delights of spring and summer are nothing without personal experience of Jesus, but when he is enjoying the presence of God 'December's as pleasant as May'. In 1:52 the emphasis shifts from the personal life to theological affirmation. This hymn is about the eternal status of Jesus as the Son of God, believed to exist even before the mountains, hills, rills (streams), skies, oceans and stars were created. (Similarly, at the end of time, according to 1:41, verse 6, 'The earth shall soon dissolve like snow/The sun forbear to shine' but God 'Will be for ever mine'.)

2 If you think back to the two earlier eighteenth-century hymns that you studied, the view of nature there was a static one. Nature is either, in Addison, an orderly testimony to the reality and power of God or, in Watts, a 'present' to be offered up in response to the amazing love of Jesus Christ. In Newton and especially Cowper, we find a much more dynamic view of nature. For them its changing and varied characteristics are symbols that illuminate the differing attributes of God and his relationship to the Christian believer. Remember one of the cultural shifts identified in Unit 1 is a growing appreciation of the anarchy of nature. While for Cowper and Newton nature is not anarchic because God is ultimately in control of it, they are very much aware of its awesome and unpredictable side (2:85, 3:15). Although their sense of God as the providential power behind nature must be clearly contrasted with a more secular Romantic outlook in which nature is perceived as having a spiritual force of its

own, we can still see significant changes in attitude in the *Olney Hymns*.

Cowper was further to develop his consciousness of the revelation of God to the believer through nature in *The Task* when he wrote:

> The soul that sees him, or receives sublimed
> New faculties, or learns at least t'employ
> More worthily the pow'rs she own'd before;
> Discerns in all things, what with stupid gaze
> Of ignorance, till then she overlook'd,
> A ray of heav'nly light gilding all forms
> Terrestrial, in the vast and the minute,
> The unambiguous footsteps of the God
> Who gives its lustre to an insect's wing,
> And wheels his throne upon the rolling worlds.
>
> (*The Task*, V.805–14, quoted in Baird and Ryskamp, 1980–95, vol.2, p.231)

Cowper realizes that the sceptical and unconverted will not see God in nature, but to those who have the eye of faith, its testimony to an overarching divine purpose is inescapable.

Now that you have read a cross-section of the *Olney Hymns*, it is helpful to stand back a little and consider other ways in which they illustrate the cultural shifts between Enlightenment and Romanticism identified in Unit 1. Certainly there is much here that is consistent with the development of more fluid notions of the self and individual identity. Both Cowper and Newton write a lot about their own lives and spiritual experience. They do so in a manner very much consistent with a shift from reason to sentiment and passion, being not afraid to express strong emotions, even though they believe that God's providence brings an underlying order to their world. The individual and intensely personal nature of Evangelical religion was both a sign of a changing cultural world and an influential mechanism by which such changes were disseminated in society, a point to which we shall shortly return in the final section of this unit. The *Olney Hymns* also well illustrate the increasing incorporation of the private and personal into public culture. Hymns began life as personal statements, but through corporate singing and widespread dissemination became very much public cultural property. 'Amazing grace' (1:41) is the most striking illustration of this process.

Above all in this text we could certainly identify much to support the growing consciousness of death and the impulse towards melancholy, immortality, the divine, mystical and supernatural. We need though to be a little careful here, insofar as religious texts in any age will be concerned in some measure with matters of this kind. It can certainly be argued, though, that the *Olney Hymns* illustrate an intensification of such moods. References to death, judgement and immortality are central and recurrent. 'Melancholy' is very much apparent, especially in Cowper's hymns. Thus, for example, in 3:73 (which is not reproduced in Anthology I) he writes that 'sorrow may well possess the mind' in this life, but affirms that he seeks 'immortal joys above'. There is, however, room for debate as to how far this mood was attributable to Cowper's depressive personality, how far to his Evangelical beliefs, and how far to the wider cultural climate. There is also a consistent and powerful sense of divine and supernatural power (including the malign force of Satan as well as the benign presence of God) behind the visible everyday world, and a sense of intense mystical encounter that is both vividly experienced and earnestly sought.

5 Hymns, religion and a changing culture

How influential were the *Olney Hymns*? The comments of one early twentieth-century scholar provide a good starting point for further evaluation:

> It [*Olney Hymns*] was the Evangelical theology put into rhyme for singing but even more for reading and remembering. It became an Evangelical handbook, printed over and over again in England and America and it exerted an immense influence.
>
> (L.F. Benson, quoted in Russell, 1963, p.16)

Certainly, if we look at the publishing history of *Olney Hymns* there is strong evidence that it was very popular. By 1836 it had already gone through 37 recorded editions, with the probability that many more copies were printed in British provincial towns and in America (Russell, 1963, p.16). In addition, many of the individual hymns quickly found their way into other hymn-books, which were a burgeoning publishing industry by the beginning of the nineteenth century, as hymn singing rapidly gained in popularity. Publishers, then as now, did not extensively reprint a work unless they were aware of a strong demand for it. The extent of this demand shows clearly that this was a book bought not only by clergy and other religious 'professionals' but also by large numbers of lay people. It would seem therefore that it was a work that fitted well with the religious and cultural climate of the period. The last decade of the eighteenth century and the first third of the nineteenth were indeed a period in which the impact of the Evangelical movement very greatly increased, partly through massive growth in Methodism, partly through its increasing permeation within the Church of England. These developments will be further discussed in the next unit.

So far in this unit we have primarily been reading *Olney Hymns* in its original immediate context as an expression, written in the 1770s, of the religious beliefs and experience of its two authors. Awareness, however, of its subsequent popularity alerts us to another way of reading the text, as a source of insight into the religious outlooks of the many thousands who used it in their personal devotional lives and congregational worship. This does not mean that we should slip into supposing that merely because people read and sang Cowper's and Newton's hymns they consciously assented to every sentiment and theological position expressed in them. It is reasonable to suppose though that they were widely found to be helpful and meaningful expressions of religious belief, and that they acquired an authoritative status within rapidly expanding Evangelical communities at the end of the eighteenth century. From a religious point of view they were consciously written for 'plain people' (Preface, Anthology I, p.233) and were hence likely to be more easily understood than the text of the Bible and prose theological writing. In a wider cultural context they were familiar to many for whom the elite culture of opera, painting, and literary and philosophical writing was largely inaccessible. The success of a hymn can indeed be measured by the criteria Newton set for himself: while memorable hymns were more than pious jingles, they were seldom great poetry (although some of Cowper's hymns showed significant distinction).

In reading the text in this way it is important to bear three factors in mind. First, there was an inevitable time lag between the initial publication of the hymns and their widespread use, and they came to be sung in contexts very different from those for which they were originally written. The full extension of the influence of the text on popular Christian beliefs outside Olney itself would not have occurred until a generation or so after its first publication, that is, some 20 years after 1800. Since then some of the hymns have continued to be widely reused and adapted. 'Amazing grace' has had a particularly interesting history, acquiring great popularity in North America in the nineteenth century as an expression of popular religious revivalism.[7]

Second, individuals, church leaders and publishers were all selective in their use and dissemination of the hymns. Numerous late eighteenth- and early nineteenth-century hymn-books included selections from the *Olney Hymns*, but few reprinted more than 25 or so of them (Leaver, 1980, pp.58–9). We see the end product of this process in our own day, in the half dozen or so of the original 384 Olney hymns that still feature in church worship. While Cowper's hymns are, in general, the better poetry, Newton's capacity to write verse that expresses profound religious convictions in deceptively simple and timeless language has ensured that

[7] It even became a feature of secular culture in the later twentieth century, for example in a 1972 hit recording by the Royal Scots Dragoon Guards, and as accompaniment to the funeral of Spock in the 1982 film *Star Trek II* (Hindmarsh, 2002).

his work has retained a central place in Christian worship. For example, look at 1:57 ('How sweet the name of Jesus sounds', p.243). The simple repetitive metre of the verses and the rather mechanical rhymes (ear/fear, whole/soul, breast/rest, Friend/End, heart/art, etc.) make it very easy to memorize, and, combined with its moving expression of personal faith, have secured its appeal across the generations. Selection also operated within hymns, as verses were omitted either because they did not appeal or in order to make a hymn shorter and more manageable. Later editors and writers were also quite ready to amend the original text if they felt it could, from their point of view, be improved. This process was even underway before *Olney Hymns* was published: in 3:15, verse 5, Cowper's original last line was 'But wait, to smell the flower'. Newton appears to have changed his friend's text to 'But sweet will be the flower', a more confident but arguably more mundane version (Watson, 1985, p.50).

Third, linkages between words and music were important in the image and popularity of hymns. Newton and Cowper – as far as is known – did not write any music to accompany their hymns, and so these were initially sung to any available tune that fitted the metre, most probably in Olney to metrical psalm tunes dating back to the sixteenth and seventeenth centuries. It is possible that they might also have been sung to livelier, more elaborate, contemporary tunes such as those in a book published by Martin Madan in 1769, but as both Cowper and Newton preferred simple musical accompaniments it is unlikely that this happened in Olney (Leaver, 1980, pp.60–3). Subsequently, words could become linked to tunes written later, perhaps many decades later, than the verses. These associations could secure enduring popularity. For example, the simple tune 'St Peter' by A.R. Reinagle (1799–1877) used from 1861 for 'How sweet the name of Jesus sounds' perfectly complements the artlessness of the words, while the linking of 'Glorious things of thee are spoken' to Josef Haydn's (1732–1809) magnificent stirring tune 'Austria' has ensured it a lasting place in rousing collective worship. The tune 'New Britain' that is now inextricably bound up with 'Amazing grace' did not become associated with the words until the 1830s, and is an American folk melody with possible Scottish origins (Hindmarsh, 2002).

Some of the music that came to be associated with the *Olney Hymns* is sung and discussed on Audio 4, tracks 1–11: *The Olney Hymns and Popular Religious Music*. This would be a good point at which to listen to it. You should also read the corresponding AV Notes.

As these tracks demonstrate, the congregational experience of hymn singing was very much shaped by the tunes as well as the words. These tunes were in themselves part of a constantly changing popular musical culture. Accordingly, we must not see hymns as merely a fixed product of the mind of particular authors at a specific moment in time. In reality, they were part of continually evolving religious traditions in which their own content, and the way in which they were read and sung, could be

Figure 10.8 Anonymous, 'The public worship of God' from The Pearl of Days, *no.12, December 1881, p.45. Photo: Mary Evans Picture Library, London.*

This image of a Victorian congregation singing, a century after the Olney Hymns *were published, prompts reflection on how the use of the texts in worship would have changed during that period. By the mid-nineteenth century, hymns had become a central and accepted part of worship in most churches, in contrast to their unofficial and informal status in Newton's and Cowper's day. The tunes used would almost certainly have been different from those familiar to Olney parishioners in the 1770s.*

very fluid. It is impossible for historians to reconstruct all the nuances of these processes, but it is very important to be aware that they were occurring (see Figure 10.8).

In order further to develop your awareness of hymns as an expression of changing attitudes and beliefs, I shall conclude this unit by asking you to look at three examples of early nineteenth-century hymns which reflect the more fully developed impact of Romanticism. These are Robert Grant's 'O worship the King' (1833), Reginald Heber's 'From Greenland's icy mountains' (1819), and James Montgomery's 'Hail to the Lord's anointed' (1821).

EXERCISE Read these three hymns (Anthology I, pp.265–9) and consider the following questions:

1 In what ways do these writers develop trends we have already identified in the *Olney Hymns*? (You may find it most helpful to think about attitudes to the natural world and God's relationship to it.)

2 What different features do you notice in these hymns which you did not encounter in the *Olney Hymns*?

DISCUSSION

1 In all three hymns there is considerable fluency in relating God to the natural world, which contrasts with Newton's somewhat wooden approach to natural imagery and extends Cowper's creative explorations. Grant uses vivid imagery drawn from the natural world – light and space, 'deep thunderclouds' (verse 2), and a gentler sense of permeating dew and rain (verse 4). In Montgomery too there are both a gentle representation of nature (verse 4) as testimony to the goodness and care of God, and more majestic and expansive ones (verses 3 and 6) that evoke the divine greatness as the ultimate source of stability in a volatile world. Heber evokes the richness of the natural world (verses 1 and 2) and (verse 4) visualizes the winds and waters as carriers of knowledge of the Messiah (Jesus).

2 A number of different features are apparent:

(a) Grant's initial portrayal of God (verse 1) is as a medieval potentate wearing his armour and situated in a splendid pavilion, a characteristically Romantic evocation of a remote historical past.

(b) These hymns have less emphasis on the personal 'I' dimension of Christianity than the *Olney Hymns,* tending rather to dwell on the attributes of God and the collective experience of believers. I would not generalize too much from this point, but it is an indication that these writers were less preoccupied than Newton and Cowper with the personal repentance and conversion characteristic of early Evangelicals.

(c) In both the Heber and the Montgomery hymns there is a strong sense both of the exotic and of the relevance of the Christian message to a world beyond the shores of Britain. This was a reflection of growing interest in foreign missions from the 1790s onwards. The unabashed sense of cultural and spiritual superiority in 'From Greenland's icy mountains' may well shock you, but it provides a vivid insight into states of mind characteristic of the period.

(d) In 'Hail to the Lord's anointed' there is a vision that goes beyond spiritual conversion to include social and political change as the outworking of Christianity. Oppression is to be broken, captives to be 'let free', help given to the 'poor and needy', and equity and justice established. Here is one kind of religious response to the sense of potential for radical change stirred by the French Revolution. Such sentiments, as we shall see, helped to inspire the campaign against slavery.

6 Conclusion

Through hymns therefore we are able to chart some of the transitions between Enlightenment and Romanticism, but we also become increasingly aware that neither of these broad phases in European culture can be neatly pigeonholed. I hope in particular that through your work on this unit you have been stimulated to revise any initial preconception you may have formed of religion being necessarily hostile to the Enlightenment. The *Olney Hymns* are indicative rather of a more ambivalent and multifaceted relationship. In tracking subsequent changes, moreover, we need to be conscious of an ongoing two-way relationship between religion and secular culture. On the one hand, we can see cultural shifts reflected in hymn texts; on the other, we need to be aware that this was an age in which religion was a dynamic and formative cultural influence in its own right. We shall develop this point in our study in the next unit of William Wilberforce's ideas and impact.

References

Baird, J.D. and Ryskamp, C. (eds) (1980–95) *The Poems of William Cowper*, 3 vols, Oxford, Clarendon Press.

Bebbington, D.W. (1993) *Evangelicalism in Modern Britain: A History from the 1730s to the 1980s*, London and New York, Routledge (first published by Unwin Hyman, 1989).

Curnock, N. (ed.) (1909–16) *The Journal of the Rev. John Wesley, AM*, 8 vols, London, Charles H. Kelly.

Ella, G.M. (1993) *William Cowper: Poet of Paradise*, Darlington, Evangelical Press.

Gilbert, A.D. (1976) *Religion and Society in Industrial England: Church, Chapel and Social Change, 1740–1914*, London, Longman.

Hindmarsh, B. (1996) *John Newton and the English Evangelical Tradition between the Conversions of Wesley and Wilberforce*, Oxford, Clarendon Press.

Hindmarsh, B. (2002) 'Amazing grace, how sweet it has sounded: the history of a hymn and a cultural icon', unpublished paper.

Kent, J. (2002) *Wesley and the Wesleyans: Religion in Eighteenth-Century Britain*, Cambridge, Cambridge University Press.

Leaver, R.A. (1979) '*Olney Hymns* 1779: 1. The book and its origins', *Churchman*, 93, pp.327–41.

Leaver, R.A. (1980) '*Olney Hymns* 1779: 2. The hymns and their uses', *Churchman,* 94, pp.58–66.

Porter, R. and Teich, M. (eds) (1981) *The Enlightenment in National Context,* Cambridge, Cambridge University Press.

Rivers, I. (2001) 'Responses to Hume on religion by Anglicans and Dissenters', *Journal of Ecclesiastical History,* 52, pp.675–95.

Russell, N. (1963) *A Bibliography of William Cowper to 1837,* Oxford, Oxford Bibliographical Society.

Watson, J.R. (1985) 'Cowper's *Olney Hymns*', *Essays and Studies,* 38.

Further reading

Bebbington, D.W. (1993) *Evangelicalism in Modern Britain: A History from the 1730s to the 1980s,* London and New York, Routledge (first published by Unwin Hyman, 1989). The standard modern history of the Evangelical movement.

Davie, D. (1993) *The Eighteenth-Century Hymn in England,* Cambridge, Cambridge University Press.

Hindmarsh, B. (1996) *John Newton and the English Evangelical Tradition between the Conversions of Wesley and Wilberforce,* Oxford, Clarendon Press. The best account of Newton and his work in historical and religious context.

Kent, J. (2002) *Wesley and the Wesleyans: Religion in Eighteenth-Century Britain,* Cambridge, Cambridge University Press. A challenge to traditional historical interpretations.

Marshall, M.F. and Todd, J. (1982) *English Congregational Hymns in the Eighteenth Century,* Lexington, University Press of Kentucky.

Ward, W.R. (1999) *Christianity under the Ancien Régime 1648–1789,* Cambridge, Cambridge University Press. An overview of religion in Europe as a whole, with particular attention to Evangelicalism and its antecedents.

Watson, J.R. (1997) *The English Hymn: A Critical and Historical Study,* Oxford, Oxford University Press. An overview of the development of hymns as literary and religious texts.

Unit 11
William Wilberforce

Prepared for the course team by John Wolffe

Contents

Study components

Weeks of study	*Supplementary material*	*Audio-visual*	*Anthologies and set books*
1	AV Notes	Audio 3 Video 2	Anthology I

Objectives

When you have completed your work on Unit 11 you should have developed:

- a knowledge of key aspects of William Wilberforce's political career and writings, and an appreciation of their historical and religious significance;
- an enhanced awareness of the relationship of Evangelicalism to cultural transitions between Enlightenment and Romanticism;
- an understanding of the contribution of religion to cultural, social and political change in Britain in the years after the French Revolution.

1 Introduction

In the early summer of 1771, John Newton was visited at Olney by two of his admirers, William and Hannah Wilberforce, a wealthy childless couple, and their 11-year-old nephew and heir, also named William (Bodleian Library, Oxford, MS Wilberforce c. 49, f. 120). Newton made a profound impression on the boy. In 1785 it was to Newton that the younger William Wilberforce (1759–1833), now Member of Parliament for Yorkshire and a close friend of Prime Minister William Pitt (the Younger), turned for counsel in the midst of a period of spiritual crisis. Wilberforce's commitment to Evangelicalism was to be a defining feature of a remarkable political career, the most notable feature of which was his long campaign for British abolition of the slave trade. Wilberforce was also concerned with spiritual and moral conditions at home, stating his views in his book *A Practical View of the Prevailing Religious System of Professed Christians ..., Contrasted with Real Christianity*, published in 1797 and very popular and influential at the time. Extracts from this text and from writings on slavery will form the subject matter of this unit. Through a study of Wilberforce you will gain insights not only into the interactions between the Evangelical movement and its wider social and political environment, but also into the impact of the French Revolution on Britain and into British relations with the non-European world, as focused by the campaign against slavery. Such an understanding will provide a context for your study, later in the block, first of Mungo Park's travels in Africa, and then of the experiences of the slaves themselves.

2 Wilberforce's early career

William Wilberforce (see Figure 11.1) was born in Hull, the son and grandson of substantial merchants who had made their fortune in trade between Yorkshire and the Baltic. His father died in 1768 and he subsequently went to live for a period with his uncle and aunt. Through them he was exposed not only to the influence of John Newton, but also to that of George Whitefield, one of the major leaders of early Evangelicalism and of the Methodist movement. His mother sought to steer him rather towards a more conventional Christianity, and appeared successful in the short term. William graduated from Cambridge in 1780 as a sociable and ambitious young man, morally upright by the standards of the day, but without any signs of intense religious commitment. He had already decided that his future lay in politics rather than in the family business, and almost as soon as he was of age he was elected MP for Hull, in September 1780. In 1784 he became MP for the county of Yorkshire, an immense and populous constituency, which gave him an important power base.

Figure 11.1 John Rising, William Wilberforce, *oil on canvas, 220 × 130 cm, Wilberforce House, Hull City Museums and Art Galleries. Photo: Bridgeman Art Library.*

This portrait depicts Wilberforce in 1789, at the time that the campaign against the slave trade was gathering momentum. The sense of chaotic, earnest energy is characteristic.

Wilberforce came into Parliament at a time of considerable political turmoil. Eighteenth-century affiliations were fluid in comparison to the modern party system. The labels 'Whig' and 'Tory' had first emerged in the religious and constitutional conflicts of the late seventeenth century, but had changed their meaning during the course of the following century. Since the accession of George III in 1760 the Tories, who had been in the political wilderness for decades, had enjoyed a recovery, being favoured by the king, who saw them as a means to assert his own influence against the aristocratic Whig cliques who had previously dominated Parliament. In the early 1780s, however, the Whigs regained ground, benefiting politically from concern about a perceived growth in royal influence and military defeat in the War of American Independence (1775–83) for which the Tory government of Lord North was held responsible. They were, though, seriously weakened by their own factionalism, which made it impossible for them to form a stable administration after North's government fell in March 1782. Following two turbulent years the king appointed as prime minister the 24-year-old William Pitt, hitherto identified with the Whigs and supportive of reforms that would remove obvious corruptions and abuses, but willing to uphold the continued constitutional influence of the monarchy. Hence he came to be perceived as a Tory. Pitt was to remain prime minister until his death in 1806, apart from a short gap between 1801 and 1804. Wilberforce was a close friend of Pitt's and his political position was a similarly broadly conservative one, committed to the essentials of the existing social order and constitutional structure, but keen to promote moderate reforms.

Wilberforce's religious 'conversion' in 1785 was profound but not instantaneous. Through the influence of Isaac Milner, an Evangelical clergyman who was his companion on extended journeys on the Continent, he first became intellectually convinced of the truth of Christian doctrines that he had doubted in the early 1780s. This process of rational argument, study and consideration was characteristic of an Enlightenment way of thinking, even if the conclusion was diametrically opposed to that of sceptical Enlightenment philosophers. Then, in November 1785, Wilberforce had an intense spiritual experience, making him feel that his own past life was futile, that he was utterly dependent on the infinite love of Christ, and that his future life must be committed to the service of God. It was in the endeavour to come to terms with these new convictions that he recalled his boyhood acquaintance with Newton, now rector of St Mary Woolnoth in the City of London, and turned to him for advice. Newton, evidently perceiving in Wilberforce a recruit to Evangelicalism of great potential influence, counteracted his impulse to withdraw into primarily spiritual concerns, and strongly counselled him to remain in politics. This advice was heeded. Moreover, although Wilberforce's new-found convictions gave him a strong strain of zealous earnestness that ran through his writings and speeches, he remained on the surface an easy-going, extrovert and likeable person, who could inspire considerable affection even from those who disagreed with him. He also remained a shrewd 'political animal' whose strong commitment to long-term visions and objectives did not prevent considerable flexibility in short-term tactics. Herein lay key reasons for his success in pursuing sometimes unpopular causes.

Wilberforce's conversion confirmed an inclination to follow an independent parliamentary career rather than to accept the constraints that would have come from seeking and holding government office. He was assisted in this respect by considerable personal wealth that freed him from any financial necessity for holding a salaried post. During 1787 the two pre-eminent concerns of the rest of his career became clear. First, he emerged as the parliamentary leader of the growing campaign for the abolition of the slave trade, complementing the activities of Thomas Clarkson (1760–1846)[8] and others who sought to stir up popular sentiment against slavery. Second, he began purposefully to promote moral and spiritual reform at home, initially through obtaining the issue of a royal proclamation 'for the Encouragement of Piety and Virtue'.

When Wilberforce made his first major speech against the slave trade in the House of Commons in April 1789, few could have anticipated that it was the start of a campaign that he would have doggedly to maintain for 18 years. During most of the period between 1789 and 1807 Wilberforce brought forward at least one anti-slave trade motion or measure every year, to be met often with defeat, sometimes with partial successes that could not be translated into effective legislation. His initial timing was unfortunate because the outbreak of the French Revolution only a few months later stirred over the next few years a growing sense of insecurity in the British political elite. War with France followed in 1793. This meant that the abolition of the slave trade was liable to be regarded with enhanced suspicion because of the potential for unforeseeable consequences, notably in relation to the economics of overseas trade and British strategic interests in the West Indies. (You will find a fuller discussion of the background to the campaign against the slave trade when you study Unit 14 later in this block.)

It was in the early years of the Revolutionary Wars that Wilberforce, currently stalemated in his campaign against the slave trade and increasingly concerned about the condition of society at home, began work on the *Practical View*. Before looking more closely at this text, however, we set the scene with reference to the state of British religion, politics and society in the aftermath of the French Revolution.

[8] Clarkson became the driving force behind the Committee for the Abolition of the Slave Trade and published a classic account of the movement in 1808.

3 Britain in the 1790s

EXERCISE As an exercise in revision and reflection, I should like you before you read further to look back at Block 1, Unit 6 on the French Revolution. Clearly, events across the Channel from mid-1789 onwards were to have a profound impact on Britain. On the basis of Unit 6, answer the following questions:

1 What specific British reactions to the French Revolution are mentioned?

2 What were the implications of the French Revolution for religion? (Try to think here about Britain as well as France.)

3 How do you think British perceptions of France changed between 1789 and 1797?

DISCUSSION 1 In Unit 6 (p.263) and in *Reflections on the Revolution in France* (Anthology I, pp.80–1) you learned of Edmund Burke's hostile reaction to the Revolution, which he perceived as a dangerous destruction of tradition and continuity in favour of abstract Enlightenment principles. On the other hand (Unit 6, p.266), there was a substantial cross-section of British opinion that initially warmly welcomed the Revolution, including Wilberforce himself, as well as much more radical individuals, such as Thomas Paine. The lines from Wordsworth that Lentin quotes (Unit 6, p.266) sum up an atmosphere of widespread excitement and a sense of new beginnings. (This might be compared, perhaps, with the feelings experienced by many in the much more recent past in response to events such as the coming down of the Berlin Wall and the ending of apartheid in South Africa.)

2 Initially, the revolutionaries in France did not appear hostile to religion in general, although from an early stage the rationalist and Enlightenment ethos of the Revolution was reflected in quite radical reform of the Roman Catholic Church. From July 1790 the imposition of the Civil Constitution of the Clergy gave rise to a growing divide between the revolutionary government and the Church. Then in 1793 and 1794 there was an outright assault on traditional Catholic belief and the attempt to establish the cult of the Supreme Being in its place. This proved to be a temporary phase, but the enduring legacy of the Revolution in France was freedom of religion, in which non-Catholics enjoyed civil equality, and the ending of the privileged status of the Roman Catholic Church as an 'estate' of the realm.

The implications for Britain are not spelt out in Unit 6, but I hope you have formed some ideas. From the point of view of the established churches the spectacle of the growing revolutionary onslaught on the French Roman Catholic Church was a double-sided one. For Protestants there were initially few regrets at the prospect of reforming what they believed to be false religion, but as it became clear that the preferred revolutionary alternative to Catholicism was not Protestantism but deism, they became much more uneasy. At the same time the constitutional adoption of the principle of freedom in religion in France gave a boost to Dissenters from the Church of England, while heightening the insecurities of the supporters of the existing Church establishment.

3 The initial British perception of the Revolution was of a moderate move away from corrupt absolute monarchy towards the kind of 'balanced' constitution on which the British elite prided itself. It was therefore welcomed by all but the most conservative. As, however, in the early 1790s more radical and violent elements gained ground in Paris, erstwhile British sympathizers tended to become much more uneasy. Their fears were confirmed by the execution of Louis XVI in January 1793, and after the outbreak of war in the following month the French and above all the supporters of the Revolution tended to be demonized as enemies. Thereafter too the minority in Britain who continued to identify enthusiastically with the Revolution were liable to be labelled as subversives and traitors.

A problem that has exercised historians for many years is, put in its most concise form: why was there no revolution in Britain in the 1790s? The question is a significant one for our current purposes, because religious factors have formed an important strand in the answers that have been given. The intellectual trend was set by the publication in 1913 of *England in 1815*, in which the French historian Elie Halévy (1870–1937) argued that the growth of Methodism in this period was a key factor in the British avoidance of revolution (Olsen, 1990). Later scholars gave their attention not only to Methodism but also to the role of the wider Evangelical movement, including Wilberforce and Evangelicals within the Church of England (for example, Kiernan, 1952). In 1984 the view was again advanced that 'evangelicalism ... may, at least for some, have averted a potentially dangerous build-up of frustration and political discontent' (Christie, 1984, pp.213–14). There is no space here to go into the detail of a very complex and protracted scholarly debate, and in any case you might reasonably feel that trying to explain why something *did not* happen is ultimately a rather confusing business! Nevertheless, some points are worth highlighting in setting the scene for our discussion of Wilberforce's writings.

The 1790s were indeed a period of substantial social and political stress. At just the time the French Revolution broke out, the so-called 'Industrial Revolution' was quickly gathering momentum, with associated rapid population growth, over-crowded and squalid living conditions, and reorganization of traditional patterns of work and daily life. Supplies of food were sometimes erratic, giving rise to riots in 1795–6 and again in 1800–1. The outbreak of war led to substantial depression and unemployment because of the loss of export markets. Those in traditional industries such as handloom weaving, whose livelihoods were being threatened by the growth of new and more efficient technologies, experienced particular hardship. There were also significant ideological and organizational rallying points for those discontented with the existing order. Thomas Paine's *Rights of Man*, published in 1791, advocated the foundation of society on an Enlightenment conception of 'natural rights' rather than on the basis of historical patterns and precedents. Paine believed that such a vision was currently being realized in France. Radical Dissenters campaigned for civil equality with Anglicans. During the early 1790s there was a substantial movement of popular radical societies campaigning for political reform, centred on the London Corresponding Society (see Figure 11.2) and, at its peak, having a presence in more than 80 English towns and cities. North of the border a General Convention of the Friends of the People in Scotland met in 1792. Apart from an extreme fringe, this was a movement for peaceful constitutional change rather than violent revolution (Stevenson, 1989).

It was also strongly and effectively opposed at a popular level by 'loyalist' organizations that upheld the existing social and political structure. Nevertheless, conservatives were alarmed by the mere existence of popular radicalism, given the backdrop of revolution and war on the Continent and occasional instances of riot and unrest at home. Pitt's government responded vigorously, prosecuting some radical leaders and in 1794 suspending habeas corpus, enabling them to hold suspected agitators without trial. In late 1795 it rushed through legislation extending the definition of treason to include any attempts to intimidate the government or Parliament, and banning 'seditious' meetings of more than 50 people. Wilberforce himself made a dramatic dash to York at the beginning of December 1795 to speak at a Yorkshire county meeting in defence of the government's policy, arguing that it was not repression but a necessary safeguard of true balanced liberty.

If you wish to refresh your memory on the political situation in Britain in the 1790s, listen again to Audio 3, tracks 1–7: *Britain and the French Revolution*, presented by Clive Emsley, and reread the corresponding AV Notes.

The 1790s also saw a rapid growth in Evangelicalism. Methodist membership increased from 56,605 in 1791 to 91,825 only a decade later (Gilbert, 1976, p.31). These figures almost certainly substantially understate the numbers of those influenced by Methodism by attending meetings, worship and preaching but not formally becoming members. Although there were some radical leanings within Methodism, as reflected in a split leading to the formation of the Methodist New

Figure 11.2 James Gillray, Copenhagen House 1795, *etching on paper, Corporation of London Libraries and Guildhall Art Gallery, London. Photo: © Corporation of London.*

A meeting of the radical London Corresponding Society in October 1795 is here vividly portrayed by the well-known caricaturist, James Gillray. Despite the movement's wish to reshape the constitution, the impression given is more of good-natured protest than of revolutionary subversion.

Connexion in 1797, the great majority of the movement was conservative or at least apolitical (see Figure 11.3). In a controversial section of his *Making of the English Working Class* (1963) E.P. Thompson emphasized the role of Methodism both in reconciling the poor to industrial work discipline and in deflecting them from revolution by turning their hopes for a better world towards the next life rather than this one.

Evangelicalism was also expanding elsewhere. The numbers of **Baptists** and **Congregationalists**,[9] many of whom were influenced by the movement, grew by more than a third between 1790 and 1800 (Gilbert,

[9] Baptists, with their distinctive insistence on adult baptism, and Congregrationalists, who stressed the autonomy of the local congregation, were two of the main groups of Protestant Dissenters whose forbears left the Church of England in the seventeenth century.

Figure 11.3 Anonymous, Love Feast of the Wesleyan Methodists, *1820, engraving. Photo: Mary Evans Picture Library, London.*

By the early nineteenth century, Methodists – at least the more respectable and conservative Wesleyan Methodists – had generally moved away from the revivalist outdoor preaching of their early years and had built permanent chapels, which became a focus for community and social order. This engraving by an unknown artist depicts a Love Feast, or Holy Communion service, around 1820.

1976, p.37). Although Evangelicals remained a small minority within the Church of England, they were nevertheless gaining ground. Wilberforce was one of a small but influential circle of prominent lay converts, who provided respectability and substantial financial resources. Moreover, even before the publication of the *Practical View*, a substantial Evangelical literary contribution was coming from the pen of Hannah More (1745–1833), a Bristol-based writer and teacher (see Figure 11.4). Her *Thoughts on the Importance of the Manners of the Great* (1788) anticipated Wilberforce by criticizing the elite for their failures of morality and social responsibility. In a series of tracts directed at the lower classes beginning with *Village Politics* (1792), she diffused an anti-revolutionary message extolling the virtues of a well-ordered society. These publications were very widely distributed during the 1790s.

Figure 11.4 Henry William Pickersgill, Hannah More, *exhibited 1822, oil on canvas, 125.7 × 89.5 cm, National Portrait Gallery, London. Photo: by courtesy of the National Portrait Gallery, London.*

4 Wilberforce's *Practical View*

The *Practical View* is significant both as a kind of 'manifesto' by a prominent figure in a religious movement of rapidly expanding influence, and as part of an ongoing process of reflection on the state of British politics and society in the aftermath of the French Revolution. Wilberforce had been working on it intermittently for four years before its eventual publication on 12 April 1797. As a busy politician he struggled to find the time for sustained writing. He had initially had a pamphlet in mind, but the project grew in the making, and the book when it appeared was a substantial one of 491 pages. It has a somewhat rambling style: Wilberforce was prone to write as he talked, offering much eloquent rhetoric and lively insight, but he had neither the time nor the inclination for systematic and tightly structured thinking. (It is important to bear in mind therefore that the extracts reproduced in Anthology I are a small part of the whole work, and slimmed-down portions even of the chapters from which they are taken.) Wilberforce's underlying concern was to communicate what he believed to be the essential features of biblical Christianity to his contemporaries, first inspiring a commitment to 'real Christianity' in them, and thereby transforming the moral, political and social state of the nation. The work was an immediate success, selling 7,500 copies and being reprinted five times within six months of its first publication. It went through nine English editions by 1811 and 18 by 1830. It was published in the United States in 1798, and translated into French in 1821 and Spanish in 1827.

In the opinion of Daniel Wilson, a prominent Evangelical clergyman in the next generation, 'Never, perhaps, did any volume by a layman on a religious subject, produce a deeper or more sudden effect' (1829, p.xvii). Its appeal was attributable in part to the prominence of its author, both as politician and as Evangelical leader, and in part to its offering of a vision for personal and national salvation at a time of considerable insecurities. In the spring of 1797 Britain found itself completely isolated in the war against France. Then, within a few days of the publication of the *Practical View*, a series of naval mutinies broke out in the fleets stationed in Spithead off Portsmouth and in the Thames estuary. In 1798 there was a rebellion in Ireland. These years were perceived by some at the time and since as a moment of real danger of revolution. In this context any book that offered a diagnosis of underlying national difficulties and a possible solution to them was likely to attract considerable interest. (There is discussion of the situation between 1797 and 1801 on Audio 3, tracks 5 and 6 which provides helpful background for your study of the *Practical View*.)

EXERCISE Look at the illustration of the frontispiece, including the full cumbersome title, *A Practical View of the Prevailing Religious System of Professed Christians, in the Higher and Middle Classes in this Country, Contrasted with Real Christianity* (Figure 11.5), and read the Introduction (Anthology I, pp.270–2). Then answer the following questions:

1 What image of himself do you think Wilberforce wanted to project through the book?

2 What further insights do you gain into his motives for writing it?

DISCUSSION 1 Wilberforce is very consciously trying to portray himself *both* as someone seriously concerned about religion *and* as an active public figure. His name and his position as 'Member of Parliament for the County of York' boldly appear on the title page. He is not sheltering behind the anonymity common among authors at this period, but deliberately using his own name, status and reputation as a means to arouse interest in the book. He is apologetic that 'busyness' deprives him of the opportunity for 'undistracted and mature reflection', but makes a virtue out of his lay status, which means that he cannot be accused of having a professional interest in promoting religion. His 'view' of the state of religion in the country is to be that of a 'practical' man, distinguished from the abstract theology written by the clergy.

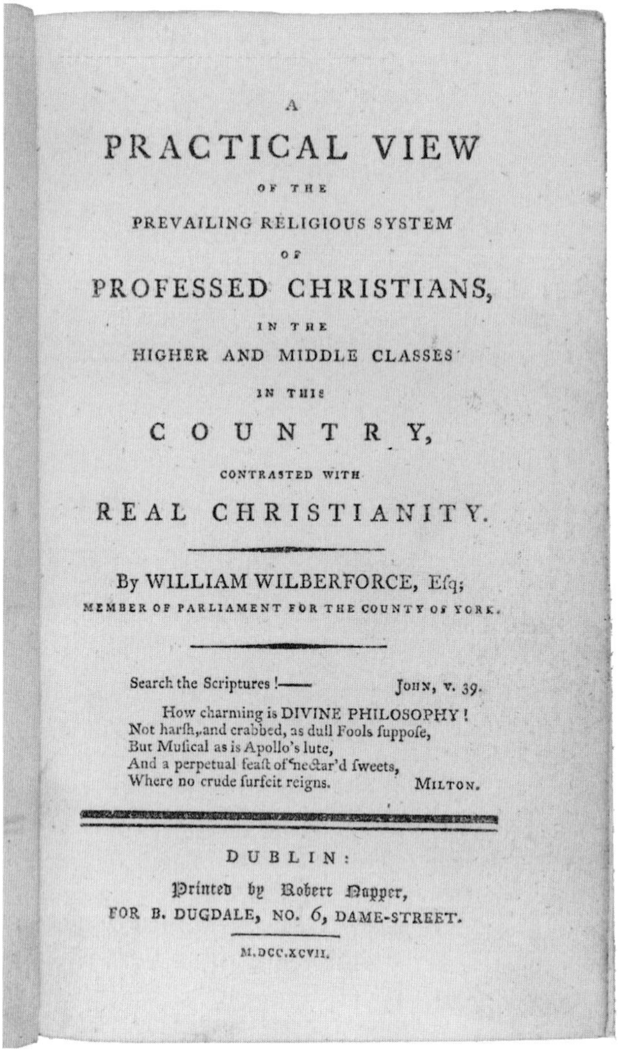

A

PRACTICAL VIEW

OF THE

PREVAILING RELIGIOUS SYSTEM

OF

PROFESSED CHRISTIANS,

IN THE

HIGHER AND MIDDLE CLASSES

IN THIS

COUNTRY,

CONTRASTED WITH

REAL CHRISTIANITY.

By WILLIAM WILBERFORCE, Efq;

MEMBER OF PARLIAMENT FOR THE COUNTY OF YORK.

Search the Scriptures !— JOHN, v. 39.

How charming is DIVINE PHILOSOPHY !
Not harſh, and crabbed, as dull Fools ſuppoſe,
But Muſical as is Apollo's lute,
And a perpetual feaſt of nectar'd ſweets,
Where no crude ſurfeit reigns. MILTON.

DUBLIN:

Printed by Robert Napper,

FOR B. DUGDALE, NO. 6, DAME-STREET.

M.DCC.XCVII.

Figure 11.5 Frontispiece of A Practical View of the Prevailing Religious System of Professed Christians, in the Higher and Middle Classes in this Country, Contrasted with Real Christianity, *1797, British Library, London. Photo: by permission of the British Library, London (shelfmark 1608/3553 T/P).*

Title page of the 1797 Dublin first edition of William Wilberforce's Practical View. *The book was published almost simultaneously in both London and Dublin.*

2 The title immediately establishes Wilberforce's central – and characteristically Evangelical – preoccupation with the dichotomy between 'real' and nominal Christianity. It also identifies his target as the 'higher and middle classes': while Wilberforce was worried about the spiritual and social state of the lower classes as well, he is not primarily concerned with them in this book. His overriding motivation is a spiritual one, calling his contemporaries to respond to the call of 'real Christianity' in this life before they have to face the judgement of Christ in the next. At the same time, though, he also believes religion to be 'intimately connected with the temporal interests of society', and accordingly that his work has an immediate relevance to the current political situation.

Following the Introduction, Wilberforce describes what he regards as an inadequate consciousness of the real teachings of Christianity among those who profess to adhere to it. This ignorance is grounded in a widespread failure to study the Bible in any depth and detail. He then expounds the Evangelical view of human nature as fundamentally corrupt, evil and depraved, as against the 'professed Christian' view that it is 'naturally pure and inclined to all virtue'. In this darkly pessimistic view of human nature, Wilberforce was also at variance with the relatively optimistic perception of humanity held by secular or deist Enlightenment writers. For him, such an insufficient awareness of sin leads to a failure to appreciate the central importance of the self-sacrifice of Jesus Christ in reconciling human beings to God and delivering them 'from eternal misery'.

In an interesting digression Wilberforce comments on the role of emotions in religion, a passage that indicates the transitional nature of this text between Enlightenment and Romantic attitudes. He observes that the 'idea of our feelings being out of place in religion is an opinion which is very prevalent', a view that he holds to be 'pernicious'. Warm feelings, he argues, are very much expressed and advocated in the Bible, and, moreover, at a human level need to be cultivated and encouraged as a basis for worthwhile achievement. 'Mere knowledge on its own', Wilberforce maintains, 'is not enough'. He therefore seems very much to be reflecting and encouraging one of the main cultural shifts with which we are concerned in this course, that 'from reason to sentiment and passion'. But in the very same passage he also shows his ties to the Enlightenment state of mind: he feels the need to justify his appeal to feelings as 'reasonable', on the grounds that it is supported by the authoritative text of Scripture and by the commonsense experience of life. And while the emotions need to be encouraged, they must also be controlled and tested in the objective examination of one's daily life and achievements. Although it might at first seem difficult to cultivate warm feelings towards an invisible deity, in fact such emotions are 'reasonable' because they are encouraged by Scripture and apparent in the experience of Christians in past ages.

In the following lengthy chapter Wilberforce expands his comparison of a perceived widespread 'inadequate' understanding and practice of Christianity with his conception of 'real' Christianity. He addresses specific issues such as Sunday observance, advocating that the day should be 'spent cheerfully' on spiritual pursuits, helping others and spending uplifting time with family and friends. He denounces the contemporary practice of duelling as 'the disgrace of a Christian society'. He criticizes a tendency to equate Christianity merely with being considerate to others and leading a useful life. Such specific spiritual exhortations and moral critique of his contemporaries build up to his reiteration of what he believes to be the 'grand radical defect in the practical system of these nominal Christians' in the next extract in

Anthology I ('Grand defect – neglect of the peculiar doctrines of Christianity', pp.272–6).

EXERCISE Read this extract now alongside my commentary below, which will help you to understand this central pivot of Wilberforce's argument and to appreciate its significance in the wider context of the course.

(p.272) After the extensive preceding discussion of moral and lifestyle issues, Wilberforce now asserts the fundamental underlying importance of doctrinal issues. The three points he emphasizes – the corruption of human nature, the atonement of the Saviour (Jesus) and the 'sanctifying influence of the Holy Spirit' – have already been at least touched on in our discussion of *Olney Hymns.* First, for Wilberforce as for Cowper and Newton, human nature is fundamentally flawed or, in theological terms, sinful. Sin comes not only from specific wrongdoing but from selfishness, neglect of doing good, and from a state of mind in rebellion against God. Sin is inherent to humanity (a doctrine known as 'original sin'), and dates back to Adam's and Eve's eating of the fruit of the forbidden tree in the Garden of Eden. This pessimistic view of human nature is clearly at variance with the more optimistic visions of human potential inherent in much Enlightenment thought, and nowhere more so than in the visionary schemes of the revolutionaries in France to create an ideal society. Second, 'the atonement of the Saviour' is shorthand for that sense of being 'Wash'd in the Redeemer's blood' that you met in *Olney Hymns* such as 'Glorious things of thee are spoken' (1:60, pp.244–5) and 'There is a fountain fill'd with blood' (1:79, p.246). God's justice means that he has to punish sinful humanity, but by dying on the Cross Jesus satisfies the need for judicial retribution. The 'sanctifying influence of the Holy Spirit' is not so much a feature of the *Olney Hymns,* but is nevertheless apparent in lines such as Cowper's 'Return, O holy Dove, return' (1:3, verse 4, p.235). In traditional Christian teaching, following the resurrection of Jesus and his ascension into heaven, the Holy Spirit was a supernatural force poured out by God on his followers at Pentecost. It empowered them to continue to follow Jesus now that he was no longer physically present on earth, and to proclaim the Christian Gospel to others. For Wilberforce it is crucial to recognize the Holy Spirit's continuing presence today as a source of strength and power for holy and obedient Christian living, which is what he means by 'sanctifying influence'. Here too, in emphasizing the supernatural dimension of religion, Wilberforce is reflecting a wider cultural shift towards Romanticism.

(p.273) Before developing the assertions of the first two paragraphs directly, Wilberforce digresses to consider two kinds of religious resolution that he considers inadequate. First, bereavement or illness

induces an awareness of mortality and leads someone to feel they have offended God. Hence they resolve to lead a more moral life in future. However, either they give up the attempt, or they set themselves too low a standard and become offensively complacent.

(pp.273–4) Second, there are those who really try hard, but become depressed by their own failures, being either driven to despair or to give up Christian belief altogether ('infidelity'). Note Wilberforce's implication that unbelief is a result of misconception and spiritual difficulty rather than an outcome of rational reflection.

(pp.274–6) The advice of conventional religious teachers that such strugglers should merely do their best and trust that all will be well is misleading comfort. Rather the Bible and, Wilberforce significantly adds, the official teaching of the Church of England itself require a much more radical approach. There needs to be heartfelt recognition of the goodness of Christ, leading to deep penitence and dependence on the grace of God for forgiveness. Holiness cannot be achieved by unaided human exertion, but requires first reconciliation to God through repentance and then the enabling power of the Holy Spirit.

(p.276) Failure to appreciate the above is the fundamental error of most nominal Christians. They need a much more profound sense of the depth of their own sinfulness, of the worth of the soul and of the costliness of Jesus' self-sacrifice. Such recognition is the essential basis for true Christian morality.

Wilberforce's whole approach is strong indirect testimony to the predominance among his contemporaries of the kinds of religious outlook he is criticizing, although objective evaluation requires a detachment from his own Evangelical zeal. Certainly his portrayal of the predominant tone of late eighteenth-century Christianity as one of undemanding endorsement of social harmony, decency and good neighbourliness rings true. A leading theological influence was that of William Paley (1743–1805) who, in his *View of the Evidences of Christianity*, published in 1794, argued that the initial revelation of Christianity in the New Testament was associated with exceptional miraculous divine interventions in the natural order. These, however, did not recur in later ages or at the present time. It followed that contemporary Christianity would be orderly and predictable. Paley was also in tune with Enlightenment thought in emphasizing the benevolence of God rather than divine judgement, and his scheme of belief had little place for the original sin that was fundamental to that of Wilberforce and the Evangelicals. Such theology gave rise to the approach of the 'modern Religionists' whom Wilberforce disliked. It was reflected in the easy-going religion evoked, for example, in the novels of Jane Austen, where clergy are portrayed as endorsing and conforming to the mores of the secular gentry (see Figure 11.6). Nevertheless, Wilberforce was unduly dismissive of the piety of some of his Anglican contemporaries: there were indications of devotion and commitment in the late eighteenth-

Figure 11.6 Richard Newton, Fast Day, *1793, engraving, 23.5 × 33 cm, British Museum, London. Photo: by courtesy of the Trustees of the British Museum.*

This 1793 engraving by Richard Newton parodies the self-indulgence of the Church of England clergy, who are portrayed tucking into a lavish dinner when they are supposed to be fasting. It caricatures reality, but points up the worldliness that Wilberforce was striving to counteract.

century Church of England that owed little to the Evangelical movement (Mather, 1985). Also, as we have already noted, Methodism was growing strongly, although primarily among the lower classes who were outside the immediate scope of Wilberforce's book.

The cultural and political climate of the 1790s provided receptive soil for Wilberforce's message. By 1797 even erstwhile enthusiasts for revolution would have had ample opportunity in the light of unfolding events in France to reflect on the extent of human 'corruption'. While Wilberforce's emphasis was thus a reiteration of a longstanding strand in Christian tradition, it also reflected the mood of the times, and a growing Romantic consciousness of the anarchic and violent potentialities of humanity. There was an increasing number of religious thinkers who took a more radical approach than Wilberforce did, believing that the current disordered state of the world presaged the apocalypse and the Second Coming of Christ. Such ideas were apparent in the visionary poetry and paintings of William Blake and in the preaching of popular prophets such as Joanna Southcott, who claimed prophetic revelations from God and believed herself to be pregnant with a child destined to be the new Messiah. By the 1820s such an outlook was gaining ground among Evangelicals. Here religion both reflected and reinforced the trend to Romanticism.

The other extracts from the *Practical View* reproduced in Anthology I come from chapter VI, in which Wilberforce broadens his perspective from the primarily spiritual emphasis of the earlier chapters to a consideration of the political implications of his analysis. In so doing he contributed to the ongoing debate on the French Revolution and the changing nature of British society and politics. The *Practical View* can usefully be compared here with another work that gave considerable prominence to religion in the aftermath of 1789, Edmund Burke's *Reflections on the Revolution in France* (1790) (which you have already encountered in Unit 6 and which is discussed further on Audio 3, track 2). To Burke the revolutionary attack on the Roman Catholic Church was one of the most disturbing features of events across the Channel, because he saw the Church as a key upholder of the continuity and tradition that he believed essential to duly regulated liberty and a safeguard against anarchy. What was important was not so much what the Church taught, but that it should remain as a source of institutional stability. The extent of Burke's alarm on this score in 1790 might seem exaggerated, because the anti-Christian phase of the Revolution was still in the future. However, to Burke, even the Civil Constitution of the Clergy went much too far because it subverted the traditional nature of the alliance between Church and State by making the former clearly subordinate to the latter. A reformed, slimmed-down and government-controlled Church would be in no position to serve as the institutional brake on ill-considered change that Burke passionately believed to be necessary.

EXERCISE Now read the first two pages of chapter VI, up to '... take up with superficial appearances' (pp.277–8). On the basis of the above summary of Burke's views, in what respects do you think Wilberforce (a) agrees with Burke and (b) disagrees with him?

DISCUSSION (a) Wilberforce strongly agrees with Burke in respect of the crucial importance of religion in general, and Christianity in particular, for political stability. You will probably have been struck by the way in which he just asserts this position, while saying 'there can be no necessity for entering into a formal proof of its truth', an indication of the extent to which it reflected a consensus among his contemporaries.

(b) Unlike Burke, Wilberforce does not feel that the mere maintenance of traditional religious institutions is sufficient. He is worried that a decline in committed Christianity will lead to adverse political consequences and hence that Christian revival is essential for political security. (You may be interested to know that Burke, who died in 1797, read the *Practical View* on his deathbed, found it comforting, and wanted to thank Wilberforce for writing it (Pollock, 1977, p.148), an indication that he had become receptive to Wilberforce's perspective.)

EXERCISE Continue to read through chapter VI of the *Practical View* (as far as '... and inspirit its efforts', pp.278–85). Again, I have provided some commentary to help you draw out the key points and appreciate their significance, particularly in helping us understand the interaction of religion and society in our period. I hope you are by now becoming more at ease with Wilberforce's style. Although his presentation is long-winded, it is not difficult to follow but it is important not to become bogged down in the detail. Accordingly, use the pointers given below to read through the text fairly quickly, appreciating the overall thrust of the argument. It is equally important though that you look properly at the text for yourself, and do not depend wholly on my summary of it.

(pp.278–82) Reasons are given as to why Christianity (or more specifically 'real Christianity' as Wilberforce perceives it) is currently in decline. Persecution, he suggests, is a stimulus to faith, but the current position of the Church is too comfortable. It has considerable civil privileges and links to 'almost every family in the community'. (By 'community' here Wilberforce again appears to be thinking only of the 'higher and middle classes'.) Commercial prosperity and general cultural progress give rise to greater materialism and a more relaxed morality, with the looser standards characteristic of the higher classes tending to diffuse downwards in the social scale. Although explicit disavowal of Christianity remains rare, it is losing its practical influence on society and morality, and outright rejection is likely to follow. Wilberforce then acknowledges that he is arguing from probabilities rather than actual observation, but claims that the reality fits the model he has presented.

In this passage Wilberforce unwittingly anticipated a key strand in the arguments of those historians and sociologists who have maintained that during the era of the Enlightenment there began an ongoing 'secularization' of the western world, with the enforced retreat of religion from the centre to the margins of daily life. The ideological critique of traditional Christianity by Enlightenment thinkers is seen as important in this process, but greater emphasis is placed on the social changes associated with the Industrial Revolution. The difficulty for religion here was not, as Wilberforce thought, increased material prosperity as such so much as its consequences in terms of what has been called the 'disenchantment' of the world. This means that industrial and urban patterns of life became increasingly mechanized and predictable, leaving less room for supernatural belief. On the other hand, the short-term consequences of industrialization for religion were often much more positive. Churches and, especially, Dissenting chapels had an important place in the social fabric of expanding towns, providing a source of meaning and community in contexts that could otherwise be very anonymous. Moreover, Christianity came to play an important role in shaping the values of the expanding middle class (Davidoff and Hall, 1987). Arguably, Wilberforce's own writing and influence were a significant factor in ensuring that in Britain at least religion responded actively to the challenge presented by industrialization rather than being overwhelmed by it.

(pp.282–3) Wilberforce briefly mentions the presence of explicit unbelief among the literary elite, encouraged by those who in his opinion should know better, but he sees this as a symptom rather than a cause of the wider trend. He sees recent events in France – clearly he has in mind the outright dechristianization of 1793–4 – as showing where such tolerance of 'infidelity' can lead. Significantly, though, his horror is not (unlike Burke's) directed at the Revolution as such, but rather at this particular phase in its development. Indeed, footnote 4 implies that he does not see the Revolution *itself* as either a consequence or a cause of moral and spiritual decline.

(pp.283–5) Wilberforce now addresses the objection that the level of religious commitment he is advocating would produce a society so preoccupied with spiritual matters that it would neglect the practical necessities of daily life. In response he first affirms the priority of following God's commands in order to prepare for heaven, but then proceeds to argue that the general prevalence of Christianity would in fact be socially useful. According to Wilberforce, who cites the authority of St Paul in his support, it is a 'gross ... error' for Christians to withdraw from their secular duties. Granted that Christianity is opposed to excessive acquisitiveness or ambition, obedience to God and trust in his overruling providence actually encourages Christians to be diligent and constructive members of society. Moreover, a nation of such true Christians would be a peaceful and respected presence in international affairs, and would only fight wars in self-defence.

Again, we can relate Wilberforce's comments here to a recurrent issue in the practice and study of religion: the tension between what are called 'world-affirming' and 'world-denying' perspectives. Throughout the history of Christianity there have been individuals and groups who have felt that obedience to God requires withdrawal from normal everyday life. These have included desert hermits in the early Church, monks and nuns in the Middle Ages and thereafter, and small groups on the more radical fringes of Protestantism. Calvinist views, such as those of Cowper and Newton, could tend to encourage a state of mind in which believers, seeing themselves as a chosen ('elect') minority, separated themselves from society. Wilberforce, however, despite his admiration for the authors of the *Olney Hymns*, was not a Calvinist. He emphatically aligned himself with those who stressed rather the obligation of Christians to be actively and constructively involved in mainstream society. His was an influential voice in setting the predominant direction of Evangelicalism (which certainly had some world-denying tendencies), and in contributing to the shaping of a nineteenth-century British culture in which secular and Christian outlooks were by no means wholly polarized.

EXERCISE Now read through the remaining extracts from the *Practical View* (pp.285–92). As you read consider the following questions, designed to focus your understanding of the passages:

1 Why, according to Wilberforce, is religion in general, and Christianity in particular, important for the well-being of society?

2 What does Wilberforce mean by 'real Christianity' (refer back if necessary to the earlier passages of the *Practical View* that you have read), and why is it a social necessity?

3 What does he think would be the consequences of a disappearance of religion, and how can these dangers be averted?

DISCUSSION 1 Even 'false Religion' (by which Wilberforce means religions other than Christianity) can safeguard good order and morality in society by providing perceived supernatural sanctions to support human law ('jurisprudence'). Christianity, however, is much more effective, primarily because its teaching checks inherent human selfishness. Note that Wilberforce takes social inequality for granted. The rich are criticized not for possessing wealth but for using it in excessive showiness or frivolousness rather than in benevolence towards others. While the poor have understandable cause for resentment when the rich flaunt their wealth or the powerful behave oppressively, they are otherwise expected to accept their situation in a 'diligent, humble, patient' frame of mind, because it has been assigned to them by the providence of God. Their life in this world ('the present state of things') is merely a period of preparation for eternal life in heaven in which rich and poor will share alike.

2 For Wilberforce, 'real Christianity' requires assent to central Evangelical doctrines of inherent human sinfulness and deliverance from divine condemnation by the atoning death of Jesus Christ on the Cross. He is insistent that the social benefits of Christianity will only be realized if adherence to it is sincere. Mere traditional respect

for an Established Church will be insufficient (another contrast between Wilberforce's position and Burke's). If the rich themselves no longer think Christianity true, they cannot expect to delude the poor into accepting it either. A rational and ethical view of life may appeal to the higher classes, but in order to win over the 'lower orders' religion needs to capture their emotions. (Although Wilberforce does not explicitly refer to Methodism, he must have been aware of its rapid growth in his own Yorkshire constituency at this very period (Baxter, 1974) and here he hints at a key reason for its appeal. More broadly he combines significant elements of a developing Romantic mindset by linking a consciousness of the presence of the 'lower orders' (an awareness of a 'working class' as such is not part of his vocabulary) to a recognition of the emotional and irrational aspects of human nature.)

3 The disappearance of religion would lead to the collapse of civil society. Given recent developments in France there can be no complacency about the dangers. These can be averted by a recognition that the root problems are moral (and spiritual) rather than political, and need to be addressed by people of status and influence setting a firm example of determined and uncompromising commitment to Evangelical Christianity. Wilberforce regards this as a matter of patriotism as well as of religion if the perceived moral poison arising in France is to be contained. The advance of true religion would bring substantial moral and political benefits quite apart from the providential blessing of God.

Wilberforce's underlying conservative inclinations and his vested interest in the existing social order led him to emphasize those aspects of Christianity that are conducive to stability rather than the more radical strands of Jesus' teaching. Nevertheless, there is no doubt of Wilberforce's absolute conviction of the reality of an afterlife and, consequently, of the spiritual perspective in which life as we know it has to be viewed. Herein was an outlook fundamentally different from that of David Hume, which you encountered in Units 4 and 5. Wilberforce's perspective though was probably much more representative than Hume's of the consensus of contemporaries. Study of it helps us to see why for social and political reasons, as well as for philosophical and theological ones, any questioning of the immortality of the soul seemed so dangerous and shocking.

The *Practical View* stirred extensive comment and debate among contemporaries. According to Daniel Wilson it was:

> at the same moment, read by all the leading persons of the nation. An electric shock could not be felt more vividly and instantaneously. Every one talked of it, every one was attracted

> by its eloquence, every one admitted the benevolence and sincerity of the writer.
>
> (Wilson, 1829, p.xviii)

The Gentleman's Magazine (vol.67, part 1, p.411), which might be regarded as representative of the polite society of 'professed Christians' to which Wilberforce addressed himself, 'sincerely' wished him success in his labours. The reviewer felt his picture both of contemporary religious practice and of true Christianity was a fair one. The Anglican *British Critic* (vol.10, pp.294–303) hailed the *Practical View* as 'one of the most impressive books on the subject of religion, that appeared within our memory'. It noted that many people were censuring the book as too severe, but they were merely trying to excuse their own indifference and in doing so confirmed the truth of Wilberforce's central contentions. It found the *Practical View* overly sympathetic to Methodism, but readily pardoned this fault as only a slight blemish on an otherwise excellent work. At the same time Dissenters influenced by Evangelicalism warmly welcomed the book's advocacy of religious convictions and practice with which they identified. *The Protestant Dissenters' Magazine* (vol.4, pp.196–8) praised the work, trusting that it would 'meet with more than common attention', although it was critical of Wilberforce's diffuse style which was thought to detract from the clarity of the argument, a frustration shared by many later readers.

Individual reactions could be profound. Arthur Young, an eminent pioneer of new methods in agriculture, bought the book and read it 'coldly at first'. He initially failed to understand the doctrinal points (if you have struggled there too, you are in good company!) but read it again and again 'and it made so much impression on me that I scarcely knew how to lay it aside'. After reading the book for a fourth time within a few months, Young was ready to dismiss criticism of Wilberforce as 'arrant nonsense' and wrote that 'my mind goes with him in every word' (quoted in Betham-Edwards, 1898, pp.287–8, 297). Similarly, when Thomas Chalmers (1780–1847), the future social reformer and leader of the Free Church of Scotland, read the book in the winter of 1810–11 it placed him 'on the eve of a great revolution in all my opinions about Christianity' (quoted in Brown, 1982, p.36).

Other commentators, however, thought the book 'fanatical' (Pollock, 1977, p.153). This perspective showed the continued prominence of a strain of Enlightenment thought in which everything must be viewed in the cool light of reason. *The Gentleman's Magazine* qualified its positive review by expressing unease lest Wilberforce's advocacy of emotion in religion should 'transport warm tempers beyond due bounds, and expose them to temptation and to censure'. The *Monthly Review* (vol.23, pp.241–8) professed itself as much a friend to religion as Wilberforce was, but firmly maintained that 'in the present day, if its authority be preserved at all, it must not be done by addressing the passions, but by appealing to reason'. The success of Wesley and Whitefield in 'reforming and civilizing' the poor depended on stirring the 'passions of the vulgar' and was no proof of the truth of their teaching. Religious practice was more important than assent to abstract doctrines, which were likely soon to be perceived as erroneous and so to lose their authority. Criticism of this kind, however, had the unintended effect of enhancing the appeal of the *Practical View* among more orthodox Christians (Wilson, 1829, p.xxi). Meanwhile, Wilberforce was denounced in pamphlets by a couple of **Unitarian**[10] writers. One held that his fundamental principles were absolutely incompatible with those of Christ himself (Wakefield, 1797, p.4), and the other attacked his doctrine as 'inconsistent with reason, unfounded in Scripture, and injurious to morality' (Belsham, 1798, pp.2–3). Nevertheless, the Duke of Grafton, a former prime minister who was sympathetic to Unitarianism, although thinking that Wilberforce laboured under 'great but involuntary errors', praised him as 'an upright, sincerely pious and beneficent character' (quoted in Betham-Edwards, 1898, pp.325–6). Such reactions revealed something of the range of contemporary perceptions of what it meant to be genuinely religious amidst the interplay of Enlightenment and Romantic cultural and social expectations.

EXERCISE

Now that you have read through the extracts from Wilberforce's *Practical View* in Anthology I, pause for a moment to review your own reactions to the text, and summarize your thoughts on the following questions:

1. What is distinctive and interesting about the text?
2. How does it fit into the processes of transition from Enlightenment to Romanticism?

DISCUSSION

1. To my mind the most distinctive characteristic of the text is the evident centrality and sincerity of Wilberforce's religious mindset and motivation, and his specific commitment to Evangelical Christianity. Moreover, he does not advocate a spiritual withdrawal from the world of mainstream politics and society, but insists that Christians should be fully engaged with it. Despite his evident unease about the current moral and political state of Britain, his religious language is too earnest to be merely a cover for some other underlying motive, such as a conservative political agenda. A text such as this is therefore an important corrective to the impression that might arise from the texts in Units 4 and 5, if studied in isolation, that this was an era in which religion was generally in retreat in the face of Enlightenment rationality. We need to recognize that the overall picture was a complex and variegated one.

[10] Unitarians were Dissenters who professed a strongly Enlightened and rational view of religion, tending to discount the supernatural and to emphasize the unity of God rather than the divinity of Jesus Christ.

Of course the question was an open-ended one, and it may be that you have developed a different line of thought, focusing perhaps on the nature of Wilberforce's response to the French Revolution, or on his perception of the structure and workings of British society. Such issues are also well worth reflecting on, but I hope you in some way still commented on the pivotal role of religion in the *Practical View*. Even if you personally find the specific religious ideas in Wilberforce's writing unattractive or difficult to understand, your study of the text should have enabled you to develop that essential insight.

2 In summary this is very much a text that combines an Enlightenment appeal to structured rationality with a Romantic one to emotion and the supernatural, although the reactions of the contemporary reviewers suggest it was perceived as emphasizing the latter more than the former. The ease with which Wilberforce moves from one mindset to another is a useful caution to us against simplistic pigeonholing of people as either 'Enlightenment' or 'Romantic' thinkers. The *Practical View* also raises for us the question of how important religion itself was as a force that promoted cultural change as well as reflecting it. There are no easy answers to such complex questions, but you might like to think further about them.

---

5 Wilberforce and slavery

In this final main section of the unit we shall be looking at extracts from two of Wilberforce's writings on slavery, the issue with which his name is most famously associated. These will also lead us into discussion of interactions between Britain and the non-European world, the main theme of the remainder of the block. Wilberforce's success as a leader of the cause stemmed from his capacity to marshal a formidable range of argumentation, including secular as well as spiritual factors, and practical considerations as well as statements of principle. In consistency with the main focus of this unit, however, we shall concentrate our attention now on Wilberforce's religious arguments against slavery. Other aspects of the debate will be developed in the following units, so we will not spend time on them at this point. As you would expect from your study of the *Practical View*, Wilberforce's religion was a fundamental feature of his anti-slavery motivation.

In his commitment to the campaign against the slave trade Wilberforce both represented and encouraged a growing identification of the Evangelical movement as a whole with the anti-slavery cause. In 1774 John Wesley had published a powerful denunciation of the trade, ending with a direct appeal to ships' captains, merchants and slave-owners to repent of their sinful involvement in it or risk incurring the wrath of God. Both the authors of the *Olney Hymns* contributed their eloquence to the campaign. In 1788 John Newton published his *Thoughts on the African Slave Trade*, in which he began by confessing his own past involvement. Although he had found it 'disagreeable' he had not had moral scruples at the time. He saw his own subsequent change of heart as perhaps representative of the nation at large. He now saw the slave trade as a wickedness that would lead to ruin and, vividly drawing on his first-hand knowledge, exposed the cruelties and degradation to which the Africans were subjected. In the same year Cowper wrote 'The Negro's complaint' (which you will encounter again in Unit 14), in which the poet perceived natural disasters as divine punishment for oppression and exploitation:

> Hark – He [God] answers. Wild tornadoes
> Strewing yonder flood with wrecks,
> Wasting Towns, Plantations, Meadows,
> Are the voice with which he speaks.

('The Negro's complaint', ll.33–6, quoted in Baird and Ryskamp, 1980–95, vol.3, p.14)

In April 1792 he addressed a sonnet to Wilberforce, encouraging him to persist in his labours:

> Thy Country, Wilberforce, with just disdain
> Hears thee by cruel men and impious call'd
> Fanatic, for thy zeal to loose th'enthrall'd
> From exile, public sale, and Slav'ry's chain.
> Friend of the Poor, the wrong'd, the fetter-gall'd,
> Fear not lest labour such as thine be vain.
> Thou hast atchiev'd a part; hast gain'd the ear
> Of Britain's Senate to thy glorious cause;
> Hope smiles, Joy springs, and though cold Caution pause
> And weave delay, the better hour is near
> That shall remunerate thy toils severe
> By Peace for Afric, fenced with British laws.
> Enjoy what thou hast won, esteem and love
> From all the Just on earth and all the Blest above.

('To William Wilberforce, Esq.', quoted in Baird and Ryskamp, 1980–95, vol.3, pp.182–3)

The campaign against the slave trade nevertheless languished in the 1790s in the face of a sense of national crisis engendered by war with France, rebellion in Ireland and unrest at home. There was a temporary peace with France in 1801, but war resumed in 1803 and was to continue until the battle of Waterloo in 1815. It was in 1804, however, that the political tide began to turn decisively in Wilberforce's favour, and in 1806 he seemed at last to be on the verge of victory. In this context early in

1807 he published his *Letter on the Abolition of the Slave Trade Addressed to the Freeholders and Other Inhabitants of Yorkshire.* Despite its title this was no short pamphlet, but a 350-page book intended to restate the abolitionist arguments used during the previous two decades in time for the parliamentary session in which, Wilberforce hoped, the measure would eventually be passed. It was formally addressed to his Yorkshire constituents, but the real target audience was the members of the House of Lords and the House of Commons on whose votes the outcome now depended.

Wilberforce began the book by affirming that his dominant motive for writing was concern for 'the present state and prospects' of Britain. He continued:

> That the Almighty Creator of the universe governs the world which he has made; that the sufferings of nations are to be regarded as the punishment of national crimes; and their decline and fall, as the execution of this sentence; are truths which I trust are still generally believed among us ... If these truths be admitted, and if it be also true, that fraud, oppression and cruelty, are crimes of the blackest dye, and that guilt is aggravated in proportion as the criminal acts in defiance of clearer light, and of stronger motives to virtue ... have we not abundant cause for serious apprehension? ... If ... the Slave Trade be a national crime ... to which we cling in defiance of the clearest light, not only in opposition to our own acknowledgements of its guilt, but even of our own declared resolutions to abandon it, is not this, then a time at which all who are not perfectly sure that the Providence of God is but a fable, should be strenuous in their endeavours to lighten the vessel of the state, of such a load of guilt and infamy?
>
> (*Letter on the Abolition of the Slave Trade*, 1807, pp.4–6)

In the body of the book Wilberforce concentrated on a systematic overview of the sufferings and hardships of the slaves. He began by looking at the situation in Africa, during which analysis he referred extensively to the evidence provided by Mungo Park's *Travels*, which you will be reading when you study Units 12–13. He then turned to the horrors of the voyage across the Atlantic, and finally and most extensively to conditions in the West Indies themselves. He argued that these would be improved by the abolition of the slave trade because the plantation owners, no longer able to obtain fresh supplies of labour, would be obliged to treat their existing slaves better. Repeatedly however, amidst the accumulation of factual evidence and carefully reasoned argument, Wilberforce's religious zeal resurfaced. Thus for him exploitation of Africa was especially reprehensible because it was a barrier against 'religious and moral light and social improvement' and was a persistent depraving and darkening of 'the Creation of God' (pp.40–2). The material sufferings of the slaves in the West Indies were bad enough, but worst of all was the denial to them of 'moral improvement, and the light of religious truth, and the hope full of immortality' (p.203).

The short extracts from the *Letter on the Abolition of the Slave Trade* in Anthology I come from part of Wilberforce's discussion of conditions in the West Indies, and then from the concluding section of the book. They enable you to get something of the flavour of the style and argument, particularly in illustrating the religious motivation for Wilberforce's campaign.

EXERCISE Read these extracts now (pp.292–4) and consider the following questions:

1 What arguments for abolition does Wilberforce put forward here?

2 How do you think his arguments were received by Parliament in 1807?

DISCUSSION 1 First, no serious attempt is made to convert the slaves to Christianity, the only thing in Wilberforce's eyes that would represent some recompense, if not justification, for their bondage. Second, whereas Christianity was instrumental in bringing about the abolition of slavery in the ancient world, Protestants are now conniving in a particularly unpleasant form of contemporary slavery, being shamed by the superior humanitarianism of Roman Catholics, Muslims ('Mahometanism') and even pagans. Third, unless the trade is abolished, the 'heaviest judgements of the Almighty' will ensue, an argument to which Wilberforce gives particular weight and with which he concludes the *Letter*. Note that when Wilberforce writes of divine judgement he is not envisaging dramatic and unexpected fire and brimstone, but rather the ongoing 'operation of natural causes' by which 'Providence governs the world'. His conception of God in this passage is thus of a rational and consistent deity who controls the world in an orderly and predictable fashion through the normal processes of nature and human society, an essentially Enlightenment rather than Romantic understanding of the cosmos.

2 Britain was at war in early 1807 (Nelson's victory and death at Trafalgar had occurred little more than a year before in October 1805). In this context of insecurity, therefore, arguments presenting the slave trade as a blot on national moral righteousness, and suggesting that decline and disaster might be the price to be paid for continuing it, were likely to fall on receptive ears. Wilberforce turned on its head the widespread perception in the more immediate aftermath of the French Revolution that significant change was too risky to contemplate: his stance now was that it was too dangerous *not* to change.

Certainly the outcome was a positive one from Wilberforce's point of view in that abolition of the slave trade in British ships and colonial possessions passed rapidly through both Houses of Parliament, and became law in March 1807. This result in part implied an increased receptivity to Wilberforce's religious arguments against slavery, but there were also other factors at work. These included the advance of liberal ideas of justice and toleration, themselves reflecting the influence of the Enlightenment, which increasingly made the oppression of Africans seem less acceptable. (This wider context is developed in the later units of this block.) Crucial too in 1807 was government support for abolition, which had been lacking at earlier stages of Wilberforce's campaign.

Wilberforce's campaign against slavery needs to be seen in the context of growing interest in the world outside Europe, a reflection of expanding colonial involvements, notably in India, and increasing cultural interchange. In the specifically Evangelical context this interest was reflected in the foundation of various missionary societies during the 1790s, including in 1799 the Church Missionary Society, in which Wilberforce himself took an active part. An earlier significant initiative had been the creation in 1791 of the Sierra Leone Company, which Wilberforce and others hoped would provide a basis for legitimate commerce and the spread of Christianity in West Africa. To twenty-first-century secular eyes there might appear something surprising in Wilberforce's simultaneous involvement in the campaign against slavery, which is still viewed as courageous progressive humanitarianism, and his advocacy of foreign missions, now often perceived as a feature of offensive western cultural imperialism. In Wilberforce's mind, however, anti-slavery and missions were not only linked but two sides of the same coin. We have already seen this outlook reflected in his concern for the Christianization of the slaves. It was evident again in 1813 when he vigorously and successfully advocated that missionaries should be allowed to operate in British India. Hindus, he thought, were 'fast bound in the lowest depths of moral and social ignorance and degradation'. He saw both missions and the campaign against slavery as opening the way to 'Christian light and moral improvement' (1813, pp.48, 106).

In 1814 the initial defeat of Napoleon seemed to Wilberforce and others to provide an opportunity to put pressure on continental European countries to join Britain in abolishing the slave trade. Wilberforce lobbied hard for the peace settlement with the new French government under the restored Louis XVIII to include immediate French abolition in exchange for the return of colonies seized by Britain during the war. He was bitterly disappointed when France only agreed to abolish in five years' time, a commitment that he feared would be unenforceable. He drew comfort, however, from the strong support for his position expressed not only by British public and parliamentary opinion, but also by Tsar Alexander I of Russia. Moreover, in March 1815 Napoleon, following his return from Elba, reversed his previous policy and decreed the total abolition of the French slave trade. The subsequent Bourbon government stood by this decision, although, as it did not actively enforce it, evasion was widespread. Meanwhile, later in 1815 the Congress of Vienna issued a declaration against the slave trade, which caused Spain and Portugal also gradually to edge towards abolition. Although slavery in the Americas was to continue for many decades and was only to end in the United States in the 1860s after a violent civil war, pressure for abolition was now gathering momentum and becoming internationalized.

In the meantime, the continuing background of armed conflict in the Napoleonic Wars until final victory over Napoleon at the battle of Waterloo in June 1815 tended to reinforce a trend within Evangelicalism towards conceiving God's intervention in the world in more apocalyptic and less orderly terms. It was a particular religious manifestation of the trend to Romanticism. There was increasing interest in the study and interpretation of the prophetic books of the Bible, particularly Daniel in the Old Testament and Revelation in the New Testament, which were held to include predictions that were as yet unfulfilled. For example, in 1815, shortly before Waterloo, James Hatley Frere (1779–1866) published *A Combined View of the Prophecies of Daniel, Esdras and St John* [Revelation], *Shewing that all the Prophetic Writings are Formed upon One Plan.* A central feature of Frere's argument was the identification of Napoleon with a 'vile person, to whom they shall not give the honour of the Kingdom' (Daniel, 11:21, Authorized Version), whose career was foretold in the Old Testament, and whose eventual defeat would usher in the end of the world. Expectation of cataclysmic divine judgement tended, if anything, to gain further ground after 1815, in the face of unrest and hardship in the aftermath of the war. In November 1817 the death in childbirth of Princess Charlotte, second in line to the throne, was widely regarded by preachers as retribution from the Almighty for the sins of the nation.

Wilberforce's final substantial published statement on slavery appeared in 1823. By this time the evident failure of the abolition of the slave trade to produce a marked improvement in the conditions of those slaves already in the West Indies led him and others to begin the campaign for the freeing of slaves in British colonies. He was now ageing and in failing health and was shortly to retire from Parliament. *An Appeal to the Religion, Justice and Humanity of the Inhabitants of the British Empire, in Behalf of the Negro Slaves in the West Indies* was therefore something of a political testament. It was intended to motivate his supporters for a sustained further period of agitation in which he himself would be unable to be an active participant. The extracts in Anthology I are particularly concerned with the religious arguments against slavery which were, if anything, even more prominent in the 1823 *Appeal* than in the 1807 *Letter.*

EXERCISE Read through these extracts now (pp.295–302) and note down answers to the following questions:

1 What are the main arguments for freeing the slaves that Wilberforce advances?

2 What does the text reveal about Wilberforce's attitudes to the non-European world?

DISCUSSION 1 (a) Slavery is inherently immoral and unjust because it degrades human beings.

(b) The slaves are unable to gain religious and moral instruction.

(c) The moral and educational condition of Blacks is worse in the West Indies than it was in Africa before they were enslaved.

(d) Slavery is an enormity inconsistent with the Christian and humane professions of the British nation.

(e) Personal independence, human dignity, and 'the consolations and supports' (p.300) of religion require emancipation from chattel slavery.

(f) Under present circumstances (with the danger of slave revolt) the protection of the colonies is a great burden on British manpower and resources. Freed slaves, on the other hand, will under Christian instruction become a 'grateful peasantry' (p.301), a basis for social and political stability in the West Indies.

(g) Above all Wilberforce is fearful of impending divine retribution if slavery continues. Significantly, he has moved away from a perception that God will operate through the predictable if inexorable workings of providence towards a consciousness of more sudden and unforeseeable judgement.

2 Wilberforce is profoundly unsympathetic to non-European cultures, making hostile comments about both Africa and India. It is evident, however, that this lack of sympathy stems primarily, if not entirely, from the fact that they are not Christian and are hence – inevitably in Wilberforce's opinion – degraded by superstition and immorality. He is though no racist, as is clear from his comparison of the good qualities of Africans in their homelands with their degraded state when enslaved in the West Indies. Non-European peoples have genuine potential to improve their lot by conversion to Christianity and/or emancipation from slavery.

Wilberforce's conviction of the central importance of Christian conversion for individuals and societies was thus a consistent theme in his writing and speaking. In 1797 in the *Practical View* he had presented a recovery of 'real Christianity' as the only effective solution to the social and political malaise that he felt afflicted Britain. In relation to slavery, while he was happy to deploy an extensive armoury of rational argument, his underlying preoccupations were that the British nation should be true to its Christian identity, and that the slaves themselves should have the opportunity to hear and respond to the Christian Gospel. Herein for him lay the path not only of religious duty but of national self-interest, because in the West Indies, as in Britain, a Christian people would also be an orderly one.

6 Conclusion

William Wilberforce died on 29 July 1833, two days after hearing that the legislation for the abolition of slavery in British dominions had successfully completed its passage through the House of Commons, a fitting conclusion to the work he had begun nearly half a century before. His adult life also coincided almost exactly with the period we are studying in this course, and offers a useful perspective from which to view some of the changes that occurred.

The *Practical View* both reflected and contributed to a major shift in religious consciousness of which the continuing growth of the Evangelical movement was the most striking manifestation. Methodist numbers may again be taken as an indicator. These showed a further steep increase in membership in England from 91,825 in 1801 to 143,311 in 1811, 215,466 in 1821 and 288,182 in 1830, which amounted to 3.4 per cent of the total adult population (Gilbert, 1976, pp.31–2). The upward trend continued in the 1830s and 1840s. These numbers may still seem relatively small in relation to the population as a whole, which was also rapidly increasing, but they represented only the committed core and Sunday attendances would certainly have been considerably higher. In the meantime, not least because of the enhanced respectability conferred by Wilberforce and his associates, Evangelicals within the Church of England became increasingly socially acceptable, and even fashionable, and their numbers also grew substantially. There are indeed grounds for seeing the impact of the *Practical View* and the wider advance of Evangelical ideology as a key strand in the process by which during the early nineteenth century an emergent middle class defined its identity against the perceived irreligion and lax morality of the aristocracy.

Such religious revival and reorientation fitted into a wider North Atlantic and European pattern. In the United States Evangelicalism grew even more rapidly than in Britain and was, if anything, even more influential in shaping cultural and social outlooks. On the Continent the years after

1815 saw a recovery in the fortunes of the Roman Catholic Church, notably in France where there was a strong reaction against the irreligion of the revolutionary years. Such trends had their own dynamics, but insofar as they represented a recovered sense of historic identity and a deeper awareness of emotion, the supernatural, and the sharp polarities of good and evil, sin and salvation, they are linked to the overall cultural shift to Romanticism.

Wilberforce's career was also of pivotal significance in terms of the relationship between Europe and the wider world. The campaign against slavery was a fundamental challenge to prevalent assumptions that 'unenlightened' non-European peoples and resources were merely subordinate and inferior and could be ruthlessly exploited. While the Christianizing impulse that drove Wilberforce and the Evangelicals carried its own assumptions of superiority over other religions and cultures, it was at the same time a powerful force for asserting the dignity and worth of every human being, of whatever race. As you turn now in the remainder of this block to examine European encounters with Africa, and to learn more about slavery from the perspectives of slaves themselves, you will come to understand more of its ambivalent, but profoundly influential, impact.

Before moving on to Units 12–13 you should view Video 2, band 3 again, as a means of consolidating and developing your understanding of Evangelicalism and suggesting links with the rest of the block and the course as a whole.

References

Baird, J.D. and Ryskamp, C. (eds) (1980–95) *The Poems of William Cowper*, 3 vols, Oxford, Clarendon Press.

Baxter, J. (1974) 'The great Yorkshire revival 1792–6: a study of mass revival among the Methodists', in M. Hill (ed.) *A Sociological Yearbook of Religion in Britain*, 4, pp.46–76.

Belsham, T. (1798) *A Review of Mr Wilberforce's Treatise*, London, J. Johnson.

Betham-Edwards, M. (1898) *The Autobiography of Arthur Young with Selections from his Correspondence*, London, Smith, Elder and Co.

Brown, S.J. (1982) *Thomas Chalmers and the Godly Commonwealth in Scotland*, Oxford, Clarendon Press.

Christie, I.R. (1984) *Stress and Stability in Late Eighteenth-Century Britain: Reflections on the British Avoidance of Revolution*, Oxford, Clarendon Press.

Davidoff, L. and Hall, C. (1987) *Family Fortunes: Men and Women of the English Middle Class, 1780–1850*, London, Hutchinson.

Gilbert, A.D. (1976) *Religion and Society in Industrial England: Church, Chapel and Social Change, 1740–1914*, London, Longman.

Kiernan, V. (1952) 'Evangelicalism and the French Revolution', *Past and Present*, pp.44–56.

Mather, F.C. (1985) 'Georgian churchmanship reconsidered: some variations in Anglican public worship, 1714–1830', *Journal of Ecclesiastical History*, 36, pp.255–83.

Olsen, G.W. (1990) *Religion and Revolution in Early-Industrial England: The Halévy Thesis and its Critics*, Lanham, University Press of America.

Pollock, J. (1977) *Wilberforce*, London, Constable.

Stevenson, J. (1989) 'Popular radicalism and popular protest 1789–1815', in H.T. Dickinson (ed.) *Britain and the French Revolution 1789–1815*, Basingstoke, Macmillan.

Wakefield, G. (1797) *A Letter to William Wilberforce, Esq. On the Subject of his Late Publication*, London.

Wilberforce, W. (1807) *A Letter on the Abolition of the Slave Trade Addressed to the Freeholders and Other Inhabitants of Yorkshire*, London, J. Hatchard and Son.

Wilberforce, W. (1807) *A Practical View of the Prevailing Religious System of Professed Christians ..., Contrasted with Real Christianity*, London, T. Cadell and W. Davies.

Wilberforce, W. (1813) *Substance of the Speeches of William Wilberforce, Esq. On the Clause in the East India Bill for Promoting the Religious Instruction and Moral Improvement of the Natives of the British Dominions in India.*

Wilson, D. (1829) 'Introduction to Wilberforce's *Practical View*' in *Select Christian Authors with Introductory Essays*, 3rd edn, Glasgow, William Collins.

Further reading

Anstey, R. (1975) *The Atlantic Slave Trade and British Abolition, 1760–1810*, Atlantic Highlands, Humanities Press. The standard account, which gives considerable prominence to the Evangelical contribution.

Gilbert, A.D. (1976) *Religion and Society in Industrial England: Church, Chapel and Social Change, 1740–1914,* London, Longman. An account of trends in religious participation with useful statistics.

Howse, E.M. (1971) *Saints in Politics: The 'Clapham Sect' and the Growth of Freedom*, London, George Allen & Unwin (first published by the University of Toronto Press in 1952). An old but still useful account of the political impact of Wilberforce and his associates.

Pollock, J. (1977) *Wilberforce*, London, Constable. The best available biography.

Schlossberg, H. (2000) *The Silent Revolution and the Making of Victorian England*, Columbus, Ohio State University Press.

Units 12–13
Mungo Park, *Travels in the Interior Districts of Africa*

Prepared for the course team by Bernard Waites

Contents

Study components

Weeks of study	*Supplementary material*	*Audio-visual*	*Anthologies and set books*
1.5	AV Notes Illustrations Book	Audio 4	Mungo Park, *Travels in the Interior Districts of Africa*

The required reading for *Travels in the Interior Districts of Africa* is as follows: author's preface and chapters I and II; chapter VI; pp.110–14, chapter X and pp.137–42; pp.175–84; pp.222–6; chapter XXII; pp.300–10; pp.330–6. Please note that chapter XXII (pp.279–90) is wrongly called chapter XXIII in your edition.

Objectives

When you have completed your work on Units 12–13 you should:

- be familiar with the scientific and institutional context of Park's *Travels*;
- be aware of the role of Sir Joseph Banks in Park's career;
- have a knowledge of Park's scientific interests and his religious beliefs, and be able to relate them to the intellectual and religious currents of his day;
- be able to use the *Travels* (a) to delineate the European 'image' of Africa in the late eighteenth century; (b) to explore European attitudes to black Africans and Moors; (c) as a point of entry into the controversy over the abolition of the Atlantic slave trade;
- be aware of the authorship of the *Travels*.

1 Introduction

In this part of the course, you will be studying Mungo Park's account of his first journey to West Africa, undertaken in 1795–7. You should have acquired the Wordsworth edition of Park's *Travels* as one of your set books, and I hope you will read it in its entirety, but that is not essential to excel in the course. To keep your workload within prescribed limits, the set reading from Park has been restricted to substantial extracts totalling about 30,000 words, which are listed on the previous page. These are the only passages with which you will need to be familiar when answering assignment and examination questions. Park presented his account in 26 short chapters and I have, in the main, selected entire chapters for you to study. Although the flow of the overall narrative is inevitably disrupted by the process of selection, I have tried to maintain the integrity of particular incidents and 'stories' within the narrative. At what point you read the selections is up to you. My advice would be to read the preface and first two chapters immediately to get a 'feel' for Park's style and the background information he gives about his journey. Then return to this unit.

2 The context of Park's journey

Why Mungo Park?

The most general and compelling reason for reading Park's *Travels* is that it will give you pleasure. Park had remarkable experiences in a part of Africa hitherto unexplored by Europeans, and he wrote about his adventures and the people he encountered in a lucid, unmannered and accessible way. Apart from the occasional use of Latin terms to refer to plant species, you should find little in Park's writing that is obscure or mystifying. Wherever his usage is unfamiliar, I have clarified it in the course of my discussion.

The more specific reasons derive from the appropriateness of Park's *Travels* for a text-based course analysing the transformation of European culture between the late Enlightenment and the rise of Romanticism. The *Travels* were published at the mid-way point of this transformation, and they are fairly representative of the cluster of values and attitudes we associate with the Enlightenment, particularly 'enlightened' enquiry into the natural world and human society. This spirit of enquiry gave renewed impulse to accumulating geographical and ethnographic knowledge of the non-European world and its indigenous societies through sponsored voyages of exploration. (Among the most celebrated was Captain Cook's expedition to the Pacific in 1768–71.) Though a solitary traveller on his first journey, Park must be seen in this wider context of sponsored exploration. He travelled under the auspices of a learned society, the African Association, and made a signal contribution to Europe's knowledge of the geography and culture of the West African interior, a part of the world inaccessible to Europeans before the 1790s. But Park was more than a dedicated traveller and sympathetic observer; he had some claim to be a natural scientist. The most characteristic feature of 'enlightened' enquiry was the desire to observe and classify the natural order systematically, and its foremost representative was the great Swedish naturalist, Linnaeus (Carl von Linné, 1707–78). By the time Park travelled in Africa, there was a Linnaean tradition of European natural history to which he was affiliated through his membership of the London Linnaean society and his association with Sir Joseph Banks (1743–1820), a member of Cook's expedition, the long-serving president of the Royal Society and the foremost patron of science of his day.

Having said that Park's *Travels* is an appropriate text because it exemplifies a spirit of 'enlightened' enquiry, it may seem odd if I add that the book also recommends itself as an expression of certain religious attitudes typical of the late Enlightenment. We normally think of science – or the scientific attitude of mind – as subverting religious belief, but, however true this proved to be in the long run, it was not generally the case in the late eighteenth century, when the natural order was almost universally taken to exhibit God's design. Natural philosophers – or, as we would say, scientists – in the Linnaean tradition saw no incompatibility between the systematic observation and classification of nature and belief in God, although their religious attitudes were informed and inflected by their scientific beliefs (and vice versa). Park's religious convictions reflected his upbringing in Scottish Nonconformity, but were not exceptional for the educated, professional elite of Protestant Europe. In studying him, we can broaden our knowledge of 'enlightened' Christianity.

The final reason for studying Park's *Travels* in this course is that the book provides an excellent entry into one of the great moral debates of his day: that over the legitimacy (or otherwise) of trading African slaves across the Atlantic in exchange for sugar, coffee, rice, cotton and other plantation crops that could only be grown in great quantities in the Americas thanks to the constant replenishment of slave labour. By the 1790s, liberal philosophers and jurists had long repudiated slavery as a violation of inalienable human rights, and political economists had condemned it as the least efficient form of labour exploitation. But this intellectual repudiation had been accompanied by the growing commercial involvement of British ship-owners, financiers, planters and stockholders in the slave-based plantation economy of the Atlantic basin. When Park first visited Africa, more African slaves were being transported in British ships than in the merchant vessels of any other nation, and more slave plantation produce was grown in colonies belonging to the British Crown than in those of any other realm. The campaign to alter radically this state of affairs by outlawing the slave trade for British nationals was especially notable for the reformers' efforts to mobilize public opinion and bring it to bear on the country's legislators. The public debate ranged far beyond the demand that a particular commerce be criminalized: it involved the compatibility (or incompatibility) of slave trading with Christianity, attitudes to race and human diversity, and the place of Africa and Africans in the world outlook of Europeans. Though he shied away from controversy, Park's renown as *the* African traveller of his day meant that both abolitionists and their opponents solicited his views on slavery and slave trading and cited his observations on African social life in their campaign literature.

Who was Park?

Park was born on 11 September 1771 at Foulshiels (see Figure 12.1), a tenant farm on the estate of the Duke of Buccleugh near Selkirk in the Scottish Lowlands, the seventh child in a family of thirteen. The parental home was a modest four-roomed cottage, which contributed to the legend of Park as 'a lad o'parts' who rose to fame from humble circumstances. In fact, the family was scarcely impecunious: Park's father (also called Mungo) became a man of some substance, who bequeathed property with a probate value of around £3,000. The Parks were Dissenters: his father had been among those who had seceded from the Established Church of Scotland in 1733 over the issue of whether lay patrons should appoint ministers. The original 'Secessionists' had upheld the Calvinist doctrine (to which you were introduced in Unit 10) that the destiny of human souls was already known to an omniscient, omnipotent God, and that human will and intervention could have no bearing on the matter. But, by the 1770s, the Secession Church had itself factionalized into the more theologically flexible 'Burghers' and the rigidly Calvinist 'anti-Burghers', and Park was brought up in the more relaxed atmosphere of the former. The minister of Selkirk Secession Church, Dr Lawson, was noted for his personal tolerance and kindliness.

Park was initially educated at home by a tutor, before attending Selkirk grammar school and being apprenticed at the age of 14 to Thomas Anderson, a local surgeon (whose daughter he was to marry on his return from Africa). In October 1788, he entered Edinburgh University, where he spent four sessions studying medicine – which he found a chore – and botany, which was then taught as an adjunct of medicine in the medical faculty. By the end of his studies, botany had become his primary intellectual interest. Park's education (and that of two brothers who also entered the professions) had to be financed by his family, but such sacrifices were not unusual among the Scottish tenant farmers. The remarks of Park's first biographer, John Whishaw, are worth quoting in this context:

> The attention of the Scottish farmers and peasantry to the early instruction of their children ... is strongly exemplified in the

Figure 12.1 Tom Scott, Foulshiels, The Park Family Home, *1884, drawing, 23 × 28 cm, The Album of Selkirk Subjects, Royal Scottish Academy, Edinburgh. (Drawn for inclusion, but not used, in* The History of Selkirkshire *by Thomas Craig Brown, 1886.)*

> history of Mr Park's family. The diffusion of knowledge among the natives of that part of the kingdom, and their general intelligence, must be admitted by every unprejudiced observer; nor is there any [other] country in which the effects of education are so conspicuous in promoting industry and good conduct, and in producing useful and respectable men of the inferior and middle classes, admirably fitted for all the important offices of common life.
>
> (1815, p.vii)

For all their staggering condescension, these comments point to something distinctive in the social culture of Lowland Scotland, particularly as viewed from England: it was a more 'open' society, with less emphasis on **ascribed status**, and a wider expectation that individuals could make their way in the world through innate talent and achievement. Scottish universities attracted students from a broader social spectrum than did Oxford and Cambridge, both because they were not barred to Dissenters and because their academic fees were lower.

Park completed his education in the summer of 1792 but did not graduate from Edinburgh, possibly because the oral examination fee was beyond his father's means at the time. Instead, he qualified professionally by passing an oral examination at the Company of Surgeons in London in January 1793. When reading Park's *Travels*, it is easy to forget that he was a medical practitioner, since he makes little mention of using his professional skills and knowledge in Africa. On the rare occasions he proffered medical advice, Africans ignored it.[11] What we know of his life indicates that for Park medicine was just a rather unpalatable means to a livelihood, not a vocation. Botany was his real passion, and he was fortunate in having as a mentor in botanical pursuits a considerably older brother-in-law, James Dickson. Dickson was a self-taught naturalist who had begun his working life as a jobbing gardener, built up a seed merchant's business in London and acquired a considerable reputation as an authority on British flora. In 1788 he, Sir Joseph Banks and other naturalists had founded the London Linnaean Society to promote botanical and zoological studies on Linnaean principles. Park had accompanied Dickson on a specimen-gathering trip in Scotland while a student at Edinburgh, and this expedition seems to have instilled in Park a sense of his true vocation. Through Dickson, Park was introduced to Banks and, thanks to that gentleman's patronage, obtained his first appointment as an assistant ship's surgeon on the *Worcester*, an East Indiaman that sailed for Bencoolen in Sumatra in February 1793.

[11] I have noted two instances: the first occurred in Bondou, when he offered to bleed the sickly king; on reflection, His Majesty declined Park's ministrations (pp.48–9). The second took place in Jarra after a young black herdsman had his leg shattered by a musket ball in an attack by Moorish cattle raiders. Park advised amputation above the knee – advice that was ignored (p.93). Neither incident suggests that the locals placed much store by western medicine.

Before embarking, Park wrote two letters to Alexander Anderson, the son of Dr Anderson and his closest friend, which express his religious faith and reveal something of his intellectual interests. In the first (dated 23 January 1793), he told Alexander that he had purchased Dugald Stewart's *Elements of the Philosophy of the Human Mind* 'to amuse me at sea. As you are in Edinburgh, you will write to me what people say of its religious character' (quoted in Lupton, 1979, p.14). Stewart (1753–1828) represented a school of Scottish philosophers who sought to dispel the scepticism and **solipsism**[12] inherent in empiricism by invoking the 'common sense' or 'natural judgement' of humankind. To those who asserted that there could be no *proof* that the external world existed or that the human agent's mind persisted over time, the 'common sense' philosophers replied that our consciousness of them is an ultimate fact, which neither needs nor is capable of proof. External reality and the continuity of the mind were self-evident principles that everyone endowed with common sense was competent to judge, and these principles were preconditions for all empirical and scientific knowledge. Furthermore, Stewart argued, common sense was the foundation of human empathy: what was self-evident to one person must be self-evident to another. Whether we should infer the overt influence of 'common sense' philosophy on Park's observations on African beliefs and psychology is a moot point, but it was part of the intellectual baggage he carried on his travels.

Park's letter continued:

> I have too much to say, and must therefore speak by halves. The melancholy, who complain of the shortness of human life, and the voluptuous, who think the present only their own, strive to fill up every moment with sensual enjoyment; but the man whose soul has been enlightened by his Creator, and enabled, though dimly, to discern the wonders of salvation, will look upon the joys and afflictions of this life as equally the tokens of Divine love. He will walk through the world as one travelling to a better country, looking forward with wonder to the author and finisher of his faith.
>
> (Quoted in Lupton, 1979, p.14)

This dour, and I think wholly unfeigned, piety was echoed in a second letter to Alexander a fortnight later (9 February 1793):

> My hope is now approaching to a certainty. If I be deceived, may God alone put me right, for I would rather die in the delusion than wake to all the joys of earth. May the Holy Spirit dwell in your heart, my dear friend, and if I ever see my native land

[12] Solipsism is the philosophical thesis that a person cannot be certain about the existence of the world outside herself; the only proposition of which she can be absolutely sure is that she herself exists.

> again, may I rather see the green sod on your grave than see you anything but a Christian.
>
> (Quoted in Lupton, 1979, p.14)

To the modern reader, these lines may suggest a sanctimonious prig with few friends, but we need to read them empathetically. People raised in Dissenting, Calvinist communities had a powerful, shared sense of belonging to the 'elect', which set them apart from those they considered not chosen by God for salvation. We should therefore not be judgemental about the self-righteousness evident in these quotations from Park's letters. Nevertheless, there is an interesting question, to which we shall return, as to whether his religious attitudes 'mellowed' on his African journey.

Park had very probably reached some understanding with Banks about gathering botanical specimens in the Indies, because on his return he presented his patron with certain rare plants. The first sentence of the *Travels* dates his home-coming to 1793, and you might wonder what Park did between then and leaving for Africa. The author had, alas, made a slip of the pen that fooled all his biographers until Kenneth Lupton checked the *Worcester*'s log: the vessel docked at Gravesend on 2 May 1794 (1979, p.17). Within three weeks of landing, Park was writing to his brother Alexander:

> I have ... got Sir Joseph's word that if I wish to travel he will apply to the African Association and ... I am to hire a trader to go with me to Tombuctoo and back again.
>
> (Quoted in Lupton, 1979, p.17)

Far from hanging around, the young man was in a hurry to make his way in the world. He was also trying to establish a reputation as a serious naturalist: on 4 November 1794, Park read a paper to the Linnaean Society on eight newly identified species of fish found in Sumatra.

Physically, and by all accounts temperamentally, Park (see Figures 12.2 and 12.3) was well suited to the rigours of African exploration: he was a strongly built man, over six feet tall, with a phlegmatic, methodical disposition. He had acquired a knowledge of navigation and geology, possessed many practical skills, and had an aptitude for languages.

Sir Joseph Banks and the institutional network of scientific exploration

Sir Joseph Banks had such a pivotal role in Park's career that it is appropriate to say something more about his place in the scientific community of the late Enlightenment. Banks was what contemporaries called a 'virtuoso': an omnivorous, massively erudite, amateur collector

Figure 12.2 Anonymous, after Henry Edridge, Mungo Park, *c.1797, watercolour and bodycolour on ivory, 8.3 × 7 cm, National Portrait Gallery, London. Photo: by courtesy of the National Portrait Gallery, London.*

Figure 12.3 Thomas Rowlandson, Mungo Park, *c.1805, watercolour, 22.9 × 15.2 cm, National Portrait Gallery, London. Photo: by courtesy of the National Portrait Gallery, London.*

whose trifling publications over a long lifetime contributed nothing original to knowledge. He had little taste for abstract reasoning but conceived of science in Baconian[13] fashion as that 'useful knowledge', acquired by induction, which was indispensable for social progress. Significantly, his interests lay in a domain – very broadly, the life sciences – in which the amateur collector continued to vie with the professional practitioner. The theoretical structure of the life sciences still invoked, around 1790, the concept of the **Great Chain of Being**, or the idea that nature formed a continuous, unchanging ladder in which each species occupied a preordained rung and differed from the species above and below it in minute ways. Banks knew of the accumulating, and by the later eighteenth century massive, evidence that subverted the notion of a Great Chain of Being, yet he was quite untroubled by the theoretical problems this posed. This was of a piece with his overall attitude to science. His critics within the Royal Society accused him of neglecting the rigorously theoretical sciences of mathematics and physics.

Banks's immense importance was as an entrepreneur and organizer of science. He gave unstintingly of his time, money and administrative talent in promoting scientific institutions and ensuring that the discoveries of scientists reached 'polite society'. As a wealthy landowner, Banks had the means to turn his London home into a research institution, with a vast library and huge collection of specimens that later formed the core of the Natural History Museum. He also had the social cachet that brought him an audience at court, the friendship of George III (who gave him charge of the Botanical Gardens at Kew) and access to government. Banks was elevated to the Privy Council in 1797 and served on two of its committees: on trade and on coin. Before the French Revolution, 'enlightened knowledge' was not generally seen in Britain as subverting the established order of Church and State, but rather as a driving force – along with commerce and manufacture – of ineluctable 'improvement'. The 'Glorious Revolution' of 1688 had – in the view of 'enlightened' opinion – endowed the United Kingdom with the ideal institutional matrix for the progress of civil society. Sharing this mindset allowed Banks to be both a patriot and a citizen of the international 'Republic of Letters': he served the imperial state and sought to extend its power and influence in the wider world, but he also corresponded throughout his life with scientists in Europe and America and was a member of over 50 foreign scientific academies. It is symptomatic of his international standing that, after his death in 1820, Banks was eulogized by the great zoologist and palaeontologist Georges Cuvier (1769–1832), before the Académie française.

[13] After Sir Francis Bacon (1561–1626), who put forward a classification of the sciences in the *Novum Organum* (1620) and developed an empiricist theory of knowledge in *The Great Instauration* (1623). Bacon's name is forever associated with the notion that scientific theories are formed inductively – through empirical observation and the accumulation of 'facts'. His influence on the Enlightenment was enormous.

Up to 1782, Banks's closest friend and most important scientific collaborator was Daniel Solander (1733–82), the Swedish botanist who had been Linnaeus' outstanding student. This partnership was crucially important in promoting Linnaean ideas among British naturalists. Linnaeus conceived of the natural world as a static, minutely graded hierarchy of coeval species, with human beings at the peak, a conception perfectly concordant with the Great Chain of Being. (When first published in 1735, the *Systema Naturae* included a classification of human varieties according to skin colour: white, yellow, red and black, with white Europeans at the pinnacle. This was much modified in subsequent editions. I revert to the issue of racial classification in the section on 'Africans and human nature'.) Though Linnaeus' basic paradigm did not involve a radical shift in scientific thinking, his binomial system of classification offered a way of organizing the accumulating body of empirical data that was both simpler and more comprehensive than its predecessors and rivals. (Basically, binomialism meant allocating plants and animals to a genus of which the species share structural characteristics: examples of binomial classification can be found on pages 8–9 of the *Travels* where three species of sorghum – or the genus *holcus* – are identified. Though it is not part of the prescribed reading, you might like to note the specific reference to Linnaeus on page 90 where Park discusses the edible berry identified in the Linnaean system as *Rhamnus lotus*.) To Banks, the Linnaean system seemed like a guiding thread through the labyrinth of nature. As well as a classificatory system, Linnaeus provided a practical example for botanical collectors: beginning in the 1740s, he had sent expeditions from Uppsala in Sweden to China, America, Java and Egypt to gather specimens and make observations. In 1771, Andreas Berlin had been despatched to West Africa, though he soon died of disease. Banks used the same method from his base at Kew: Francis Masson was sent to the Cape of Good Hope and Henry Smeathman to the Banana Islands off Sierra Leone, where he made the first substantial collection of West African plants and insects.

The African Association

The African Association to which Sir Joseph applied on Park's behalf was typical of the institutional network of learned societies supporting exploration and specimen gathering. It had originated in a dining club of 12 gentlemen *savants* (six were Fellows of the Royal Society) who, in June 1788, resolved:

> that as no species of information is more ardently desired, or more generally useful, than that which improves the science of Geography; and as the vast Continent of Africa, notwithstanding the efforts of the Antients, and the wishes of the Moderns, is still in a great measure unexplored, the Members of this Club do form

> themselves into an Association for Promoting the Discovery of the Inland Parts of that Quarter of the World.
>
> (Quoted in Hallett, 1964, p.46)

The Association's members numbered 95 by 1790 and were overwhelmingly men of independent means. They included leading campaigners for the abolition of the slave trade, most notably William Wilberforce, but also prominent opponents of abolition. In practice, the Association never involved itself either way in the abolition issue, nor with the commercial interests, hoping to substitute 'legitimate commerce' for slave trading. Nor did it concern itself with the missionary activity just under way in West Africa. Philanthropic committees and an association of African merchants either already existed or were soon set up to cater for these sectional interests. The African Association's primary purpose was the accumulation of geographical knowledge, though it had the secondary purpose of ensuring that this knowledge served national interests.

That said, the Association must be seen in the broader context of British interest in West Africa following the loss of the American colonies. To the political class, the region appeared a suitable dumping ground for convicts and a place where the black 'Loyalists' who had fled to Nova Scotia after the War of American Independence could be relocated. More speculatively, it was considered a potential market for British manufactures. Philanthropists were looking for coastal enclaves to establish settlement colonies, mostly of emancipated slaves though one utopian scheme envisaged a mixed-race community of British artisans and black freedmen. All told, there were a dozen such colonizing projects in the 1780s and early 1790s, though none showed any grasp of West Africa's epidemiological realities. To give one example: out of 350 men sent to a penal settlement on the Gold Coast in 1782, only seven were alive and on duty in 1785. The African Association distanced itself from both official and private initiatives, but advocated a more coherent and interventionist policy on the part of the state. It was instrumental in securing the appointment of a British consul at Senegambia[14] (who is mentioned on page 2 of the *Travels*) and after Park's return became an openly imperialist pressure group.

But the Association's political role was subordinate and largely subsequent to its primary purpose. *A Plan for the Association*, written by its secretary, Henry Beaufoy MP, for publication in 1790 bemoaned the fact that:

[14] Senegambia is the name given to the region drained by the Senegal and Gambia rivers, and roughly comprises the modern states of Senegal and the Gambia.

> the map of [Africa's] Interior is still but a wide extended blank, on which the Geographer, on the authority of Leo Africanus,[15] and of the Xeriff Edrissi the Nubian Author,[16] has traced, with a hesitating hand, a few names of unexplored rivers and of uncertain nations.
>
> (Quoted in Hallett, 1964, p.101)

These Arab authorities had been dead for centuries, and to Beaufoy it was scandalous that an age priding itself on its enlightenment should be so ignorant about a large portion of the world. The Association's members could not conceive of the European penetration of the African continent being anything but beneficial for its benighted denizens. Its *Proceedings* of 1790 concluded with an earnest hope that Europe's material and moral superiority – which was unquestioned among the educated elite – would 'rub off' on Africans as the interior was opened up to legitimate commerce:

> [O]f all the advantages to which a better acquaintance with the inland regions of Africa may lead, the first in importance is, the extension of the commerce and the encouragement of the manufactures of Britain ... [I]f, on the system of the Moors ... associations of Englishmen should form caravans, and take their departure from the highest navigable reaches of the Gambia ... there is reason to believe, that countries new to the fabrics of England, and probably inhabited by more than a hundred millions of people, may be opened gradually to her trade ... [The Association's members] cannot be indifferent to the reflection that ... by means as peaceable as the purposes are just, the conveniences of civil life, the benefits of the mechanic and the manufacturing arts, the attainments of science, the energies of the cultivated mind, and the elevation of the human character, may in some degree be imparted to nations hitherto consigned to hopeless barbarism and uniform contempt.
>
> (Quoted in Hallett, 1964, pp.101–2)

– which nicely encapsulates 'enlightened' Europe's self-esteem.

[15] [Leo the African (*c*.1483–*c*.1552) was a Moor who had travelled widely in the Sudan and was subsequently captured by Christian corsairs in the Mediterranean. He was taken to the court of Pope Leo X where, in the 1520s, he wrote *A Geographical History of Africa*. An English translation was published in 1600. For Europeans, it was the most important source of knowledge of the physical and political geography of the Western Sudan until Park initiated the era of exploration.] (Author's note.)

[16] [Xeriff Edrissi – more usually known as Sharif Idrissi – was a leading scholar in the 'golden age' of medieval Arab geography. His compilation of African geography, based on the accounts of itinerant merchants and scholars, dates from 1154.] (Author's note.)

Arab authors referred to the sub-Saharan region stretching from the Atlantic to the Nile as the *Bilad al-Sudan*, 'the land of the black men'. From them, Europeans had gleaned that the western Sudan was – or had been – a region of major states, with substantial cities connected by a great inland river, the Niger, that served as a commercial waterway. They were uncertain as to where the river rose, the direction in which it flowed and its outlet to the sea. Some believed that the Niger was a tributary of the Senegal river, others that it joined the Congo. The Association focused its efforts on determining the river's course and followed a policy of sponsoring individual explorers, of whom three were commissioned prior to Park. But an equally important step taken by the Association to remedy its geographical ignorance was to ask Major James Rennell, Britain's leading cartographer, to compile a new map of Africa. More accurate maps, which excluded purely decorative and mythical features and conveyed the maximum topographical information in the clearest way, had been a tangible product of the Enlightenment's rational and critical spirit. The French cartographers, Guillaume Delisle (1675–1726) and J.B. Bourgignon d'Anville (1697–1782), had effected a qualitative leap in map-making techniques. Rennell was indebted to d'Anville's earlier attempts at scholarly reconstruction when he drew up the map included in the Association's Report of 1790 (see Plate 12.1 in the Illustrations Book). You should study this carefully and compare it with the maps drawn by Rennell in *c.*1798 and then in 1799 (Plates 12.2 and 12.3), after Park returned with fresh information, for there is no better way of seeing how knowledge of West African geography became more extensive and precise. The cartographical errors that remained were partly a matter of human frailty. On Rennell's map of Park's journey, we have overlaid a transparency of a modern map (Plate 12.4) that shows the actual course of the Niger, the location of major towns and modern international frontiers. From it you will see that, on the basis of the information Park gave him, Rennell drew the course of the river too far to the east, although the direction of its flow is reasonably accurate, as are the spatial relations between major towns. The reason for this discrepancy is that, in the course of his travels, Park lost count of the days of the month and consequently introduced a systematic bias into his navigational reckonings.

Banks, the indefatigable committee man, was the Association's treasurer and, with Beaufoy, ran the organization by controlling its steering committee. They were the only members present at the committee meeting on 23 July 1794 that resolved 'to accept Mr Park's offer of services as a geographical Missionary' (quoted in Hallett, 1964, p.158). You will find Park's 'very plain and precise instructions' on page 3 of the *Travels*, so they need not be repeated here. The same meeting agreed his financial terms:

> from the First of August, To the time that Mr Park shall proceed to the Gambia, he shall be allowed by the Association 7/6 per day ... [F]rom the commencement of his Journey from the Gambia

> to the Niger, to the day of his return to Europe, or to some European settlement, provided the day of this return shall not exceed Two years from the day of his departure from the Gambia, Mr Park shall be allowed by the Association the sum of 15/- per day ... [Furthermore] £200 shall be paid by the Association for the purchase of such goods as, in the opinion of the Committee, will be requisite for the expenses of Mr Park's journey from the Gambia to the Interior Countries of Africa.
>
> (Quoted in Hallett, 1964, p.158)

Park was supposed to accompany Mr Willis, the newly appointed consul for Senegambia, but the latter's departure was so long delayed that Park joined a vessel belonging to Messrs Eden and Court. The Association allowed him £55 to defray the expense of his passage and outfit, in addition to the £200 already noted.

Park's pay of five guineas a week while journeying in Africa was much more than he could have expected to earn as a country doctor, but generous terms were necessary if men of calibre were to be recruited for such a hazardous enterprise. Of Park's three predecessors, two had perished in the Association's service. John Ledyard, an American adventurer who had served with Captain Cook, died in Egypt while trying to approach the Niger from the east. Major Daniel Houghton, who is mentioned several times in the opening chapters of the *Travels*, had ventured overland from the head of navigation on the Gambia in early 1791. After sending back some useful despatches, he wrote a brief note from Bondou on 1 September saying he had been robbed of all his trade goods by the son of a local potentate, but was 'in good health on his way to Tombuctoo'. He then disappeared and was soon rumoured to have been murdered. But, before vanishing, Houghton had provided the vital information – given to him by a Muslim sherif[17] in Bambouk – that the Niger flowed eastward from Timbuctoo, towards the centre of Africa, and that it carried considerable commercial traffic.

3 Our man in Africa

The 'image' of Africa in the 1790s

This section is based on chapters I and II of the *Travels*; if you have not already done so you should read them now.

[17] A sherif originally meant a descendant of Mohammed through his daughter Fatima, but was more generally applied to any man of noble status. Confusingly, the same term was applied to a religious dignitary. (Alternative spellings are 'shereef' and 'sharif'.)

EXERCISE I want you to use Park's description of the states and societies bordering the Gambia to build up a composite 'image' of the estuarial Africa well known to Europeans when he landed there. Imagine yourself reading these chapters when the book was first published in 1799 and consider the following questions:

1 Is African society on the Gambia, as described by Park, wholly alien to your own?

2 Are you given an impression of barbarous, 'tribal' peoples without writing, coinage or settled agriculture and with only rudimentary political organization?

3 What social institutions and practices do we learn about?

4 How would you sum up relations between the Europeans on the Gambia and local Africans?

DISCUSSION 1 A contemporary would have recognized several basic points of similarity between the societies as described by Park and his or her own. For a start, they were not 'stateless' or 'acephalous' societies, but small kingdoms with recognized frontiers, in which royal authority was highly effective. (We should note, however, that they were not despotic; the sovereign's power was 'by no means unlimited', p.15.) Most people appear to have lived in towns or large villages. There were sharp points of difference between Africa and Europe: polygamy was the norm (p.19) and slavery was widespread. Park estimated that three-quarters of the population were in a servile state (p.19), though he emphasized that African slave-owners did not have the absolute power over their household and field slaves exercised by white plantation owners. But, overall, the Gambia must have seemed a reasonably familiar part of the world. This is not surprising: Europeans had been trading there for nearly two and a half centuries; Portuguese and English were quite widely understood.

2 Park does not use the term 'tribe' in these chapters, and his more usual expression for an African political collectivity is 'nation' (e.g.: 'I should ... give some account of the several Negro nations which inhabit the banks of this celebrated river', p.12). The Africans he describes grew a wide range of food and industrial crops in their fields and gardens (pp. 8–9) and manufactured their own cotton cloth. They had adopted cowries as a medium of exchange and internal commerce was well developed. The products of the interior (iron, gum, shea butter) were traded for salt from the coastal states (pp.21–2). Although there was no native system of writing, the spread of Islam had led to the introduction of the written word and the Muslim code of law. Overall, we are not given the impression that social life was 'barbarous'.

3. We learn about judicial institutions and practices (the hereditary magistracy, open-air courts, professional advocacy), civic institutions, the institution of slavery, and the practice of valuing imported commodities in terms of a standard iron 'bar'.
4. The essential feature of Afro-European relations, it seems to me, was that Europeans traded on the Gambia on the sufferance of African political authorities, and African merchants were the commercial equals of the Europeans with whom they dealt.

EXERCISE What practical steps did Park take prior to his journey into the interior? What light do they throw on the dangers of African exploration and the frame of mind with which Park approached his task?

DISCUSSION Park took the eminently practical steps of 'seasoning' himself and learning Mandingo (now usually referred to as Malinké) before setting out for the Niger. Both testify to what I would call his level-headed professionalism. Malinké was and remains the most widely spoken language in Senegambia and what is now Mali. You will have gathered, I am sure, that 'seasoning' was the practice of acquiring some immunity to the endemic local diseases before venturing into the interior.

To add a little medical context: the disease barrier was the most formidable obstacle to the European penetration of tropical Africa and the main reason why colonial settlement was so sparse before the late nineteenth century. In this respect, the American tropics were much kinder to incomers than Africa: the mortality rate among white troops stationed in West Africa in the 1830s was roughly five times that of those in the West Indies. Here we have an essential part of the explanation of why Europeans shipped slave labour from one tropical region to another, rather than establishing plantations in Africa itself. By Park's day, it was well known that incomers were most likely to die from 'fever' during their first months of residence, and that those who had contracted a non-fatal bout of sickness improved their long-term chances of survival. The 'smart fever' that laid Park low at the end of July was very likely *falciparum malaria*, the most lethal variant of the disease, and you will have gathered that Park did not have our understanding of its aetiology. He could have protected himself with infusions of chinchona bark, a natural source of quinine, which was enjoying something of a vogue among travellers in exotic climes at this time. I can shed no light on why he did not do so.

There is a potent image in our culture of Africa as 'the dark continent', and it is tempting to project this image back on to the eighteenth century. According to P.D. Curtin's classic study of British ideas about Africa in this period, that would be a mistake:

> 'The image of 'darkest Africa', either as an expression of geographical ignorance, or as one of cultural arrogance, was a nineteenth-century invention… [R]elative to their knowledge of the world in general, eighteenth-century Europeans knew more and cared more about Africa than they did at any later period up to the 1950s.
>
> (1964, p.10)

For all the gentlemen *savants* of the African Association bemoaned their indebtedness to dead Arabs for their exiguous knowledge of the interior, Africa occupied a large place in European treatises on world history and geography. In the encyclopaedic *Universal History* (published in 65 volumes between 1736 and 1765) two of the 16 volumes in the 'Modern History' section were devoted to Africa. The treatment was as extensive as that given to east, south-east and south Asia combined. Moreover, the substance of the Africa volumes was the history, manners and customs of Africans themselves. Similarly, C.T. Middleton's *New and Complete System of Geography*, published in two volumes in 1779, devoted more space to Africa than it did to all of Asia, and three times as much space as it gave the Americas. West Africa alone received more detailed treatment than India. The continent was not a dark void in Europe's cultural map of the world.

The Gambia itself had once been a major centre of English, Scottish and (more latterly) North American enterprise in West Africa, but was a commercial backwater by the 1790s. In 1711–20, Senegambia had supplied about 31,000 slaves to the Atlantic trade, which was 9 per cent of total overseas slave exports in that decade. In the 1790s, the region supplied 7,000 slaves, which was less than 1 per cent of total Atlantic exports (Lovejoy, 1983, Table 3.4). Under its charter, the Royal African Company had enjoyed a monopoly on British trade with the Gambia and maintained a fort on James Island, not to overawe the local Africans – on whom the garrison depended for food and water – but to protect British interests against the French, based at St Louis at the mouth of the Senegal. When individual traders were licensed to trade with West Africa around 1730, the company was granted a state subsidy to defray the costs of its fort. Francis Moore, a company 'writer' or commercial agent, had published a fascinating account of trade and society on the river in 1738. (Park refers to this book on p.20 of the *Travels*.) It was evidently a much more bustling thoroughfare in Moore's day. He reckoned that up to 2,000 slaves a year were being funnelled into the Gambia for the Atlantic trade by a hundred or so African merchants. Most were prisoners of war, and a high proportion would have been captured during the Muslim *jihads* in the interior. But the opportunity to sell slaves in return for highly valued imports of cloth, guns and liquor was also a strong

temptation for the powerful to enslave petty offenders in local society. As Moore noted:

> Since this slave-trade has been used, all punishments are changed into slavery; there being an advantage on such condemnations, they [that is, powerful Africans] strain for crimes very hard, in order to get the benefit of selling the criminal. Not only Murder, Theft and Adultery are punished by selling the criminal for a slave, but every trifling crime is punished in the same manner. There was a man brought to me to be sold for having stolen a tobacco-pipe.
>
> (1738, p.42)

In Moore's time, not all slave exports were destined for the New World plantations. Many young captives were taken to Cadiz and Lisbon, where there was a fashion for black household servants. What proportion of total exports they constituted is difficult to say, but the Iberian demand for boys and girls was such that 'there is scarce any difference between the prices of young slaves and grown ones' (Moore, 1738, p.45). This specialized trade was largely curtailed in the 1760s when slave imports into metropolitan Portugal were banned.

During the Seven Years' War (1756–63) Britain had overrun most of the French posts in Upper Guinea. In 1764 these were joined with the settlements on the Gambia to form the crown colony of Senegambia, with a constitution modelled on that of the British colonies in North America. This was the first attempt made by a British government to assume responsibility for the administration of an area of African territory and its inhabitants. It proved a complete failure. French merchants based at Goree retained much of the trade and evaded the duties on which the colonial administration relied for its revenue. With exiguous financial resources and limited manpower, there could be no question of effective occupation of the hinterland. During the War of American Independence the French recaptured most of their former posts in Africa and, at the peace of Versailles (1783), the British presence here was once again restricted to the Gambia. The Crown relinquished its responsibilities to the Company of Merchants Trading to West Africa. This was not a monopoly corporation and did not itself engage in trade, but was an association that enabled its members to share the costs of protection and other externalities.

When Park arrived, the slave trade was in the hands of three individual merchants (Dr Laidley and the Ainsley brothers) trading on their own account. They saw only about three small British ships a year. The principal supply areas for the Atlantic trade were thousands of miles away, in West Central Africa and the hinterland of the Bight of Biafra. This needs to be borne in mind when considering Park's more general observations on the relation of the Atlantic slave trade to slavery *within* Africa.

Africans and human nature

This section is 'triggered' by some passages in chapter VI, which is your second reading from Park. I have provided a passage linking this chapter to the earlier part of Park's narrative, and you will need to read that first to grasp some of the events recounted in the chapter.

Linking passage

1795

Park left Laidley and the Ainsley brothers on 3 December and headed east for the kingdom of Woolli. For about the first month of his journey he followed a route taken by previous European travellers; not until 18 February did he reach the vicinity of Major Houghton's death. Park's travelling companions when he set out were Johnson, an emancipated slave who had spent time in England and was hired as an interpreter; Demba, a slave boy who spoke Serer in addition to Malinké, and who had been promised his freedom by Laidley if he behaved himself; a Muslim blacksmith who had worked for Laidley and was returning home to the kingdom of Kasson; and three Muslim freemen (two of whom were slave merchants). It was surmised that Houghton's substantial baggage train had attracted the rapacity of African potentates so Park had been instructed to travel with the minimum of trade goods. To a remarkable degree, he depended on Laidley's credit with African slave merchants based hundreds of miles in the interior. Park did not, unfortunately, escape the predatory taxation of travellers by kings and their officials; on 25 December, he was relieved of half of his goods on the orders of the King of Kajaaga and found himself unable to procure provisions for want of money. But, in a touching incident, he experienced the spontaneous kindness of an old female slave who gave him a meal of groundnuts while he sat upon the Bentang (or public platform) in Joag:

> This trifling circumstance gave me peculiar satisfaction. I reflected with pleasure on the conduct of this poor untutored slave, who, without examining into my character or circumstances, listened implicitly to the dictates of her own heart. Experience had taught her that hunger was painful, and her own distresses made her commiserate those of others.
>
> (p.62)

On several occasions in his travels, Park was to be profoundly grateful for the charity of ordinary African women, and for contemporary readers these were the most moving moments in his narrative – a point I want you to bear in mind when considering the reception of Park's book. Immediately after this incident, Park was befriended by Demba Sego Jalla, the nephew of the King of Kasson, a neighbouring state that was preparing for war with Kajaaga. Park and his party then travelled to Teesee, in Kasson, in Demba Sego's company.

EXERCISE Now read chapter VI and answer the following questions:

1 This chapter provides interesting evidence that Park was traversing West Africa's major cultural frontier. What was it? How would you describe relations between Africans living on the frontier? How was the frontier advancing, according to the evidence of this chapter?

2 In this chapter, Park gives his readers an unambiguous account of his understanding of human nature; summarize it in your own words and say how it affected his attitudes to Africans. I am persuaded by Park that he was not just voicing a conventional sentiment; are you?

3 Contemporary readers may well have felt that Park had unintentionally contaminated himself morally while travelling in Africa. Why was that?

DISCUSSION

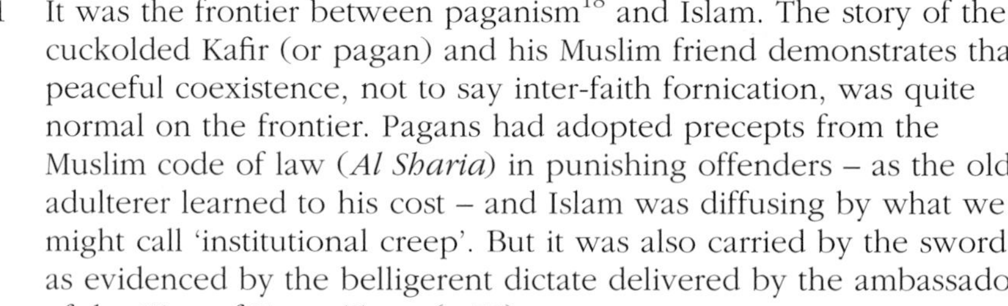

1 It was the frontier between paganism[18] and Islam. The story of the cuckolded Kafir (or pagan) and his Muslim friend demonstrates that peaceful coexistence, not to say inter-faith fornication, was quite normal on the frontier. Pagans had adopted precepts from the Muslim code of law (*Al Sharia*) in punishing offenders – as the old adulterer learned to his cost – and Islam was diffusing by what we might call 'institutional creep'. But it was also carried by the sword, as evidenced by the belligerent dictate delivered by the ambassador of the King of Foota Torra (p.71).

2 Park had no doubt that all humans had a common nature and that Africans formed the same emotional bonds and experienced the same sympathies as did Europeans. Africans may have been uninhibited by the restraints of civilized society – and so were 'rude children of nature' – but beneath the skin they were no different from Europeans in their attachments and affections (p.74). What persuades me that this is not simply a conventional utterance is the detail that follows. The welcoming crowd gathered round the returning blacksmith are real people, who had never seen a European before, and were initially suspicious of Park's uncommon appearance, but intrigued by his outlandish clothes.

3 To continue his journey, Park had to draw on Laidley's credit with Salim Daucari, a local slave merchant who regularly traded with the Gambia (p.75). To a modern reader, Park seems curiously blind to

[18] By 'paganism' Park meant what many scholars now call 'indigenous religions', that is, locally-based religions other than Christianity, Judaism and Islam. In our own day, the term 'pagan' is also commonly used for someone who has no religion. In these units, however, Park's usage is followed.

any moral conflict between believing all humans had a common nature and depending on the 'kindness and attention' of a man who traded in human beings. The matter requires further research, but I suspect that contemporary abolitionists would have had the same response.

To gloss the last point: Park was quite non-judgemental about slavery and slave trading within Africa, as you may have noted from his account of the absconded slave who was severely flogged on being recaptured (p.67) and similar incidents. This moral detachment is one of the strengths of the *Travels* as a documentary record; Park simply recorded what he saw, without saying whether it was right or wrong.

Park's sympathies for ordinary Africans and his lack of the racial arrogance exhibited in later European commentaries on African life prompt the obvious question as to how representative he was of educated opinion of his day. There is, unfortunately, no brief answer. The attitudes of late eighteenth-century Europeans to racial diversity are difficult to summarize in a way that does justice to their complexity and fluidity over time. A barrier to our understanding is the virtually irresistible temptation to read into Enlightenment discussions of race both precursors of the scientific racism of the later nineteenth century and anticipations of our own racial egalitarianism. Such hindsight establishes false continuities: eighteenth-century attitudes to racial diversity arose within a framework of understanding that was completely disrupted by the triumph of evolutionary science in the nineteenth century. In Park's day, theology was a constraint on or, to put it less pejoratively, a positive source of all knowledge that we would regard as lying in the domain of the 'human sciences'. Racial variation in humans was often classed with species variation in the Great Chain of Being, without any clear distinction between nature and culture. The first anthropological classifications of human variation were the work of naturalists (such as Linnaeus) attempting to fix the place of human kind(s) in the order of creation. Up to the end of the eighteenth century, naturalists could not shake off the theological dogma that all species had been created perfect and in their present form were 'degenerations' from the original ideal.

I won't pretend this is easy to grasp, and it may seem awfully remote from Park's 'common sense' sympathies for the Africans he encountered. Still, we cannot answer the question 'How representative was he?' without looking at the wider intellectual context in which he wrote. I will sketch in the historical background with a very broad brush and then focus on ideas and controversies within Britain and the scientific community with which Park was familiar.

The orthodox Christian view was that all humans could trace a common descent to Adam and Eve, and so partook of a common nature and original sin. On the authority of Genesis, black people or those of mixed ancestry were believed to be descendants of Noah's second son, Ham, whose particular sin of filial irreverence made the term Hamite (or Chamite) one of obloquy. With the revival of classical learning, educated Europeans had frequently supplemented precepts drawn from the Bible with the Aristotelian notion of innate human differences that fitted men and women for their place in the social order. Aristotle had contended that, since many were slaves by nature, it was both natural and in their interest that they be subject to men who could make the necessary moral judgements for them. Here was a justification for chattel slavery, which was an accepted institution throughout Europe up to the sixteenth century (and way beyond in the Mediterranean).[19] The Aristotelian view did not presuppose that only blacks were peculiarly fitted for slavery, but by 1500 there were recognized prohibitions throughout Europe against enslaving Christians, or more particularly European Christians, for sale or economic purposes. European felons could be condemned to galley slavery in the Mediterranean; convicts and captive European rebels could be despatched as slaves to American colonies; but the notion of reducing Europeans who were not felons or rebels to the status of chattel was abhorrent.

With the development of transatlantic sugar plantations that were viable only with coerced labour, Europeans had to confront the question as to which groups of outsiders were 'suitable' for enslavement. One option was to enslave Native Americans, but their dreadful susceptibility to imported disease and refusal to be habituated to routine tasks made them an unsatisfactory source of coerced labour. The most economically rational course would have been to enslave the many thousands of destitute Europeans – who were already subject to draconian laws against beggary and vagabondage – and to transport them across the Atlantic, along with the convicts, rebels and indentured servants. But white enslavement was excluded by the cultural prohibition against treating Europeans as chattel. Instead, Europeans resorted to the second-best option of purchasing slaves on the African coast, where there was a ready supply. Slavery was a ubiquitous feature of African life and for many centuries blacks had been marched across the Sahara for sale in the slave marts of the Muslim world. *The long-term consequence of resorting to Africa for slaves was to elide, in a way unique to the Euro-American world, the concept of slavery with that of race.* In the planter-dominated, caste-conscious societies of Brazil, the Caribbean, and the southern American states, people of black African descent were known only as slaves or emancipated slaves. And, despite communities of free blacks in Europe's seaports and elsewhere, black skin, hair texture and facial features were intimately associated in art, literature and plebeian culture with slave status. Stereotypes of 'the Negro' reflected the elision of race and slavery. As one abolitionist was to remark despairingly in an attack on slavery, 'Negroid features and complexion, regarded as the

[19] Chattel slavery persisted in Sicily as late as 1812.

natural badges of inferiority, seem to mark [blacks] out for slavery' (quoted in Barber, 1978, p.60). The words 'noir' and 'black' were virtual synonyms for 'slave' in the eighteenth century.

As I have already indicated, the European philosophical tradition had decisively repudiated slavery before the Atlantic slave plantation economy controlled by Europeans reached anything like its full extent. Most 'enlightened' thinkers followed John Locke in rejecting innate qualities of mind, and therefore had no truck with Aristotle's notion that a large class of humanity was innately fitted for bondage. Human nature was generally conceived of as uniform, although this abstract commitment to uniformism was challenged in two ways. First, increasing ethnographic knowledge demonstrated the sheer diversity of human society, and prompted the question why a supposedly invariant human nature gave rise to such variety of institutions and customs. Second, by the mid-eighteenth century European intellectuals were convinced that their own civilization had progressed far beyond all others in its technological and cultural accomplishments. This collective self-esteem was particularly marked when Europeans compared black societies with their own, and it led some to argue that innate differences between black and white were the cause of cultural differences. Hence the tension in the Enlightenment's understanding of racial variation: in an abstract way, blacks partook of a common human nature; when encountered in the flesh they were 'naturally' different and 'naturally' inferior.

We should note in passing that slavery had been both challenged and defended from *within* the Protestant tradition since the seventeenth century. Puritanism had encouraged a new humanitarianism, of which the Quakers were the best-known representatives, but also reinforced 'literalism' or reading the Scriptures as the literal truth. Passages in the Bible can be cited both to condone and to condemn slavery. Those wishing to justify the institution could – and frequently did – cite Leviticus, 25:44.[20] As one historian has remarked, this passage 'can only have suggested to the reflective but still literal mind that slavery had a place in the divine economy' (Anstey, 1975, p.186). Opponents of slavery could cite the books of the prophets Joel and Amos, where those who enslave are threatened with divine retribution. The ambiguities in the Bible, and its openness to conflicting interpretations, meant that fundamentalist Protestants were found on both sides of the ideological conflict over the abolition of the slave trade. The majority of theologians saw no scriptural impediments to slavery; it is indicative of their acceptance of the institution that the Society for the Propagation of the Gospel had its own slave plantation in the West Indies. In 1788, a pro-slavery clergyman, the Reverend Raymond Harris, published *Scriptural Researches on the Licitness of the Slave Trade. Shewing its Conformity with the Principles of Natural and Revealed Religion. Delineated in the*

[20] 'Your male and female slaves are to come from the nations around you; from them you may buy slaves' (New International Version).

Sacred Writing of the Word of God. An increasingly articulate minority found slavery utterly repugnant because it conflicted with a moral duty to act with compassion and benevolence to others, irrespective of their status and colour. By the 1780s, many slavery opponents were Evangelical Christians persuaded that Holy Scripture proved that the institution was ever detestable in the sight of God. They saw in the redemption of the Chosen People from Egyptian bondage a paradigm of their personal salvation.

What I have said so far implies that the ideological defence of slavery entailed the racist categorization of Africans as innately inferior to Europeans, and possibly as a different type of human. There were certainly conspicuous examples of this rationalization in the years when slavery was widely questioned, but before abolitionism was a formally organized movement. The most frequently cited was Edward Long's *History of Jamaica*, first published in 1774. Long was a West Indian planter and judge with many years' experience overseeing African slaves, who assured his readers that:

> In general, [Africans] are void of genius, and seem almost incapable of making any progress in civility or science. They have no plan or system of morality among them. Their barbarity to their children debases their nature even below that of brutes. They have no moral sensations; no taste but for women, gormondizing, and drinking to excess; no wish but to be idle ... In so vast a continent as that of Afric ... we might expect to find a proportionable diversity among the inhabitants ... But, on the contrary, a general uniformity runs through all these various regions of people; so that, if any difference be found, it is only in degrees of the same qualities; and, what is more strange, those of the worst kind ... Whatever great personages this country [i.e. Africa] might have anciently produced ... they are now degenerated into a brutish, ignorant, idle, crafty, treacherous, bloody, thievish, mistrustful and superstitious people ... [A]lthough they have been acquainted with Europeans, and their manufactures, for so many hundred years, they have, in all this series of time, manifested so little taste for arts, or a genius either inventive or imitative.
>
> (Long, 1970, vol.2, pp.353–6)

As slaves of Europeans, Long argued, Africans acquired industrious habits and useful skills, and their characters were chastened by discipline and exposure to true religion. But he did more than repeat the clichés of the West Indian interest; he had the trappings of scientific learning. He used the concept of natural gradation in the great chain of creation to call into question the fundamental unity of humankind:

> When we reflect on the nature of [Africans], and their dissimilarity to the rest of mankind, must we not conclude that they are

> different species of the same *genus*? Of other animals, it is well known, there are many kinds, each kind having its proper species subordinate thereto; and why shall we insist, that man alone, of all other animals, is undiversified in the same manner, when we find so many irresistible proofs which denote his conformity to the general system of the world?
>
> (Long, 1970, vol.2, p.358)

In effect, Long denied the biblical account of human beings' common descent from Adam and Eve and put forward a theory of polygenesis. The genus *homo* was, he claimed, divided into three species with different origins: Europeans and similar types; 'Negroes'; and 'orang-outangs'. By this time, naturalists were beginning to conceive of a species as a group of organisms capable of interbreeding, and the manifest fact of miscegenation was a problem for polygenesism. In support of it, Long claimed mulattos were either infertile hybrids or that their descendants degenerated into infertility. The evident falsifiability of this claim did not stop Long's book from being widely read by the naturalists. Polygenesists recycled his ideas over the next three-quarters of a century, and American pro-slavery publicists often referred to his work.

The credence given to polygenesis and innate African inferiority among the British general reading public in the 1780s and 1790s is more difficult to gauge. Abolitionists clearly saw them as false notions they had to confront. When Thomas Clarkson composed his *Essay on the Slavery and Commerce of the Human Species*, he was at pains to confute the reasoning that 'the Africans are an inferiour link of the chain of nature, and are made for slavery' (1788, p.116). Clarkson accepted that 'In their own country ... [Africans] are mostly in a savage state. Their powers of mind are limited to few objects. Their ideas are consequently few' (p.118). But, he argued, this 'uncultivated state' (p.118) was no different from that of Europeans before they were civilized. Most 'experts' would have agreed: their explanations for what was perceived as African inferiority were basically environmentalist. The article on 'Negro' in the 1797 edition of the *Encyclopaedia Britannica* imputed a string of 'notorious vices' to 'this unhappy race' ('idleness, treachery, revenge, cruelty, impudence, stealing, lying, profanity, debauchery, nastiness, and intemperance') but attributed these to the 'influence of climate and the modes of savage life' or to the degrading effects of slavery. The article also added that 'there is good reason to believe that [blacks'] intellectual endowments are equal to those of the whites who have been found in the same circumstances' (quoted in Davis, 1984, pp.132–3). Environmentalist accounts such as this were more consonant with prevailing orthodoxies than Long's ideas. We must recall that the British state and society were institutionally Christian and few questioned the biblical account of creation. Polygenesis contradicted what was a central religious dogma for the great majority. After abolition of the slave trade became a national issue in late 1787, defenders of slavery rarely deployed the theory of different racial origins and blacks' innate 'fitness' for bondage in their polemical literature. Polygenesis was part of the ideological background, but too heterodox to be entertained by more than a minority of 'advanced' thinkers.

By the 1790s, the most authoritative scientific account of racial variation was to be found in the work of Johann Friedrich Blumenbach (1752–1850), the German polymath generally acknowledged as the founder of scientific anthropology. Blumenbach's doctoral dissertation at the University of Göttingen was a pioneering work of physical anthropology entitled *De Generis Humani Varietate Nativa* ('Concerning the Natural Variety of the Human Race'). In it he proposed a division of humankind into four main types or races: the Caucasian (or European), the Mongolian (or Asian), the Ethiopian (or black African) and Native Americans. Blumenbach regarded Caucasians as the original strain and the latter three as 'degenerations' resulting from the influence of climate, food and mode of life. The use of this derogatory term makes

Blumenbach sound like a precursor of scientific racism, but it seems that he used it in a technical sense to mean 'variation'. Against the polygenesists, Blumenbach insisted that 'There is but one species of the genus man' (quoted in Gascoigne, 1994, p.153). In subsequent decades, Blumenbach developed and refined his classification of human types, drawing extensively on anatomical data received through the good offices of Sir Joseph Banks, with whom he corresponded over several decades. (The fact that Hanover, where Blumenbach resided, shared its ruling house with Britain facilitated the despatch of specimens.) The refinements of Blumenbach's classificatory system need not concern us. What is pertinent, however, is that he became known as a staunch advocate of the unity and the physical and mental equality of humankind. He insisted that there were no sharp distinctions between human types: the differences between them 'run so insensibly, by so many shades and transitions one into the other that it is impossible to separate them by any but very arbitrary limits' (quoted in Gascoigne, 1994, p.153). By the 1790s, Blumenbach's name was well known in British scientific circles and his articles were being translated for the British scholarly journals. In one of them, he argued 'That the negroes, in regard to their mental faculties and capacity, are not inferior to the rest of the human race' (*The Philosophical Magazine*, 1799, III, pp.141–7).

One last point worth adding to this already complex discussion is that, although black Africans frequently encountered prejudice and abuse in Britain and other European countries, this was not a universal experience. By the later eighteenth century, it was not uncommon for wealthy Africans living in the Gambia and Senegal to send their sons to Britain and France to acquire a European language and commercial skills. In the later 1780s, there were about 50 African trainees residing in or around Liverpool. Christianized, educated Africans could move in polite society, and we know of a few who married 'respectable' British women and lived unmolested lives. European merchants in the Africa trade valued literate African converts as intermediaries with the local society. The Company of Merchants Trading with West Africa appointed Philip Quaque, a Fantee who had been educated and ordained in England, as their official chaplain on the Gold Coast; he became the most highly paid member of the company's staff, except for the governor himself. When defending the concept of black equality, Blumenbach cited examples of black court musicians, black Protestant clergymen, black university teachers, and black correspondents of scientific academies; he even mentioned a black person serving as a councillor of state to the King of Prussia (*The Philosophical Magazine*, 1799, III, pp.141–7).

EXERCISE Read back over this discussion and try to answer the following question: 'How representative was Park of educated opinion in his attitude to Africans?'

DISCUSSION I shall keep my specimen answer brief. Park was one of a tiny number of Europeans who had lived among Africans for any length of time as an equal. In this, he was quite atypical. But a commitment to an all-inclusive human nature *in the abstract* was not unusual among people of his class, background and religious persuasion. The idea of common descent was not only a powerful religious myth; it had the authority of the best scientific minds writing in those discourses in which racial difference was constructed and comprehended. Sceptics were perhaps more likely to entertain notions of African inequality on the putative grounds of their different descent. But Park was not a sceptic; nor were the vast majority of his educated contemporaries. For an age that thought in terms of natural rights, a common human nature was morally charged with a common equality.

In Moorish captivity

This section is based on pp.110–14, chapter X, and pp.137–42. Again, I have provided a linking passage.

Linking passage

After leaving Kasson, Park's direct progress to the Niger was frustrated by the imminent war involving the neighbouring pagan states of Kaarta and Bambarra to the east. The King of Kaarta (whom Park calls Daisy Koorabarri, though the name is now written as Desse Koulibali) received Park courteously, but advised him to return to Kasson to await the end of hostilities. This would have meant travelling inland during the rainy season, which Park was loath to do, so he pressed for an alternative. Daisy suggested taking a circuitous route to the Niger via the Moorish kingdom of Ludamar to the north, though he cautioned that this was 'by no means free from danger' (p.87). On 18 February, Park and his companions passed through the frontier village of Simbing. En route, they had witnessed the depredations of Moorish cattle raiders who terrorized the sedentary pagan villagers. The inhabitants of the first substantial town in Ludamar, Jarra, were predominantly 'Negroes' who preferred 'a precarious protection under the Moors, which they purchase by a tribute, rather than continue exposed to their predatory hostilities' (p.101). In Jarra, Park was still able to obtain funds on Laidley's account from a local slave merchant, which testifies to the commercial trust linking Europeans on the coast with African traders in the interior. Park sent a message and a handsome gift to Ali, the sovereign of Ludamar, asking for permission to pass through his territory. Johnson, Park's interpreter, was so fearful of the Moors that he resolved to return to the Gambia; Demba, the slave boy, insisted on accompanying Park. On 7 March, Park and Demba were apprehended by a party of Moors who had been sent by Ali to take them to his desert-edge camp at Benowm (see Figure 12.4).

Figure 12.4 A View of Ali's Tent at the Camp of Benowm, *from Mungo Park,* Travels in the Interior Districts of Africa*, 1799, 2nd edn, British Library, London. Photo: by permission of the British Library, London (shelfmark 681.e.21).*

EXERCISE

Now read from 'About five o'clock [on 12 March] we came in sight of Benowm ...' (p.110), plus chapter X, then attempt the following questions:

1 Does Park's account of his reception by the Moors warrant his description of them as 'a people who study mischief as a science, and exult in the miseries and misfortunes of their fellow creatures' (p.114)?

2 How would you describe Park's survival strategy while he was in Ali's camp? What light does this throw on Park's character (or perhaps one should say the characterization of himself that he wanted to convey to his readers)?

3 Park recounts two incidents when he was the object of the attention of Moorish women (pp.120–1, 124–5). What appeal do you think such incidents would have had to Park's contemporary readers? What might we infer about notions of literary taste and decorum at the time when Park was writing?

4 What prejudice – virtually universal among late eighteenth-century Europeans – would have been confirmed when they read Park's account of the Moors?

DISCUSSION

1 My response would be 'not entirely'. Park's account of his reception seems to have been coloured by his recollection of the whole period of his captivity, when he suffered the privations of thirst and hunger (partly because the Moors insisted he observe Ramadan). To me, the Moors seem to have exhibited the understandable curiosity of a relatively isolated people who had never seen a European and were astonished by his outlandish dress. Their hostility towards Christians is well attested in other sources, but the incident with the wild boar could be interpreted as a crude practical joke.

2 Park initially believed himself to be under threat of death, mutilation or blinding, and to survive he adopted a strategy of Christian forbearance. I think this was in character, but was also part of the self-portrait he wanted to convey to the reader.

3 The appeal of these incidents is that of the *exotic*; they would have been wholly foreign to the experience of late eighteenth-century British readers who would, I suspect, have felt a pleasurable *frisson* in learning about manners and customs so different from their own, particularly as they involved relations between foreign women and a European man. You may have been puzzled as to what exactly was dashed in Park's face, but it is pretty clear that it was a bowl of bride's pee. Notions of taste and decorum constrained the way Park related this incident, but they were less restrictive than those prevailing in the production of 'polite' fiction.

 4 The prejudice against Islam. 

EXERCISE Park gives a more extended account of the Moors' society and culture in chapter XII, and concludes that they are 'at once the vainest and proudest, and perhaps the most bigoted, ferocious, and intolerant of all the nations on the earth' (p.147). To a modern reader, this reeks of ethnocentricity, or a failure to understand other societies in terms of their own moral and cultural standards. It is worth asking whether Park's loathing for the Moors was such that he was unable to write about them objectively. Read pp.137–42 (up to '... too good a beard for a Christian') and form your own assessment. Why might Park have been particularly offended by the treatment of women?

DISCUSSION As is his wont, Park makes many factual observations whose accuracy I am inclined to take on trust. Some of them bear quite favourably on the Moors: they practise the normal range of handicrafts (weaving, leatherwork, ironwork), a fact that does not seem entirely consistent with the assertion that 'the majority of the people are perfectly idle' (p.142). The Moors prize literacy, and all boys are taught to read and write parts of the Koran. They administer criminal justice promptly and decisively. It is a matter of fact that corpulence in women was (and still is) much admired in traditional desert societies. The – to us – disgusting practice of force-feeding girls with kouskous and milk to fatten them up is perfectly credible. You cannot be expected to have known this, but it is worth adding that Park and his 'enlightened' contemporaries regarded the way a society treated women as a key indicator of its moral 'progress'. By this criterion, the Moors were indeed backward. As far as we know, Park portrayed the role of these quasi-nomadic, desert fringe peoples in the political ecology of the Sahel[21] quite accurately. Park's account of them was affected by his own experience of captivity and a European's normal prejudice against Islam, but still seems to me reasonably objective.

If Park's contemporary readers were xenophobes looking for a reflection of their own prejudices in his narrative, they would have found it in his depiction of the Moors, not black Africans. The rudeness and barbarity of the Moors are frequently contrasted with the humanity and gentleness of 'Negro' villagers (as on p.108). Park was too conscientious a reporter not to record his captors' occasional courtesies, and he evidently found some favour with Fatima, Ali's principal consort. But the composite portrait of the Moors is unredeemed by any suggestion of 'noble savagery'. Anti-

[21] Sahel, from the Arabic *sahil* meaning 'shore', refers to the transitional zone between the southern edge of the Sahara and the tropical forest. Park spells it 'Saheel'.

Muslim prejudice certainly coloured this portrait, but was not its primary inspiration. As you will learn, Park owed his life to a black Muslim, and elsewhere he openly acknowledged Islam's educative role in West Africa.

Park had a particular reason for detesting the Moors: when he was eventually released from captivity on 28 May, Ali insisted on retaining the boy Demba as part of his slave entourage (pp.149–50). The lad had served Park devotedly, and they were evidently fond of each other. He did his utmost to have the boy redeemed, though with what success we do not know. Moreover, Park appears to have suffered some trauma in Ali's camp, which he spared his readers. Years after returning home, memories of his captivity were still giving him nightmares. In 1804 he told Walter Scott, who had become a close friend, that certain incidents had been omitted from the book in order not to shock the credulity of the public. It is pointless speculating as to what they might have been.

Reaching the Niger

This section is based on the second half of chapter XV, pp.175–84.

Linking passage

After his release by Ali, Park spent a month in or near Jarra under constant threat of being taken into captivity again by the Moors. The town had become embroiled in the war between Kasson and the neighbouring states and towards the end of June was threatened by Daisy's advancing army. Park witnessed its hurried evacuation by 'the poor inhabitants, who were thronging after me, driving their sheep, cows, goats, etc ... There was a great noise and crying everywhere upon the road' (p.156). On 1 July, after a hair-raising encounter with three Moors, Park eventually headed east for Sego alone, and with not much more than the clothes he was wearing. His horse had 'been reduced to a perfect Rosinante' (p.157 – a reference to Don Quixote's cadaverous nag in Cervantes' celebrated comic novel). For a fortnight, he made his way through Fulani (or as Park says, Foulah) country, avoiding the Moors and begging for food from villagers. On 11 July, he met up with some fugitives from 'the tyrannical government of the Moors' (p.172) who were transferring their allegiance to the King of Bambarra.

EXERCISE Now read from 'Next day we continued our journey ...' (p.175) to the end of the chapter and attempt the following questions:

1 Park encountered a coffle or caravan of 70 slaves on 19 July; where was it going? What significance do you attach to its destination and composition in terms of the slave-trading economy of Senegambia?

2 What image of himself does Park convey in the subsequent passages?

3 What impression does the reader gain of Sego and its hinterland? How would this have influenced contemporary perceptions of Africa?

4 How would the incident narrated on pp.181–2 have influenced contemporary perceptions of black Africans?

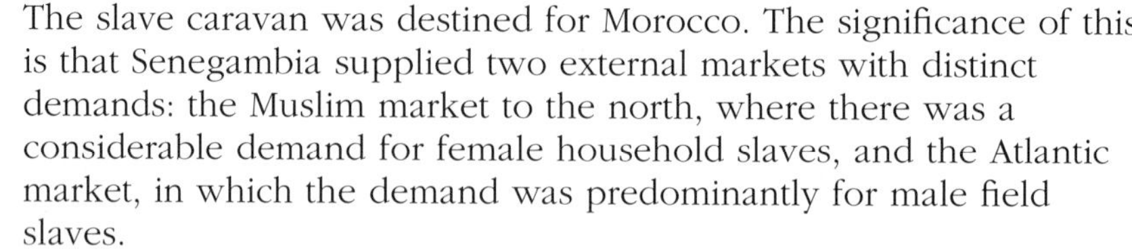

DISCUSSION 1 The slave caravan was destined for Morocco. The significance of this is that Senegambia supplied two external markets with distinct demands: the Muslim market to the north, where there was a considerable demand for female household slaves, and the Atlantic market, in which the demand was predominantly for male field slaves.

2 By this stage of his journey, Park was destitute, his horse was on its last legs, and he had become a figure of fun for African villagers. Given the earlier reference to Rosinante, we might read a suggestion of Don Quixote into this pen-portrait. Nevertheless, Park assures his readers of his Christian dedication to his mission: having drunk from the Niger, he gives thanks to the Almighty. So we might add a hint of Bunyan's Pilgrim.

3 Sego and its hinterland presented 'a prospect of civilisation and magnificence' (p.180) which Park had little expected to find in the African interior. The reader is given the impression of a substantial urban complex on both banks of the Niger, with whitewashed, clay-built houses, mosques in every corner, and quite broad streets. A great number of people were waiting for public ferries to cross the river. Even without supporting evidence, we can surmise how this description would have influenced perceptions of sub-Saharan Africa: it could no longer be considered wholly barbarous.

4 The incident is bound to have strengthened the perception that black Africans were as kind and charitable as common folk anywhere. I think it would be fair to add that the incident lent itself to sentimentalization: these were humble women who had taken Park in, fed him and given him somewhere to sleep while they extemporized a song lamenting his circumstances. To cap it all, they were spinning far into the night. You would be forgiven for thinking: 'Too good to be true.'

Questions 3 and 4 required you to speculate, though not I think unduly. For confirmatory evidence as to how impressions of Africa and Africans were affected by Park's account, it is worth citing the biographical memoir John Whishaw composed quite near the event:

> In addition to these discoveries relating to the physical state of Africa, others were made by Park scarcely less important, in what may be termed its *moral* geography; namely, the kind and

> amiable disposition of the Negro inhabitants of the Interior, as contrasted with the intolerance and brutal ferocity of the Moors; the existence of great and populous cities in the heart of Africa; and the higher state of improvement and superior civilization of the inhabitants of the Interior, on a comparison with the inhabitants of the countries adjoining to the coast.
>
> (1815, p.xx)

We know that contemporaries were deeply affected by the incident on pp.181–2. It was celebrated in an excruciatingly sentimental parlour song ('A Negro Song', 1799), with words by the Duchess of Devonshire and music by G.G. Ferrari.

The consolation of religion

This section is based on the entry for 25 August, pages 222–6.

Linking passage

Park was refused permission by the King of Bambarra to cross to the south bank of the Niger, but was given 5,000 cowries as a token of royal hospitality. Park reckoned this was equivalent to £1, but provisions for himself and horse were so cheap it should have sufficed for 50 days' living expenses. He rode westward towards Jenné, but on 27 July (or thereabouts, because the dating of the narrative becomes confusing at this point) Park's mount collapsed and refused to rise. Assuming the animal was moribund, Park went down-river by canoe as far as Silla, which proved the easterly limit of his journey. On 29 July, Park recognized he could go no further: he was sick, exhausted, and his stock of cowries was insufficient to hire a canoe for any length of time. Moreover, he was informed that the territory ahead was in the control of hostile Moors. He decided to return to the Gambia, though not before he had gathered as much information as he could about the towns and kingdoms on the Niger. Quite unexpectedly he recovered his horse from a friendly 'dooty', but torrential rains flooded his path and much of his journey was spent wading through creeks. His difficulties were compounded by the fact that he was rumoured to be a spy and some village headmen refused him hospitality. On 25 August, he set out from Kooma (where he had been well received) for Sibidooloo in the company of two shepherds.

EXERCISE Now read the entry for that day and summarize in your own words what the passage on pp.225–6 (from 'After they were gone ...' to the end of the chapter) tells us about Park's religious beliefs.

DISCUSSION The passage brings out both the strength of Park's religious convictions and how his intellectual interest in the natural world complemented his faith. Having been stripped of his clothes by Fulani bandits, and robbed of his horse and meagre possessions Park had good reason to despair. He was 500 miles from the nearest European settlement in a vast, rain-sodden wilderness 'surrounded by savage animals, and men still more savage'. What sustained his spirits was 'the influence of religion'. Parlous though his situation was, he still felt under 'the protecting eye of that Providence who has condescended to call himself the stranger's friend'. Park's confidence that he was in God's care was reinforced by his acute observation of the natural world around him. His attention was drawn to the delicate construction of a tiny moss, which he 'could not contemplate ... without admiration' (p.225). He reasoned that God, who had created a plant so perfect though apparently unimportant, could not be unconcerned with the situation and sufferings of a man formed after his own image.

The religious attitude articulated in this passage can be related to two broad developments in Protestant theology in the later eighteenth century: the doctrine of divine providence and the perception of the natural world as the handiwork of God. I must hasten to add that neither was novel, but the arguments for both were systematized and rationalized during the Enlightenment, partly in reaction to the deism fashionable in intellectual circles. Deists believed in the existence of God the creator on rational grounds but rejected 'revealed religion'. Knowledge of God could not come through divine agency because, deists contended, once the world had been created, God had withdrawn from his creation and was essentially unknowable. To use a favoured image (and one which you encountered in Unit 10) the divine watchmaker had left the mechanism he had constructed to run by itself. Deists believed in a providential order in the sense that this was 'the best of all possible worlds', but this belief was different from the Christian concept of a benevolent God *actively providing* for humanity. In rebutting deism, Protestant thinkers linked divine providence to the idea of progress. The growth of scientific and technical knowledge, the burgeoning of commerce, the efflorescence of civil society – all were taken as the manifestation of a great providential purpose and as evidence that God was progressively revealing himself to humankind. Nature was interrogated for evidence of God's design, and knowledge of nature was thought to bring people closer to knowledge of God.

Clearly, we must not *over*-contextualize what we read in Park, lest his personal convictions become lost in the religious *Zeitgeist*.[22] The background is helpful for understanding the man; it should not overwhelm him. There is suggestive evidence that the unattractive self-

22 *Zeitgeist*: the spirit of the age.

righteousness – or so it seems to me – exhibited in his letters to Alexander Anderson (quoted on pp.94–5, above) was modulated by his time in Africa. For example, he showed a sensitivity to the integrity and nuances of indigenous religious belief that seems out of character with his earlier, arrogant dogmatism. From talking to so-called pagans, Park concluded that, without exception, they believed in a single divine creator and preserver of all things who had ordained a future state of reward and punishment for humankind (p.253). The pagan conception of the deity closely resembled that held by deists in 'enlightened' Europe: the pagan God was so remote and exalted that it was 'idle to imagine the feeble supplications of wretched mortals [could] reverse the decrees, and change the purposes of unerring Wisdom' (p.253). Contemporaries reading Park's description of the African belief system could not have but been struck by its basic similarity with their own.

Linking passage

After the robbery, Park made his way to Sibidooloo where the Mansa, or the local lord, was able to effect the restitution of his horse and clothes. Recurrent sickness (possibly yellow fever because of the discoloration of his skin) now made travelling painfully difficult and near famine conditions in the countryside meant that poor villagers could spare nothing for a European mendicant. Park observed an emaciated mother who was compelled to sell her five-year-old boy into slavery so that she could provide for the rest of her family. Park finally abandoned his horse and made his way to Kamalia, where illness and destitution forced him to halt (see Figure 12.5). He owed his life to a Muslim slave-trader, Karfa Taura, who was collecting a coffle of slaves with the intention of selling them to the Europeans on the Gambia as soon as the rains were over. For the price of a prime slave, Karfa agreed to look after Park over the coming months and then lead him to the Gambia. 'Thus was I delivered by the friendly care of this benevolent Negro from a situation truly deplorable' (p.235). Again, we must note that Park seemed strangely unperturbed by the moral dilemma in which he found himself.

Park spent nearly six months in Kamalia, convalescing and deepening his knowledge of Mande society and culture. In this, he was much assisted by a Muslim schoolmaster, Fankooma. To his undisguised pleasure, Park found that literate black Muslims shared part of the religious culture in which he had been reared: they were familiar with much of the Judaic tradition through Arabic versions of the Pentateuch, the Psalms and the book of Isaiah. The stories of Genesis, the Flood and the House of David were already known to educated Mande such as Fankooma (p.292) – a fact which caused Park to bemoan the indifference of the Europeans on the coast to proselytizing Christianity among Africans. Park's enquiries resulted in three chapters of ethnographic description that are interpolated into the narrative: chapters XX and XXI are devoted to Mande customs, beliefs and handicrafts, and chapter XXII to slavery.

Figure 12.5 A View of Kamalia, *from Mungo Park,* Travels in the Interior Districts of Africa, *1799, 2nd edn, British Library, London. Photo: by permission of the British Library, London (shelfmark 681.e.21).*

(Through a typographical error, this is called chapter XXIII in your edition.) You should now read the chapter on slavery.

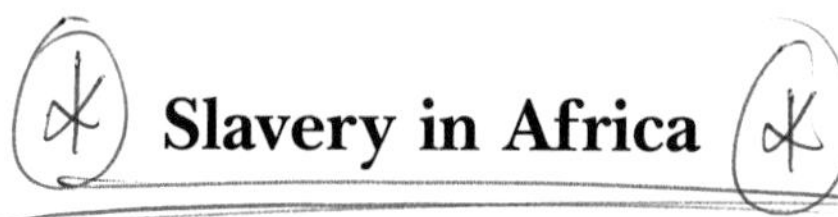

Slavery in Africa

This section is based on chapter XXII, pages 279–90.

EXERCISE

1 What social class and economic institution were unknown in Africa? Do you think their absence was a cause or a symptom of widespread slavery? What consequence did it have for the social division of labour? (If you are puzzled, consider these remarks from p.262: 'As the arts of weaving, dyeing, sewing, etc., may easily be acquired, those who exercise them are not considered in Africa as following any particular profession, for almost every slave can weave, and every boy can sew.')

2 What broad distinctions does Park draw between slaves in Africa? What was the main social source of freely marketable slaves? What were the advantages for slave-traders of captives who had been slaves from birth?

3 What distinction does Park make between wars in Africa? How would you describe the relationship between social violence and slavery?

4 Apart from war, what were the other main sources of slavery? How does Park's testimony differ from that of Francis Moore with respect to one source?

5 In the final paragraph on p.290, Park manifests a sharp difference of opinion between himself and the abolitionists. Summarize this difference in your own words.

DISCUSSION

1 The class of free wage-earners and the institution of a labour market were unknown in Africa. This was almost certainly a symptom of widespread slavery, which appears to have antedated the emergence of a market economy with significant production for exchange. (I would add that most scholars now attribute the ubiquity and persistence of slavery in sub-Saharan Africa to the abundance of land and the continent's chronic under-population: there was no landowning class and political power was accumulated by coercing people into dependency, not – as in Europe – by controlling territory.) One consequence of ubiquitous slavery was an undifferentiated social division of labour: the only specialized craft occupations were leatherworking and iron smelting and working.

2 Park distinguishes between domestic slaves, who could be sold by their masters only under strict conditions, and prisoners of war who could be marketed without restraint. Capture in war was the main source of marketable slaves, but captives could be distinguished between those born in a servile condition and freemen. The former were more prone to be taken captive, rarely ransomed, and their advantage to slave-traders was that they were less likely to try to escape and more resigned to enslavement.

3 Park distinguishes between wars that were formally declared by rulers and usually terminated in a single battle, and chronic slave raiding between feuding nations and groups. The second, in particular, resulted in vicious circles of social violence and enslavement.

4 Famine, debt and the punishment of criminals were the other main sources of slavery. According to Park, the only offences punished by enslavement were murder, adultery and witchcraft. His testimony on this point differs sharply from that of Francis Moore, who referred to enslavement for petty offences. The most cogent explanation for their apparently conflicting testimony is that things had changed since Moore's day when the greater external demand for slaves acted as an inducement to enslave for trivial misdemeanours.

5 Abolitionists argued that outlawing the Atlantic slave trade would have an 'extensive and beneficial' effect *within* Africa. It would, they

p279-290

claimed, remove a major incentive for powerful Africans to enslave the weak, curtail the vicious circles of social violence and enslavement, and encourage the development of free wage labour. Park was deeply sceptical about these claims, reasoning that slavery in Africa predated the Atlantic slave trade and would continue if and when that trade were prohibited.

There is no reason to doubt the general accuracy of Park's observations on African slavery and slave-trading. We cannot avoid drawing the conclusion that the Atlantic trade functioned for as long and as smoothly as it did thanks largely to African initiative and enterprise. Europeans provided the major external demand, but the 'supply side' of the market was controlled and regulated by native merchants. When confronted with this unpalatable fact, students sometimes ask: 'Why did Africans enslave other Africans for sale overseas?' The question presupposes that they thought of themselves as Africans, which of course they did not. Before the twentieth century, only Europeans (or Euro-Americans) were conscious of Africa as a geographic entity and only they conceived of its inhabitants as 'Africans'. The diverse peoples of Africa lacked a common cultural canopy, such as the world religions provide, and never articulated a notion of universal human rights. Islam, the most dynamic religion in Africa, preached the equality of all true believers, but condoned slavery as a form of religious 'apprenticeship' and accepted the legitimacy of enslavement in the course of *jihad*. Until Christianity began to win converts, slavery was an unquestioned part of the human condition in Africa. In most states, organized society was inconceivable without coerced dependence. Basically for this reason, Park's prognosis in the final paragraph of chapter XXII proved correct: outlawing the Atlantic trade made little difference to slavery within Africa. From about 1830, African slave-owners responded to the growing European demand for palm products, groundnuts and other commodities by putting their slaves to work. Over vast areas slavery became a mode of production that was suppressed only by the European colonial conquests, and then very slowly.

It is worth adding here that Park's prognosis was most unwelcome to opponents of the Atlantic slave trade, as was his ostentatious refusal to condemn the trade in the *Travels*. The *facts* Park recorded were frequently cited in abolitionist tracts. The third (1804) edition of *A Concise Statement of the Question Regarding the Abolition of the Slave Trade*, which was the summa of the abolitionist case, drew extensively on Park's evidence. But his silence on the principle at stake cast a pall over his reputation. According to Whishaw, 'his name [was] constantly mentioned in the list of persons conversant with Africa who were not friendly to the Abolition; his authority was always appealed to with some triumph by the advocates of the Slave Trade' (1815, p.xxv). This was unfair to Park, who 'uniformly expressed a great abhorrence of slavery

unfortunately for Park

and the Slave Trade whenever these subjects occurred in conversation' (Whishaw, 1815, p.xxxiv). The explanation given by his friends for his public silence was that he looked on abolition as a measure of state policy, then under consideration in Parliament, on which it would have been improper for him to offer a private opinion to the reading public. An alternative and perhaps more likely explanation is that he was unduly influenced by the man who helped edit the *Travels*: Bryan Edwards, MP, a leading apologist for the Atlantic slave trade. We will return to this in section 4.

With the slave caravan

This section is based on the entries for 19 to 25 April inclusive, pp.300–10. They deal with the first stages of the 500-mile march from Kamalia to the Gambia. They have been selected both for their intrinsic interest and because Park's contemporary readers considered the incidents described among the most poignant in the *Travels*.

EXERCISE We can reasonably assume that there was nothing out of the ordinary in what Park describes in these pages. Use the information he gives us to write a couple of paragraphs saying how a slave caravan was organized and controlled, what conditions its participants endured, and how refractory slaves were disciplined. Pay particular attention to the story of Nealee: what does this tell us about the attitude of African slave-owners towards their slaves?

DISCUSSION When this caravan left Bala, it comprised 73 people, 38 of whom were free people and their domestic slaves, while 35 were slaves being marched for sale on the Gambia. Small numbers joined the caravan en route. We do not know whether the typical caravan would have comprised marketable slaves and free people and their attendants in roughly equal proportions, but we can surmise that at least one freeman or domestic slave was required to guard four chattel slaves and to provide security against bandits. It appears that none of the freemen in this caravan carried firearms. Donkeys were used as pack animals, though the slaves provided much of the porterage. Unless they were in dire straits, everyone walked. A caravan would aim to halt each night at a town or village where supplies could be purchased, though this was not always possible.

Park refers to five slave merchants setting out in the caravan, and they were probably joined by two more, so we can deduce that, on average, each owned about half a dozen marketable slaves. In other words, these were petty traders who had come together for mutual protection. The coffle included six singing men, whose function was to regale the marchers and obtain a welcome from the villages at which the caravan called. Karfa was the caravan's acknowledged leader: after it had crossed the river Kokoro, it was he who ordered the whole company to 'keep close together and travel in their proper station' (p.306). His authority was buttressed by that of his friend, the Muslim schoolmaster, and religious ritual had an essential part in the organization and control of the caravan. Departure was preceded by both 'a long and solemn [Muslim] prayer' (p.301) and an elaborate ceremony suggestive of animistic practice. A prayer was said prior to taking the road to Kinytakooro, and it would seem that everyone in the caravan ate a handful of meal that had been 'blessed' by the schoolmaster.

The coffle included male and female slaves, though we do not know in what proportions, and some were evidently mere girls and boys. Each slave bore a heavy head load, which consisted of provisions and – I would hazard – trade goods. They usually travelled roped round the neck in groups of four, though lame and exhausted slaves were untethered and allowed to make their way more slowly under the eye of a freeman or domestic slave. For those who had spent 'years in irons' (p.301) – please note! – before being marched to the coast, the brisk pace and tyrannous distances were agonizing. A day's march could be anything up to 30 barefoot miles on stony paths. At any sign of recalcitrance, slaves were put in irons. Early in the journey a woman and girl slave, who had been severely whipped for dilatoriness, may have attempted suicide by eating clay – a practice that was 'by no means uncommon', according to Park (p.303). These tiny details illustrate both the savage discipline that kept a coffle in order and the desperate measures some slaves took to end their misery.

At a casual reading, the story of Nealee demonstrates wanton cruelty; considered more closely it reveals the solicitude of the slave vendor for his human property. Slaves did not come cheap. Nealee represented a substantial fraction of Karfa's working capital; he did everything in his power to retain her in the coffle. When she complained of pains in her legs, she was relieved of her load. When she was attacked by bees, the slave merchants picked out the stings, washed her and rubbed her with bruised leaves. When the whip would not induce her to walk, she was first placed on a donkey and then carried on a litter. Only when every attempt to carry her forward proved ineffectual was she left to die. Her fate was not lightly dismissed: '[it] made a strong impression on the minds of the whole coffle' (p.310). The caravan's pastor, the schoolmaster, spent the whole of the ensuing day fasting in consequence of Nealee's death. Human life was valued.

The middle passage

This section is based on the final pages of the *Travels*, covering Park's return to Pisania in early June 1797 and his voyage home via the West Indies, pp.330–6.

Linking passage

After Nealee's death, the caravan proceeded without major incident through the Jallonka wilderness towards the Gambia. As they approached the coast, it became evident to Park that the international slave trade had subtle market mechanisms: the price offered by European traders was low, so African slave merchants were preparing to withhold the supply until it rose, though they had to calculate whether a future return would cover the extra costs of maintaining their slave holdings in the meantime. (Why the international price was low we are not told; presumably it was because warfare and the Santo Domingo slave revolution had disrupted the pattern of demand.) Vendors also had to consider the composition of their slave holdings: on two occasions, slaves from the coffle were exchanged for local slaves because this was mutually advantageous to their owners.

EXERCISE Now read from 'Being now arrived within a short distance of Pisania ...' (p.330) to the end of the chapter and attempt the following questions:

1 What expedient did Karfa adopt – at Park's suggestion – when it became evident there was little demand for slaves?

2 What final impression is given of Karfa's character? How would the characterization have 'worked' on readers in Park's day?

3 Assuming that Park's voyage to Antigua was reasonably typical for an American vessel, what do we learn about the 'middle passage'?

DISCUSSION 1 Karfa hired some huts to accommodate his slaves, and a piece of land on which they could grow their own food, while waiting for their price to rise.

2 The final impression is of a man devoted to Park and overawed by the accoutrements of 'civilized' life and the technical accomplishments of Europeans. Park describes him as possessing 'a mind *above his condition*' (p.334). He is an exemplary African whose worthiness holds out the possibility of 'progress from rudeness [meaning ignorance and incivility] to refinement' (p.334). This characterization of Karfa must have flattered the cultural self-esteem of Park's readers, while it reminded them that Africans partook of a common human nature. That this paragon of benevolence was

responsible for poor Nealee's death was 'air-brushed' from Park's pen portrait.

3 The 'middle passage' took a grievous toll in lives of both slaves and seamen. Between 25 and 27 of the ship's cargo and crew died of illness on what was a comparatively short voyage to Antigua. This was quite normal. Slave merchants reckoned to lose about 15 per cent of a shipment on the 'middle passage'; mortality among seamen was greater than in any other trade. Park was right to maintain that conditions would have been less severe on a British slaver: in 1789, Parliament had enacted the first regulations of the trade in response to the mass campaign demanding abolition. A limit was placed on the number of slaves that could be carried per ton of ship, and bounties were instituted for captains and surgeons who landed slaves alive. The measure led to a sharp fall in mortality. North American slaving vessels were notoriously unseaworthy because the trade attracted merchants and owners with little working capital who needed to make quick profits.

---

4 Writing and publishing the *Travels*

The question of authorship

Up to this point, I have treated the *Travels* as a document of record and neglected its status as a literary text. It is now time to ask how it came to be written and who, in fact, was the author (or authors). These questions do not in any way impugn the factual observations in the book. We can take it on trust that Park's experiences were accurately recorded and that he made nothing up, but this does not mean that the narrative is devoid of literary skill and technique. If, for example, you refer back to the story of the cuckolded Kafir and the lecherous Muslim priest on pp.68–9, you will see that it is told with economy and wit. Alliteration is used most effectively to catch the reader's attention and to create a heightened sense of immediacy, as in this sentence:

> The culprit was tied by the hands to a strong stake; and a long black rod being brought forth, the executioner, after flourishing it round his head for some time, applied it with such force and dexterity to the Bushreen's back, as to make him roar until the woods resounded with his screams.

Did Park write this? Most probably not. Shortly after his return from Africa, he was put in touch with the new secretary of the African Association, Bryan Edwards, so that an account of his travels could be presented to its members in time for their meeting on 26 May 1798. Edwards worked from memoranda supplied by Park, but brought to the task considerable experience as a professional author. He had spent 25 years in the Caribbean before returning home and writing *A Civil and Commercial History of the British West Indies.* This was a well-documented, cogent and elegantly written defence of the plantation system and the slave trade that supported it. Partly on the strength of his *History,* Edwards was elected to Parliament in 1796, where he soon distinguished himself as the most intellectually able of the 'West Indian' spokesmen. The *Abstract* of Park's journey that Edwards wrote was incorporated wholesale into the *Travels*; indeed, some incidents are described in almost the same words in both texts. However, large sections of the final narrative are not even sketched in the *Abstract*, and there is little of the general descriptive material that appears in chapters XX–XXIII.

Soon after the *Abstract* was completed, Park began work on the definitive version of the *Travels.* He was not a naturally fluent writer, and was given considerable editorial assistance by Edwards with at least the first eight chapters. Such arrangements were not unusual when publishing travel literature. Explorers' accounts were frequently 'ghosted' by professional writers; for example, a Dr Hawkesworth was the real author of Captain Cook's *Voyages.* When Park sent Edwards his early drafts, the latter evidently found them pretty tedious. On 22 October, he wrote to Banks:

> Previous to [Park's] captivity, there is such a sameness in the Negro manners and the occurrences which he relates are so unimportant that it requires some skill in composition and arrangement to make the reading supportable. How I have acquitted myself you can best judge, I hope for Park's sake, you will not spare correction out of tenderness for me.
>
> (Quoted in Hallett, 1964, p.165)

But Edwards fairly quickly revised his estimation of Park's literary abilities, for he wrote to Banks on 30 January 1799:

> Park goes on triumphantly – He improves in his style so much by practice that his journal now requires but little correction; and some parts, which he has lately sent me, are equal to anything in the English language.
>
> (Quoted in Hallett, 1964, p.165)

While this would seem to settle the question of the authorship of the latter half of the *Travels* in Park's favour, the issue remains as to whether he deferred unduly to Edwards in expressing (or withholding) certain opinions with respect to slavery in Africa and the likely impact of abolishing the Atlantic trade. Whishaw asserted that most of chapter XXII 'may be confidently pronounced, from the peculiar character both of the style and sentiments, to have proceeded from the pen of Mr Edwards' (1815, p.xcviii). I cannot share Whishaw's confidence for two reasons. First, we have the conflicting evidence (known to Whishaw) of George Hibbert, the anti-abolitionist MP, who knew Park through membership of the Linnaean Society:

> I have read and heard that we are to look to Park's facts, and not to his opinions; and that it has been insinuated that his editor, Mr. Edwards, has foisted those opinions into the book. It happened to me once to converse with Mr. Park, at a meeting of the Linnaean Society, when this very topic was started; and he assured me that, not being in the habits of literary composition, he was obliged to employ some one to put his manuscript into a form fit for the public eye; but that every sheet of the publication had undergone his strict revision; and that not only every fact, but every sentiment of it was his own.
>
> (Substance of three speeches in Parliament on the Bill for the Abolition of the Slave Trade (1807), quoted in Whishaw, 1815, p.xcx)

Second, we have Edwards's opinions on African slavery and the likely impact of abolition in his *History of the British West Indies* with which we can compare those expressed in the *Travels*, and in crucial respects they differ. Edwards was too respectful of his readers' intelligence to deny the evils of slavery and, during a Commons debate, wished 'most sincerely that the slave trade was suppressed' (quoted in Anstey, 1975, p.257) – but gradually. His rationale for the trade was that European enslavement was preferable to African enslavement:

> To attempt the defence, in all cases, of a traffic thus supported [by violence and war] would be an outrage to the feeling of humanity; and yet this much may be said in its favour, that the wretched victims who are slaves in Africa, are, by being sold to the whites, removed to a situation far more desirable, even in its worst state, than that of the most fortunate slaves in their native country. It is universally allowed, that the condition of these poor people, under their own governments, is deplorable in the extreme. Their property is without security; their persons have no protection; and they exist entirely at the disposal of a master, who may treat them ill, and even put them to death at his pleasure, without being amenable to any law.
>
> (Edwards, 1794, vol.2, p.404)

There is no suggestion of this rationale in the *Travels*, and the tenor of Edwards's remarks on African slavery differs significantly from Park's nuanced analysis. While waiting for the coffle to assemble in Kamalia, Park observed that, although discontented slaves were bolted by the ankle to a thick length of wood, 'In other respects, [their] treatment ... during their stay at Kamalia was far from being harsh or cruel' (p.297).

Only a perverse reader could come away from Park's description of the slaves awaiting embarkation (pp.330–1) convinced that they were bound for a better life. I think we can take it that the views on slavery in the *Travels* were Park's.

The rewards of authorship

Late eighteenth-century publishers and booksellers worked with a speed and efficiency that put the modern industry to shame. Park was still writing the book in February 1799; the first edition appeared on 5 April. It was published and retailed by George Nicol (1761–1829), the bookseller to the king who had brought out other works of travel (including an edition of Cook's *Voyages*). The first quarto edition had a print run of 1,500 copies, which sold out within a week, such was the public interest in Park's exploits. The book included the map Rennell had constructed on the basis of Park's information and several handsome engravings, which may account for its being priced at £1.11.6. (The average earnings of a London artisan were then 18 shillings per week.) The African Association continued to pay Park seven shillings and sixpence per day up until 25 May and generously waived its rights over the *Travels*. Park received the impressive sum of 1,000 guineas for the first edition, as well as his deferred salary of £615. Nicol's profit came from subsequent editions: the second and third appeared in the summer and autumn of 1799, and the fourth in 1800. French and German translations also appeared in 1800.

More research needs to be done on the reception of the *Travels* in the literary periodicals, but the evidence we have indicates that the reviews were very favourable. The reviewer in the *Annual Register* praised the author for describing things as he saw them and for having 'consulted his senses rather than his imagination'. There was nothing that strained the reader's credulity and 'no exaggerated picture of his sufferings and dangers' (quoted in Lupton, 1979, p.114). Others welcomed the insights into African culture and society: the notice in *The Gentleman's Magazine* concluded: 'The Negroes of these districts are not to be considered as an uncivilized race; they have religion, established governments, laws, schools, commerce, manufactures, *wars*!' (quoted in Lupton, 1979, p.112). The book's reputation was cemented by its literary qualities: Whishaw attributed its 'distinguished success' not only to the subject matter, but also to its merits as a composition: 'the clearness of the descriptions, the natural and easy flow of the narration, and the general elegance of the style' (1815, p.xxx). The European renown of the *Travels* can be judged from the entry in the *Biographie Universelle*, published in Paris in 1822. Here we read:

> A judicious and accurate observer, as well as an intrepid traveller, Park gives us a faithful picture of the manners of the Moors and Negroes. The tone of truth which pervades his narrative, his style

at once simple and graceful, and the splendour of his discoveries, secured the success of his book, which in a short time ran through several editions, and was translated into most of the languages of Europe.

(Quoted in H.B., 1835, p.138)

5 The political impact of the *Travels* and the origins of Park's second African journey

While Park was away, Britain had been waging a global war with France and, in this context, the African Association's role as an imperial pressure group had become more pronounced. The knowledge Park had gained of West Africa's geography was inevitably taken as an incentive to extend Britain's political power in the region. We have striking evidence for this in Banks's address to the Association on 25 May 1799, when the *Abstract* Edwards had prepared was formally presented to the members. Banks painted a glowing prospect of the commercial and imperial advantages to be won now that Park had opened a gate into the interior. The overland passage from the navigable waters of the Gambia to those of the Niger could, Banks asserted, be secured by 500 troops. Once embarked on the Niger, 200 men with field pieces 'would be able to overcome the whole Forces which Africa could bring against them'. The trade that the Moors conducted with the Niger towns produced, Banks surmised, 'an annual Return of about a Million Sterling – much of it in Gold'. He went on:

> If Science should teach these ignorant savages, that the Gold which is Dust at the mouth of the river must be in the form of Sand at a high part of the Current, of Gravel in a still more elevated station, or of Pebbles when near the place from whence it was originally washed ... is it not probable that the Golden harvest they are already in the habit of gathering might be increased an hundred fold? As increased Riches still increase the wants of the Possessors, and as Our Manufactures are able to supply them, is not this prospect, of at once attaching to this country the whole of the Interior Trade now possessed by the Moors, with the chance of an incalculable future increase, worth some exertion and expense to a Trading Nation? ... It is easy to foretell that if this country delays much longer to possess themselves of the Treasures laid open to them by the exertions of the Association, some Rival Nation will take possession of the Banks of [the Niger].
>
> (Quoted in Hallett, 1964, pp.168–9)

Shortly after delivering this address, Banks approached the government on behalf of the African Association with a proposal for 'securing to the British Throne, either by conquest or by Treaty, the whole of the coast of Africa from Arguin to Sierra Leone, or at least to procure the cession of the River Senegal, as that River will always afford an easy passage to any Rival Nation' (quoted in Gascoigne, 1998, p.180). Banks urged that a charter company, vested with military and political powers, be formed to carry the march of empire into the interior. His memorandum envisaged the conversion and better government of the natives and the greatest practicable diminution of slavery. In short, he was proposing a comprehensive annexationist and 'civilizing' policy.

The governing elite had more pressing strategic priorities than West Africa, and was unreceptive to the arguments for a preclusive imperialism in the region. Banks's memorandum was pigeonholed. Three years passed before the War Office advised Banks that it was contemplating an official expedition to trace the course of the Niger to the sea. The main purpose was exploration, although there was a strong subsidiary interest in 'heading off' French advances from the Senegal. Park was the obvious choice to lead such an expedition, and once again Banks was instrumental in securing his appointment.

After innumerable delays, Park started inland on his second African journey in early May 1805. This expedition had the same purpose as the first, but there the resemblance ended. In its personnel and equipment, the second mission was a military safari. Park was accompanied by 44 Europeans, mostly soldiers who had volunteered for the trip, but including four carpenters, a draftsman, a Lieutenant Martyn to command the troops, and Park's brother-in-law. The instructions were to use conciliatory measures on every occasion, but the party had sufficient weaponry not to be intimidated by small African forces. It was equipped with the materials needed to build and rig two 40-foot boats, each with a beam of eight feet and drawing two and a half feet of water. A large store of trade goods, needed for purchasing provisions and mollifying kings, was provided; it included 460 yards of good quality cloth. Each man was in charge of at least one pack donkey, and more were purchased en route.

The expedition set out in the hot season, when the rains were imminent, and the journey quickly became a nightmare struggle against the disease environment. By the time they reached Bambakoo (now written Bamako) on the Niger on 19 August, only 11 Europeans survived. The rest had died of illness. By November, only five Europeans (including Park) still lived, and one was deranged. They improvised a 40-foot boat, and embarked on the Niger on the 15th. Park consigned the journal he had kept until that time, together with letters to his wife, Banks and Lord Camden (the secretary for war and the colonies), to the keeping of a native guide, who brought them to the Gambia, whence they were sent to Britain. According to the account of another guide who accompanied

Park down-river, the vessel was attacked at the Bussa rapids in modern-day Nigeria, where Park and his companions drowned while attempting to escape.

The modest fillip given to imperial expansion in West Africa in the early 1800s, partly as a result of Park's acclaim, was dissipated by the failure of his second expedition. Official interest in sponsoring further exploration of West Africa lapsed until the Colonial Office employed Hugh Clapperton and Dixon Denham to explore Hausaland, in northern Nigeria, in the early 1820s. The course of the lower Niger was not finally established until the Lander brothers, who were also engaged by the Colonial Office, made their way by canoe from Bussa to the sea in 1830. The river flowed into the great delta where Europeans had been trading for centuries without suspecting that a huge inland waterway lay beyond the ganglion of creeks and streams.

6 Conclusion

Open University students are, I know, pressed for time, but I would be disappointed if, having studied substantial extracts from the *Travels*, you had no desire to read the book in its entirety. My overriding purpose has been to get you to engage with an enjoyable text. The generic appeal of travel writing is that it gives us the vicarious pleasure of peregrination – that is, travel in foreign parts – without having to endure its hazards. Eighteenth-century travel writing bore a family resemblance to the picaresque fiction then popular – both were loosely plotted, involved low-life characters and constantly shifting locations – but, unlike fiction, travel writing had the status of a truthful record and was supposed to be 'enlightening'. (Recall Park's preface: 'As a composition, [the book] has nothing to recommend it but *truth* ... [though] it claims to enlarge, in some degree, the circle of African geography', p.xxiii). The eighteenth-century elite travelled abroad for pleasure but not pure hedonism; travel was a way of cultivating the mind and needed to be taken seriously. Lord Chesterfield fussily instructed his son while the dear boy was in Italy 'to extract the spirit of every place you go to. In those places, which are only distinguished by classical fame, and valuable remains of antiquity, have your Classics in your hand and in your head; compare the ancient geography, and descriptions, with the modern; and never fail to take notes' (*Letters to His Son*, April 19, O.S., 1749).

Travel writing mediated the notion of travel as enlightenment, but it also resonated with an older tradition of travel as act of religious devotion. The pilgrim is the archetypal traveller in Christian culture; pilgrims' tales were among the earliest of literary genres in the European vernaculars. Bunyan's *Pilgrim's Progress* was reputedly the most popular book in English after the Bible. The pilgrim was a cultural type with whom every Christian could identify. There were affinities between Park's journey and a pilgrimage: he was on a 'quest'; his faith restored his sense of purpose when he was in the slough of despair; reaching the Niger was akin to accomplishing a religious mission. It is not altogether fanciful to suggest we identify with Park because we recognize the pilgrim in him.

Apart from being a pleasurable text, the *Travels* remains an enduringly valuable piece of reportage. Some of Park's observations on African life and culture and on Islam were mistaken; for example, he took *Al Sharia*, or the *Sharia*, to be the name of a particular book, whereas it is the whole body of Islamic law. But his mistakes were a matter of honest misinterpretation; none arose from sheer prejudice. Indeed, it is striking how far he was able to suspend his antipathy to Islam to give a rounded picture of its educative and normative role in the western Sudan. More than any other traveller in Africa, Park helped revise the image of its peoples and cultures entertained by the educated reading public. Most were willing to credit Africans with all the attributes of an abstract human nature and to presuppose that their 'barbarism' was a consequence of climate and 'mode of living'. Park demonstrated that they were ordinary human beings, as is amply confirmed by the slave narratives that you will study in the next two units.

When you have completed your work on these units, you should listen to the discussion on Audio 4, tracks 12–20: *Mungo Park*, in which three Africanist scholars evaluate Park's observations on slavery in Africa, religion and the social roles of women from the perspective of modern scholarship. You should also read the corresponding AV Notes.

References

Anstey, R. (1975) *The Atlantic Slave Trade and British Abolition 1760–1810*, Basingstoke, Macmillan.

Barber, Anthony J. (1978) *The African Link: British Attitudes to the Negro in the Era of the Atlantic Slave Trade, 1550–1807*, London, Frank Cass.

Blumenbach, J.F. (1799) 'Observations on the bodily conformation and mental capacity of the Negroes', *The Philosophical Magazine*, vol.III, pp.141–7.

Clarkson, T. (1788) *Essay on the Slavery and Commerce of the Human Species* (first published 1784).

Curtin, P.D. (1964) *The Image of Africa: British Ideas and Action, 1780–1850*, Madison, University of Wisconsin Press.

Davis, D.B. (1984) *Slavery and Human Progress*, Oxford, Oxford University Press.

Edwards, B. (1794) *An Abridgement of Mr. Edwards' Civil and Commercial History of the British West Indies*, 2 vols, London, Parsons and Bell.

Gascoigne, J. (1994) *Joseph Banks and the English Enlightenment: Useful Knowledge and Popular Culture*, Cambridge, Cambridge University Press.

Gascoigne, J. (1998) *Science in the Service of Empire: Joseph Banks, the British State and the Uses of Science in the Age of Revolution*, Cambridge, Cambridge University Press.

H.B. (1835) *The Life of Mungo Park*, Edinburgh, Fraser and Co.

Hallett, R. (ed.) (1964) *Records of the African Association 1788–1831*, London, Thomas Nelson and Sons.

Long, E. (1970) *History of Jamaica*, 3 vols, London, Frank Cass (first published 1774).

Lovejoy, P.E. (1983) *Transformations in Slavery*, Cambridge, Cambridge University Press.

Lupton, K. (1979) *Mungo Park the African Traveller*, Oxford, Oxford University Press.

Moore, F. (1738) *Travels in the Inland Parts of Africa*, London.

Whishaw, J. (1815) 'The account of the life of M. Park', prefixed to the *Journal of a Mission to the Interior of Africa*.

Further reading

Blackburn, R. (1988) *The Overthrow of Colonial Slavery 1776–1848*, London, Verso.

Clarkson, T. (1808) *History of the Rise, Progress and Accomplishment of the Abolition of the Slave Trade by the British Parliament*, 2 vols, London, (Frank Cass reprint, 1968).

Davis, D.B. (1966) *The Problem of Slavery in Western Culture*, Ithaca, Cornell University Press.

Unit 14
Slave writings (1)

Prepared for the course team by David Johnson

Contents

Study components

Weeks of study	*Supplementary material*	*Audio-visual*	*Anthologies and set books*
1	Illustrations Book	–	Anthology I

Objectives

After reading Unit 14 you should:

- be able to discuss the history of Britain's role in Atlantic slavery in the period 1770–1807;
- understand the arguments for and against slavery in this period;
- appreciate the textual strategies of 'persona' and 'genre' employed in Cugoano's slave writings;
- understand the role of Enlightenment thought in Cugoano's writings.

Aims

The aim of these two units on slave narratives is to provide a perspective from beyond Europe on the key concerns of the period 1780–1830. We shall examine how the slave narratives of the eighteenth century (Quobna Ottobah Cugoano) and those of the nineteenth century (Robert Wedderburn and Mary Prince) both utilize and extend the ideas of the Enlightenment and Romanticism. Unit 14 introduces the arguments about slavery and abolition in the age of Enlightenment, and then proceeds to analyse Cugoano's *Thoughts and Sentiments on the Evil of Slavery* (1787). Unit 15 introduces the wider contexts of slavery and abolition in the age of revolution, and analyses Wedderburn's *The Horrors of Slavery* (1824) and Prince's *The History of Mary Prince* (1831). In reading Cugoano, Wedderburn and Prince, we consider not only *what* they wrote, but also *how* they expressed their ideas. In other words, we examine the variety of textual strategies employed in their writings to express their opposition to slavery.

1 Introduction

In 1783 the first petition submitted to the British Parliament for the abolition of slavery was unanimously rejected, with King George III's leading minister Lord North speaking for both Houses of Parliament when he declared that slavery 'was necessary to almost every nation in Europe' (quoted in Drescher, 1999, p.5). Four years later, the freed African slave Quobna Ottobah Cugoano disagreed vehemently with North's view in his pamphlet *Thoughts and Sentiments on the Evil of Slavery*. Cugoano declared that 'it ... is ... the incumbent duty of all men of enlightened understanding, and of every man that has any claim or affinity to the name of Christian, that the base treatment which the African Slaves undergo, ought to be abolished' (Anthology I, extract 1, p.130). Very few observers in the 1780s would have given any chance to Cugoano's views prevailing over those of Lord North, but within 30 years, in 1807, the House of Commons voted by 283 votes to 16 in favour of abolishing the slave trade.

In this unit, we look closely at extracts from Cugoano's writings, and ask the following questions:

1 What were the historical conditions that enabled Cugoano to make his bold denunciation of slavery in 1787?

2 What textual strategies, literary forms and rhetorical devices does Cugoano draw upon in *Thoughts and Sentiments*?

3 To what extent does Cugoano utilize the terms, values, assumptions, ideas and arguments of Enlightenment thought in his writings?

The full text of Cugoano's *Thoughts and Sentiments* is just over 100 pages in length, and ranges widely over a complex variety of abolitionist arguments, with sudden shifts in focus and tone, and unexpected transitions from one **genre** of writing to another. It is also punctuated with lengthy quotations from other abolitionist writers (not always acknowledged), and is written in the convoluted style of the eighteenth-century pamphleteer. We have reprinted four extracts from Vincent Carretta's excellent recent edition of *Thoughts and Sentiments* in Anthology I. You are required to read extract 1 (the first ten pages of the text) and extract 4 (the final ten pages) for this unit; extracts 2 and 3 are optional extra reading and include further passages characteristic of Cugoano's writing. In the discussion and analysis to follow, I focus mainly on passages from extracts 1 and 4, but at times also refer to passages in extracts 2 and 3, and to passages from *Thoughts and Sentiments* not included in Anthology I. Finally, note that like many eighteenth-century writers, Cugoano's spelling is inconsistent and eccentric. Rather than peppering quotations from his writing with '[*sic*]' after each spelling error or silently modernizing his spelling, I have simply retained his original text.

Before we start to read Cugoano's text, however, we need to consider the question: What were the arguments that Cugoano had to address in *Thoughts and Sentiments*, both those in favour and those against slavery? Take notes of the discussion that follows.

2 Slavery in the age of Enlightenment

In the Introduction to Block 3, we outlined the historical genesis and rapid growth of the Atlantic slave system from the sixteenth to the eighteenth centuries. Before examining the arguments for and against slavery, however, it is important to register the role that slavery played in sustaining the British economy, its impact on the millions of African slaves, and the increasing opposition to it in the final third of the eighteenth century.

Profits from the slave trade and slave plantations were immense. In the early eighteenth century, the return on capital invested in West Indian sugar plantations was about 20 per cent, and although this figure had decreased to 12 per cent by 1775, it remained significantly higher than the 3.5 per cent return on English farming land. The historian Ronald Segal points out that the £10,000 per year enjoyed by the wealthy Mr Darcy in Jane Austen's *Pride and Prejudice* would have been dwarfed by comparison to the riches of slave-owners like William Beckford, who inherited £1m. from West Indian plantations (1995, p.41). Indeed, the wealth of the slave-owning classes was of such an order that, by the eighteenth century, slave-traders and plantation owners exerted a defining influence upon Britain's national economy, with cities such as Bristol, Liverpool and London especially dominated by slaving interests. Their profits were invested in a variety of ways. In the early eighteenth century, certain Bristol merchants invested profits from slavery in the development of industrial and manufactured goods, as in the case of Thomas Goldney II's (1664–1731) support for the inventor and ironworker Abraham Darby (1678–1717). Goldney's capital, earned originally from a single slave-trading voyage, provided Darby with the financial support for his efforts in producing the high quality iron that was to be indispensable in Britain's Industrial Revolution. Other avenues of investment for the Bristol slave merchants included the arts and learning, as well as banking, as the historian S.I. Martin explains:

> At the same time that residents such as Henry Bright were shipping slaves from Angola to St. Kitts in decks no higher than 4 ft 2 in, they were also investing in the Theatre Royal and new private libraries and becoming patrons of banks.
>
> (1999, p.52)

A number of high-street banks in Britain today are descended from banks that were founded in the eighteenth century on profits from the slave trade. For example, the Heywood brothers of Liverpool used their fortunes from the slave trade to establish their own bank, Arthur Heywood Sons and Co., which was subsequently absorbed into the Bank of Liverpool, then into Martin's Bank, and ultimately into Barclays Bank. A final form of investment favoured by the beneficiaries of the slave trade was in the political system itself. Often starting out from the margins of society, the slave merchants used their newly acquired wealth to penetrate the ranks of the landowning aristocracy, thus acquiring the status that enabled them to purchase direct political influence in Parliament. As a result, by 1800 there were at least 50 MPs representing the interests of the slave merchants and traders.

This accumulation and concentration of wealth in the hands of a small elite in Britain was achieved at a terrible cost. Estimates vary, but there is now general agreement among historians that between 1550 and 1807 10–12 million Africans were transported as slaves to the Americas, in addition to the approximate 17 million abducted in the trans-Saharan slave trade. Britain dominated the trade, transporting 3 million slaves between 1700 and 1807, followed by the French, who transported 1.15 million during the same period. The slave trade reached its peak in the final decades of the eighteenth century – during the age of Enlightenment – with between 80,000 and 100,000 slaves transported annually from Africa to the Americas up until Britain's abolition of slavery in 1807. Even after abolition, slave-trading continued illegally, and slave ships were still plying their trade in the middle of the nineteenth century. The impact on Africa was devastating: by 1850, the population of Africa was 25 million, but historians have calculated that *without* the slave trade the figure would have been between 46 and 53 million. Furthermore, the external demand for slaves precipitated a fundamental restructuring of African societies, with smaller social units replaced by large, highly centralized kingdoms controlled by those Africans involved in providing slaves for European traders. The mortality rate for slaves on the notorious '**middle passage**' from Africa to the Americas was high – between 10 and 20 per cent, a figure that translates as at least 1 million deaths during the Atlantic slave trade. Conditions for slaves working on plantations were so harsh that one-third of slaves died within three years of arrival, the average life expectancy for plantation slaves was eight years, and there was a 5 per cent annual *decrease* in the number of slaves working on the plantations throughout the eighteenth century. The statistics, of course, only tell part of the story, and we return to consider the hardships of slave existence in our discussions of Cugoano, Wedderburn and Prince.

Opposition to slavery came from two sources, namely from the slaves themselves and from the abolitionist organizations in Europe, and particularly in Britain. As regards slave resistance, the first major uprising in this period was Tacky's Revolt in Jamaica in 1760–1, when about 400 rebel slaves burnt plantations, and were only finally suppressed after months of fighting. Far more damaging was the protracted and ultimately successful uprising in the French colony of Santo Domingo that we have already noted in Units 7–8. In a campaign that started in 1791, the charismatic slave leaders, first Toussaint L'Ouverture and, after his death, General Jean-Jacques Dessalines, transformed the slaves into a formidable army that finally drove the French from the island in 1804 in a defeat that cost France some 60,000 lives. The historian C.L.R. James emphasizes the connections between French Enlightenment thought and the Santo Domingo/Haiti slave uprising – Toussaint read and was inspired by the anti-slavery writings of Abbé Guillaume Raynal (1713–96). The connection is vividly acknowledged in the portrait by Anne-Louis Girodet-Trioson of Jean-Baptiste Belley standing in front of a bust of Raynal (see Figure 14.1). Belley was a member of the delegation from Santo Domingo which successfully convinced the French National Convention to abolish slavery throughout the French colonies in 1794. However, according to James, although the 'ex-slaves of the San Domingo Revolution established their affinity with the population of revolutionary France' (1989, p.356), that affinity disappeared when Napoleon reintroduced slavery, and was replaced by determined opposition to France:

> For self-sacrifice and heroism, the men, women and children who drove out the French stand second to no fighters for independence in any place or time. And the reason was simple. They had seen at last that without independence they could not maintain their liberty, and liberty was far more concrete for former slaves than the elusive forms of political democracy in France.
>
> (1989, p.357)

The uprising in Santo Domingo, however, was exceptional, and in the rest of the Caribbean the slave economies survived for many more years.

As regards opposition to slavery from abolitionists, campaigns against the slave trade were coordinated increasingly by energetic groups such as the Committee for Effecting the Abolition of the Slave Trade and the Committee for the Relief of the Black Poor (both formed in 1786). One key strategy used by the abolitionists was the submission of public petitions to Parliament. By 1790, there were more anti-slavery petitions than those for any other political cause in Britain, as large numbers of people gave their support – the petition launched in 1787 in Manchester, for example, attracted 10,700 signatures out of a population at the time of 50,000. Further strategies to mobilize public opinion against the slave trade were for abolitionist speakers to travel throughout Britain giving public lectures, and for books and pamphlets exposing the horrors of the slave trade to be published and distributed cheaply. The most important critiques of slavery published in the 1780s included the former West Indian slave-owner Reverend James Ramsay's *An Essay on the Treatment*

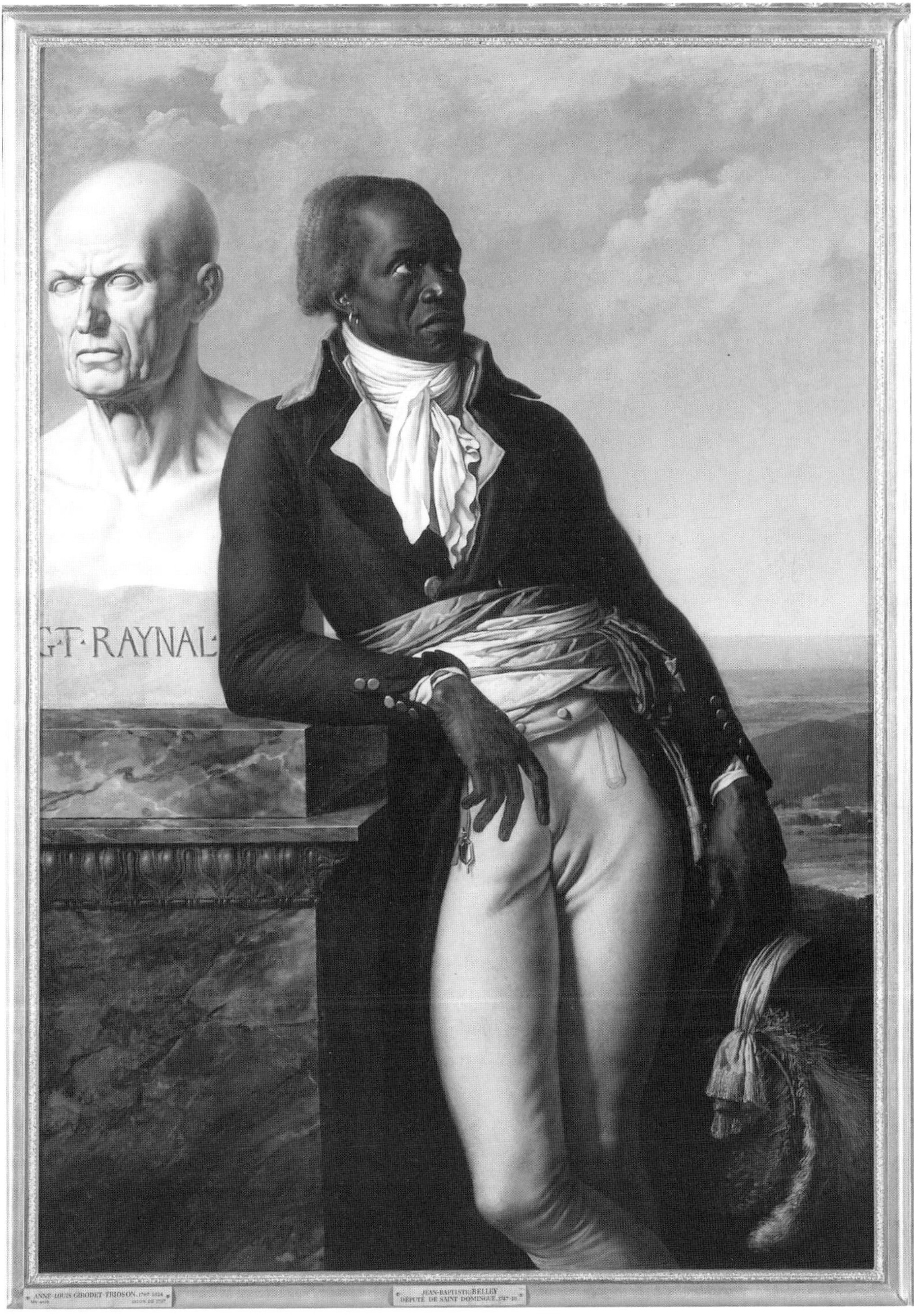

Figure 14.1 Anne-Louis Girodet-Trioson, Jean-Baptiste Belley, *1797, oil on canvas, Châteaux de Versailles et de Trianon. Photo: © RMN.*

and Conversion of African Slaves in the Sugar Colonies (1784) and abolitionist leader Thomas Clarkson's *An Essay on the Slavery and Commerce of the Human Species, Particularly the African* (1786). Abolitionist efforts were answered angrily by pro-slavery supporters, with publications such as the West Indian planter James Tobin's *Cursory Remarks upon the Reverend James Ramsay's Essay* (1785) and Gordon Turnbull's *An Apology for Negro Slavery* (1786) contesting every abolitionist claim and reasserting long-entrenched defences of slavery. It is to the specific arguments for and against slavery that we now turn.

What were the arguments in favour of slavery?

It is important to register that, however repellent slavery might appear to us today, in the eighteenth century it enjoyed wide acceptance right up until about 1760. The historian David Brion Davis points out that:

> [even in the] 1760s there was nothing unprecedented about chattel slavery, even the slavery of one ethnic group to another. What was unprecedented by the 1760s and 1770s was the emergence of a widespread conviction that New World slavery symbolized all the forces that threatened the destiny of man.
>
> (1975, p.41)

This remarkable shift in the moral consciousness of Europe from at least tacit support to outright rejection of slavery was furiously contested. The debates of the time provide the immediate context of the three slave writers we examine in Units 14–15, and in order to appreciate the distinctiveness of their respective contributions, we need now to consider the arguments they sought to counter, as well as those they tried to support.

The political and economic arguments in favour of slavery are distilled in the following evidence collected in the 1805 Report of the Committee of the House of Assembly of Jamaica, appointed to inquire into the Proceedings of the Imperial Parliament relative to the Slave Trade:

> [A]t a moment when all Intercourse with [Great Britain] was proscribed in the most opulent and commercial states of Europe, and both Force and Artifice were being employed to exclude her from the others, when Great Britain was preparing to meet the mightiest Host that ever had been arrayed against her, and was engaged in a Contest for national Existence, of which her youngest son might not see the Termination, her Statesmen adopted Measures more fatal to her Prosperity, than all the rancorous Hatred or insidious Guile of her arch Enemy could have accomplished or hoped, and by Laws and Regulations, by withholding from the West Indian Colonies a necessary Supply of Labourers.
>
> (Quoted in Drescher, 1999, p.34)

The first part of this sentence emphasizes the threat posed to Britain's survival by France, both commercially and militarily. In commercial terms, France had denied Britain access to most European markets, and was using all available means to exclude it from the few that remained open; in military terms, France's armies threatened to vanquish Britain. The second part of the sentence argues that at this most unpropitious moment any movement to reform Britain's slave economy would favour France, and drastically weaken Britain's capacity to check the march of its imperial competitor. In other words, the argument was that Britain's political establishment since the sixteenth century had protected the slave-owning classes of the West Indies and, as a result, Britain had, by the eighteenth century, come to enjoy global pre-eminence. The corollary of this argument was that any attempt on the part of Parliament to dismantle the slave economy would assuredly lead to Britain losing that ascendancy and being subordinated to France. Furthermore, as Britain's pro-slavery lobby pointed out with relish, Napoleon's attitude towards slavery was dictated not by humanitarian considerations, but by what he thought served France's best interests – hence his ultimately costly decisions to reintroduce slavery in the French Caribbean colonies in 1802 and again in 1814.

Pro-slavery Members of Parliament received substantial support for their views from political commentators, historians and journalists. One of the most influential texts that popularized the pro-slavery position was Edward Long's *History of Jamaica* (1774). You have already encountered Long's ideas in some detail in the units on Mungo Park, so we need only repeat his main arguments in brief. Long argued that slavery enriched *all* classes of British people; that West Indian slavery was essentially benevolent; that slaves in the Caribbean were better off than the poor in England and than Africans who remained in Africa; and that the effect of enslaving Africans and compelling them to work on plantations had the ultimate effect of civilizing them. What lent Long's ideas greater authority at the time was the fact that he drew upon the scientific vocabularies of Linnaeus' *Systema Naturae* (1735) and Comte de Buffon's *Histoire Naturelle* (1749) in order to justify his rigid organization of humanity into a strict racial hierarchy, with Africans at the bottom. As you saw in Units 12–13, he presented as scientific fact his opinion that all Africans were intrinsically 'brutish, ignorant, idle, crafty, treacherous, bloody, thieving, mistrustful and superstitious people' (Long, 1970, vol.2, p.353), thus seeking to diminish British sympathy for the plight of slaves.

As regards the religious arguments, Christian theology until the eighteenth century tolerated slavery. St Augustine's views set out in *The City of God against the Pagans* (413–26) provided a defence of slavery for Christians that was repeated with little variation until it was challenged in the eighteenth century. According to Augustine:

> By nature, then, in the condition in which God first created man, no man is the slave either of another man or of sin. But it is also

> true that servitude itself is ordained as a punishment by that law which enjoins the preservation of the order of nature, and forbids its disruption ... The apostle therefore admonishes servants to be obedient to their masters, and to serve them loyally and with a good will, so that, if they cannot be freed by their masters, they can at least make their own slavery to some extent free. They can do this by serving not with cunning fear, but in faithful love, until all unrighteousness shall cease, and all authority and power be put down, that God may be all in all.
>
> (Quoted in Dyson, 1998, pp.943–4)

To paraphrase: slavery is not sanctioned in the original 'City of God', but in the world after the Fall the highest law of God becomes the preservation of order. Those who transgress this law by disrupting the existing order are justly enslaved as punishment. Once enslaved, the transgressors of God's law of order have a duty themselves to preserve that order by obeying and serving their masters 'in faithful love'. The long-term hope remains that ultimately 'all unrighteousness shall cease', God's authority will be restored in full, and (it is implied) slaves might then be free once again. Augustine's views on the condition of slavery survived the Reformation unchanged, and indeed remained the official line of the Roman Catholic Church until abolition in the nineteenth century, although this was complicated by efforts among Dissenting missionaries to convert slaves to Christianity. A more ambivalent Christian attitude to slavery was typified by the Bishop of London, Dr Beilby Porteus (1731–1808), who condemned the particular form of the Atlantic slave trade as a sin, but still clung to the traditional Christian justifications for human bondage, and accordingly stopped short of demanding immediate abolition.

Arguments in support of slavery from literary and philosophical figures during the Enlightenment repeated substantially the same ideas as the economic, political and religious writers. For example, Dr Samuel Johnson's biographer James Boswell was a staunch supporter of slavery. Boswell warmly approved the slave societies of classical Greece and Rome, and argued that:

> [t]o abolish a status which in all ages God has sanctioned, and man has continued, would not only be robbery to an innumerable class of our fellow subjects; but it would be extreme cruelty to the African Savages, a portion of whom it saves from massacre, or intolerable bondage in their own country, and introduces into a much happier state.
>
> (1933, vol.2, p.256)

Boswell thus synthesizes many of the main arguments for slavery: that God has approved it; that to end it would impoverish 'our fellow subjects'; and that Africans suffer far worse privations in Africa than they do on the slave plantations. Opposition to the abolitionist cause did not come only from literary figures from Britain's ruling establishment; the radical journalist William Cobbett (1762–1835), author of *Rural Rides*, was also an outspoken critic of the abolitionists. Cobbett shared the racist views of figures like Boswell, describing blacks as 'degraded brutes' (quoted in Drescher, 1999, p.72). His main objection to abolition was that he believed British workers were worse off than West Indian slaves, a sentiment frequently expressed both in pro-slavery propaganda and in satirical political cartoons (see Figure 14.2). On this view, the struggle for abolition was therefore an annoying distraction from the more urgent political struggles for workers' rights in Britain itself.

Another variant on Boswell's views on slavery can be found in the writings of the Scottish Enlightenment philosopher, David Hume. According to one of Hume's recent editors, his *Treatise of Human Nature* (1739–40) is 'by common consent the greatest work of philosophy to have appeared in the English language' (Flew, 1988, p.vii). Hume was dissatisfied with the *Treatise*, and reworked it several times in a number

Figure 14.2 James Gillray, Philanthropic Consolations after the Loss of the Slave Bill, *1796, etching and engraving printed in brown ink, 25.8 x 36 cm, British Museum, London. Photo: by courtesy of the Trustees of the British Museum.*

This print depicts William Wilberforce and the Bishop of Westminster with two black women. It plays on British fears of miscegenation, and suggests that the motives of the abolitionists were less high-minded than they claimed.

of different editions of *An Enquiry Concerning Human Understanding* (1748, 1772, 1777), with the final edition appearing the year after his death. As you discovered in Unit 4, Hume was suspicious of the intuitive reasoning of French Enlightenment thinkers, and proposed an alternative version of reason based upon empirical methods of experience, scientific observation and the application of certain (mainly mathematical) principles of abstract reasoning. Recall the concluding lines of Hume's *Enquiry*:

> If we take in our hand any volume, of divinity or school metaphysics, for instance, let us ask: *Does it contain any abstract reasoning concerning quantity or number?* No. *Does it contain any experimental reasoning concerning matters of fact and existence?* No. Commit it then to the flames, for it can contain nothing but sophistry and illusion.
>
> (Flew, 1988, p.195; italics in original)

Hume's conclusion stands as a resounding affirmation of one particularly influential strand of Enlightenment reason, and his intellectual efforts for the most part were in profound sympathy with the modernizing impulses in British political life of the eighteenth century. Hume was also critical of slavery in classical antiquity, arguing that domestic slavery 'rendered [every man of rank] a petty tyrant, and educated amidst the flattery, submission, and low debasement of his slaves' (quoted in Carretta, 1999, p.179). However, at the same time that Hume was declaring an unflinching commitment to his empiricist version of reason and criticizing classical slavery, he was expressing support for New World slavery and repeating views of Africans that coincided precisely with those of the anti-abolitionists. In the second edition of his essay 'Of national characters' (1754), Hume adds in a footnote:

> I am apt to suspect the negroes and in general all other species of men (for there are four or five different kinds) to be naturally inferior to the whites. There never was a civilised nation of any other complexion than white, nor any individual eminent either in action or speculation. No ingenious manufactures amongst them, no arts, no sciences. On the other hand, the most rude and barbarous of the whites, such as the ancient Germans, the present Tartars, have still something eminent about them, in their valour, form of government, or some particular ... In Jamaica, indeed, they talk of one negroe as a man of parts and learning; but it is likely he is admired for slender accomplishments, like a parrot who speaks a few words plainly.
>
> (Quoted in Eze, 1997, p.33)

Hume wrote this note several decades before the debate over slavery ignited, but when it did, the pro-slavery faction seized upon his words as formidable philosophical support for their political campaigns.

Conversely, abolitionist campaigners, including Cugoano, set out to discredit Hume's views. We shall return to Cugoano's reply to Hume in due course, but first need to consider the abolitionist arguments assembled to refute the defenders of slavery.

What were the arguments against slavery?

The economic, political, religious and philosophical arguments in favour of slavery were all vigorously contested in the latter half of the eighteenth century. The first major figure to question the economic vitality of slavery was another Scottish Enlightenment philosopher, Adam Smith. Smith opposed the long-entrenched economic system of **mercantilism**, which rested upon the state (or the king) granting trade monopolies to certain favoured companies, thus protecting them from competition. Britain's trade in slaves had initially been governed by mercantilist principles, with the Royal African Company in the sixteenth century granting an exclusive charter to trade in slaves, but by the 1720s this charter proved unenforceable, and more efficient slave-traders swiftly overtook the Royal African Company. As the eighteenth century proceeded, mercantilist forms of protectionism in other sectors of the economy also came under pressure, as the world economy increasingly came to be organized in terms of the 'survival of the fittest', profit-driven logic of the market. Smith embraced this tendency and argued further that slave labour *retarded* the maximizing of profit because it was ultimately more expensive than **free labour** (or '**free trade**'):

> But though the wear and tear of a free servant be equally at the expense of the master, it generally costs him much less than that of a slave. The fund destined for replacing or repairing, if I may say so, the wear and tear of a slave, is commonly managed by a negligent master or careless overseer. That destined for performing the same office with regard to the free man, is managed by the free man himself ... It appears, accordingly, from the experience of all ages and nations, I believe, that the work done by freemen comes cheaper in the end than that performed by slaves.

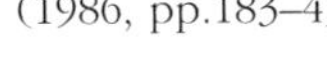

(1986, pp.183–4)

In his search for a more rational and enlightened method for running the West Indian sugar economy, Smith therefore argued not so much in terms of common humanity as in terms of utility and economic profitability. He maintained that not only were free labourers better workers than slaves, but they were also cheaper because the cost of sustaining free labourers was borne by the labourers themselves, whereas the slave-owner had to pay the 'wear and tear' expenses of keeping the slaves working.

Political arguments against slavery had to counter the belief energetically promoted by the slave-owners that an end to the slave trade would necessarily undermine Britain's national interests, and thus directly serve the interests of France. The prominent abolitionists Henry Brougham (1778–1868) and James Stephen (1758–1832) responded directly to this argument. Brougham rejected the coupling of slave profits and British economic survival, and concluded that:

> the [slave] trade does not occupy any considerable part of the national capital [and] the profits are of the description least beneficial to the country ... [T]he fruit of our iniquity has been a great and rich empire in America. Let us be satisfied with our gains, and being rich, let us try to be righteous – not indeed by giving up a single sugar cane, but by continuing on our present state of overflowing opulence, and preventing the further importation of slaves.
>
> (Quoted in Blackburn, 1988, p.302)

According to Brougham, the plantation owners and slave-traders vastly exaggerated their profits from slavery in order to protect their own narrow interests as opposed to Britain's national interests. From a position of considerable wealth and strength, Britain might therefore without any risk afford to 'be righteous' and terminate the slave trade. Stephen contrasted Britain's dynamic abolitionist campaign in the 1790s with France's continuing harsh treatment of slaves in the Caribbean, suggesting that '[t]hose who hate, oppress and murder the labouring poor in one part of the world [cannot] really wish to make them free and happy in another' (quoted in Blackburn, 1988, p.303). He concluded confidently that rather than deriving benefit from retaining slavery, France was likely to suffer both economic hardship and moral decay. Stephen's prediction proved to be accurate: as noted earlier in this section, the slave uprisings in Santo Domingo/Haiti in the decades immediately after the French Revolution were to cost France 60,000 lives with no discernible economic return to compensate for the massive losses.

Religious arguments against slavery had to counter the Christian Church's loyalty to the status quo, which was expressed as support for slavery along the lines drawn by St Augustine. The Quakers were the first to criticize slavery. Although there were wealthy Quaker plantation owners who had grown rich on slave labour, the Quaker doctrine that all men are brothers in the Fatherhood of God prompted individuals to speak out against slavery from as early as the seventeenth century. For example, in 1671, George Fox, the founder of the Quakers, urged slave-holding Quakers in Barbados to 'cause their overseers to treat mildly and gently with the negroes, and not to use cruelty towards them' (quoted in Sandiford, 1988, p.52). Despite Fox's own generous sentiments, the Quakers only collectively threw themselves behind the abolitionist cause after the Seven Years' War (1756–63), and by that stage their endeavours were supported by the Methodist and Evangelical revivals. The competing Christian sects disagreed over minor doctrinal details but shared certain core convictions. First, they agreed that all people, black and white, were equal in sin and in their capacity for spiritual redemption. The Methodist preacher George Whitefield, for example, in his *Letter to the Inhabitants of Virginia and Maryland* (1740) asks:

> Think you that your children are any better by nature than the poor negroes? No, in no wise. Blacks are just as much and no more, conceived and born in sin, as White Men are.
>
> (Quoted in Sandiford, 1988, p.53)

Second, Christian abolitionists agreed that individual liberty was an inalienable, God-given natural right that was to be enjoyed by all races. This conviction is expressed by the Methodist leader John Wesley in his *Thoughts on Slavery* (1774) as follows:

> Liberty is the right of every human creature, as soon as he breathes the vital air; no human law can deprive him of that right which he derives from the law of nature.
>
> (Quoted in Sandiford, 1988, p.53)

Third, Christian abolitionists agreed that slavery fundamentally undermined the African's passage from the darkness of ignorance to the light of Christian conversion and salvation. For example, William Wilberforce, the leader of the abolitionist movement in Parliament, acknowledged Britain's devastating effect on Africa:

> ... all improvement in Africa has been defeated by her intercourse with Britain; when we reflect that it is we ourselves that have degraded them to that wretched brutishness and barbarity ... What a mortification we feel at having so neglected to think of our guilt, or attempt any reparation.
>
> (Quoted in Sandiford, 1988, p.60)

Only with the abolition of slavery could the African's entry to the universal Christian brotherhood be possible.

There were many literary figures who lent their talents to the abolitionist cause, including most of the major writers of British Romanticism: William Cowper, Samuel Taylor Coleridge, William Wordsworth and William Blake. Of these luminaries, Cowper – whose contribution to the *Olney Hymns* we discussed in Unit 10 – undoubtedly wrote the most poetry on the subject of slavery, and through his writings made the greatest contribution to the anti-slavery movement. Cowper's most famous poem *The Task* (1785) includes the following lines:

> I would not have a slave to till my ground,
> To carry me, to fan me while I sleep,

And tremble when I wake, for all the wealth
That sinews bought and gold have earned.
No: dear as freedom is and in my heart's
Just estimation priz'd above all price,
I had much rather be myself the slave
And wear the bonds, than fasten them on him.

(*The Task*, II.29–36, quoted in Baird and Ryskamp, 1980–95, vol.2, pp.139–40)

Cowper's sympathy for slaves here is such that he declares that he would rather be enslaved himself than own and be served by a slave. Thousands of copies of Cowper's best-known poems on slavery, including 'The Negro's complaint' (1788), were distributed by the abolitionists, and also set to music and sung in the streets as popular ballads. The anti-slavery sentiments in 'The Negro's complaint' are conveyed by Cowper writing in the voice of a slave. The argument in the first stanza is that the cruel experience of being traded as property never destroys the slave's humanity:

Forced from home and all its pleasures
Afric's coast I left forlorn
To encrease a stranger's treasures
O'er the raging billows borne
Men from England bought and sold me,
Pay'd my price in paltry gold,
But though slave they have enroll'd me
Minds are never to be sold.

('The Negro's complaint', ll.1–8, quoted in Baird and Ryskamp, 1980–95, vol.3, p.13)

The second stanza concludes with the declaration that '[s]kins may differ, but Affection/Dwells in White and Black the Same' (lines 15–16, p.13), and in the third stanza, the contrast between the suffering of slaves and the indolence of Britain's slave-owners is highlighted:

Think, ye Masters iron-hearted
Lolling at your jovial boards,
Think how many backs have smarted
For the sweets your Cane affords.

(lines 21–4, p.13)

With great bitterness, the slave goes on to ask: 'Is there One who reigns on high?/Has he bid you buy and sell us/Speaking from his throne the sky?' (lines 26–8, p.14), and in the next two stanzas the hypocrisy of Christian justifications for slavery is exposed. Cowper's skilful combining of pathos and anger in 'The Negro's complaint' culminates in the final stanza when the slave suggests that it is not the slaves whose humanity is annihilated by slavery, but rather that of the masters:

> Slaves of Gold! Whose sordid dealings
> Tarnish all your boasted pow'rs
> Prove that *You* have Human Feelings
> 'Ere ye proudly question *Ours.*
>
> (lines 53–6, p.14; italics in original)

The italicized collective pronouns 'You' and 'Ours' effectively clinch the reversal of terms Cowper proposes, with humane sentiment identified not with white British merchants ('You'), but rather with black African slaves ('Ours').

As regards the philosophical arguments in favour of abolition, a number of Enlightenment thinkers disagreed with Hume's negative ideas about Africans and his sympathy for slavery. The major eighteenth-century works critical of slavery included Montesquieu's *De l'esprit des lois* (*On the Spirit of the Laws*, 1748), Francis Hutcheson's *System of Moral Philosophy* (1755) and Abbé Guillaume Raynal's *Philosophique et Politique Histoire des Deux Indes* (*Philosophical and Political History of the East and West Indies*, 1770). For Montesquieu, natural law demands universal equality, and slavery therefore defied natural law: 'As all men are born equal, slavery must be accounted unnatural' (quoted in Sandiford, 1988, pp.48–9). For Hutcheson, too, natural justice insists that 'each man is the natural proprietor of his own liberty' (quoted in Blackburn, 1988, p.48), and slavery must therefore be condemned because it fails to respect this universal right. Far more influential than Montesquieu and Hutcheson's works, however, was Raynal's *Histoire*, which went through 55 editions in five languages in the 30 years after it was first published. The sections on slavery in the *Histoire* were written by Jean de Pechmeja (1741–85), an early utopian socialist, who had lived in the French colonies and who brought an acute anger to bear on the debate. Invoking standards of justice, humanity and reason, New World slavery is rejected in violent terms: 'Whoever justifies so tedious a system, deserves the utmost contempt from a philosopher and from the negro a stab with his dagger' (quoted in Sandiford, 1988, pp.50–1). Furthermore, his abhorrence for slavery in the colonies provides the basis for a critical assault on the corrupt metropolitan institutions of Crown and Church. It is important finally to register, however, that there were substantial limits to Montesquieu, Hutcheson and Raynal's critiques of slavery. All three focused their criticisms on the cruel excesses of the slave trade, and stopped well short of proposing immediate emancipation. Even Raynal, the most radical of the three, argued strategically in subsequent editions of the *Histoire* for a 25-year apprenticeship programme for slaves leading to gradual emancipation that would both protect France's colonial interests and transform the slaves into more cost-effective free labour.

3 Quobna Ottobah Cugoano

Cugoano (1757–*c*.1800) was born among the Fantee people of what is today Ghana, and was raised in the Fantee royal household. At the age of 13, he was kidnapped by fellow Africans, sold into slavery, and transported to the West Indian island of Grenada, where he experienced first-hand the brutalities of slave existence. At the end of 1772, Cugoano was taken to England by the wealthy slave-owner Alexander Campbell, and in the following year, was baptized and assumed the name 'John Stuart'. It is not clear when Cugoano left Campbell, but by the 1780s he had acquired an education and was working as a personal servant for the fashionable painters Richard and Maria Cosway (see Figure 14.3), and mixing with prominent figures in London society. He directed his energies to campaigns to improve the plight both of slaves in Africa and the West Indies and of blacks in Britain, writing letters of appeal to public figures such as Edmund Burke, the Prince of Wales, and even George III himself. Cugoano worked closely with abolitionist leaders – among them Thomas Clarkson and Granville Sharp – delivering public lectures on his experiences of the middle passage and plantation slavery, and helping in the major court cases of the decade that first strove to address slave atrocities. The first edition of Cugoano's *Thoughts and Sentiments on the Evil of Slavery* appeared in 1787 at a key moment in the escalating campaign against slavery. After the publication of the second edition in 1791, Cugoano disappears from historical view, although there is one unreliable source who records meeting him and his English wife at the start of the nineteenth century. At the time, Cugoano's *Thoughts and Sentiments* did not sell quite as well as the works of his two black contemporaries, *Letters of the Late Ignatius Sancho, An African* (1782) and *The Interesting Narrative of the Life of Olaudah Equiano or Gustavus Vassa, the African* (1789). However, from our point of view, the fact that Cugoano's work engages in far more detail with the ideas of the Enlightenment than either Sancho's or Equiano's compensates for its relative lack of popular appeal.

EXERCISE Now read extract 1 from Cugoano's *Thoughts and Sentiments* in Anthology I (pp.129–42). As you read through the text, keep the following points in mind:

1 What **textual persona** does Cugoano assume in these opening passages? In other words, how does he describe himself in the text? To focus your thoughts on this question, you might find it helpful to circle every occasion on which he uses the first person ('I' or 'we').

2 Cugoano uses a combination of genres, or kinds of writing, notably political tract, autobiography and religious sermon. Identify the different genres, and the shifts from one genre to another.

Figure 14.3 Richard Cosway, The Artist and his Wife, *1784, etching, Whitworth Art Gallery, University of Manchester.*

The black servant here is almost certainly Cugoano.

3 How does Cugoano engage with Enlightenment thought? Note in particular where he uses key terms such as 'enlightenment' and 'reason'.

We shall now discuss in detail each of these questions in turn.

What textual persona does Cugoano assume?

It is important to clarify at the outset the conceptual distinction between Cugoano, the historical figure who wrote *Thoughts and Sentiments*, and the textual persona Cugoano assumes, the 'I' of the text. As regards the historical figure, there are interesting questions about Cugoano's authorship of *Thoughts and Sentiments* because, as in the case of Mungo Park's *Travels*, subsequent editors and critics think they detect signs of collaboration in Cugoano's work. For example, Paul Edwards, the editor of the 1969 edition of *Thoughts and Sentiments*, suggests that fellow ex-slave Olaudah Equiano revised and corrected Cugoano's writing, and cultural historian Keith Sandiford suspects that a third contributor might have supplied the 'passages of florid rhetoric and advanced argumentation' (1988, p.96). For both Edwards and Sandiford, however, the key point remains to treat the work as written and approved by Cugoano, even if collaborators were involved. What we are principally interested in here, though, is not this kind of historical speculation about how much help Cugoano received in writing *Thoughts and Sentiments*, but rather how he represents himself in the text – in other words, in understanding what textual persona he assumes.

Cugoano begins his *Thoughts and Sentiments* in the elaborate style typical of the English eighteenth-century public pamphlet by lavishly acknowledging his sponsors in the abolitionist movement as men 'worthy of universal approbation and imitation' (p.130). For Cugoano, the abolitionists combine the laudable attributes of 'enlightened understanding' (p.130) and a sincere Protestant Christian faith because they stand up courageously against slavery, a crime he describes as unequalled anywhere 'except the annals of the Inquisition and the bloody edicts of Popish massacres' (p.130). He explains the aims of his pamphlet as follows:

> What I intend to advance against that evil, criminal and wicked traffic of enslaving men, are only some Thoughts and Sentiments which occur to me, as being obvious from the Scriptures of Divine Truth, or such arguments as are chiefly deduced from thence, with other such observations as I have been able to collect.
>
> (p.131)

With these promises, Cugoano thus aligns himself with the values of both Christianity ('the Scriptures of Divine Truth') and the Enlightenment (by committing himself to the scientific methods of deduction and observation). He acknowledges the difficulty of an African trying to claim these allegiances. For most Europeans, Africans were simply incapable of appreciating either Christian or Enlightenment ideals, and Cugoano summarizes their prejudices as follows:

> That an African is not entitled to any competent degree of knowledge, or capable of imbibing any sentiments of probity; and that nature designed him for some inferior link in the chain, fitted only to be a slave.
>
> (pp.131–2)

Cugoano stoutly rejects these racist prejudices:

> But when I meet with those who make no scruple to deal with the human species, as with the beasts of the earth, I must think them not only brutish, but wicked and base; and that their aspersions are insidious and false: And if such men can boast of greater degrees of knowledge, than any African is entitled to, I

> shall let them enjoy all the advantages of it unenvied, as I fear it consists only in greater share of infidelity, and that of a blacker kind than only skin deep.
>
> (p.132)

Setting out tentatively with an apology for the defects of his education, Cugoano swiftly switches from defence to attack. He points out that the faults in his writing are as nothing compared to the thousand-fold more serious faults of slave-owners who might choose to criticize his prose. He paraphrases the prejudices held by the slave-owners – that Africans cannot acquire knowledge and are suited only to servitude – and then angrily rebuts them by describing slave-owners as 'brutish', 'wicked', 'base', 'insidious' and 'false' (p.132). Cugoano characterizes any 'greater knowledge' slave-owners might enjoy as no more than a 'greater share of infidelity', and then concludes with the egalitarian declaration that 'if a man is bad, it makes no difference whether he be a black or a white devil' (p.132).

In these opening paragraphs, we learn a great deal about the textual persona Cugoano assumes. First, he defines himself emphatically as a Christian and, more specifically, as a Protestant Christian repelled by the Catholic record of the Inquisition and 'Popish massacres'. Second, he declares his credentials as a man of the Enlightenment. He does this not only by directly identifying his project with the progressive abolitionist forces of 'enlightened understanding', but also by displaying the discursive abilities of an Enlightenment intellectual. Cugoano's ornate writing style serves in part to refute the racist belief that Africans cannot achieve European standards of learning, and his command of the English language and knowledge of English culture demonstrate not only his own competence but also the potential of all Africans. Third, he defines himself as a black African. Cugoano is aware of the negative connotations attached by white slave-owning Britain to the identity of 'black African', but he rejects these prejudices confidently. He turns the terms of abuse directed at Africans by the slave-owners against themselves – where they accuse black Africans of a lack of knowledge, for example, Cugoano argues that it is the slave-owners who in their cruelty demonstrate an even greater ignorance. There is a fourth identity that Cugoano assumes in these opening passages, which is that of 'abolitionist'. In his extravagant praise of prominent abolitionists and by dedicating his own efforts to supporting their cause, Cugoano takes on the identity of abolitionist campaigner himself.

Before moving on to discuss the genres of writing employed by Cugoano and the ways in which he engages with Enlightenment thought, I want you to read a passage from extract 3 in Anthology I (reproduced in the exercise that follows) and consider whether Cugoano assumes in addition the identity of 'Briton'. The context of this passage requires a brief explanation, as it follows on from Cugoano's short description of the notorious *Zong* case. In 1781, the captain of the slave ship *Zong*,

Luke Collingwood, ordered 133 slaves to be thrown overboard in order to claim insurance for their loss at sea. Upon returning to Britain, the insurance company refused to pay up, and despite compelling evidence that the slaves were sacrificed for motives of greed alone, the British judge found in favour of Collingwood and the Liverpool ship owner, William Gregson, and ordered the insurers to pay Gregson £30 per slave. The case was publicized widely by the abolitionist Granville Sharp, and it came to symbolize all that was evil about the slave trade and the indifference of the British establishment. The artist J.M.W. Turner, whose own early career had been sponsored by a West Indian slave-owning MP, later depicted the *Zong* tragedy in his 1840 painting *Slavers Throwing Overboard the Dead and Dying, Typhoon Coming On* (see Plate 14.1 in the Illustrations Book).

Cugoano was understandably angered by the *Zong* case, as it epitomized for him the attitudes towards slaves of not only the slave-owners and traders, but also the British courts and, by extension, the British public.

EXERCISE Now read the passage below. As you do so, circle each time Cugoano uses the first person plural, and try to work out who 'we', 'us' and 'our' refer to. Also circle each time Cugoano uses the third person plural, and try to work out who 'they' or 'them' refer to.

> But our lives are accounted of no value, we are hunted after as the prey in the desart, and doomed to destruction as the beasts that perish. And for this, should we appear to the inhabitants of Europe, would they dare to say that they have not wronged us, and grievously injured us, and that the blood of millions do not cry out against them? And if we appeal to the inhabitants of Great-Britain, can they justify the deeds of their conduct towards us? And is it not strange to think, that they who ought to be considered as the most learned and civilized people in the world, that they should carry on a traffic of the most barbarous cruelty and injustice, and that many, even among them, are become so dissolute, as to think slavery, robbery and murder no crimes? But we will answer to this, that no man can, with impunity, steal, kidnap, buy or sell another man, without being guilty of the most atrocious villainy.
>
> (Extract 3, p.151)

DISCUSSION The pronoun 'we' in the first three sentences ('we are hunted after', 'we appear to the inhabitants', and 'if we appeal') refers to 'we the enslaved Africans'. However, the 'we' in the final sentence ('we will answer to this') refers to 'we the abolitionists'. In other words, Cugoano identifies first with the African slaves and then with the abolitionists. Whether the shift from the first to the second sense of 'we' is intentional is less significant than the fact that in both cases Cugoano in his choice of pronoun expresses a personal identification with a constituency *outside* the British and European establishment.

In the second sentence, the pronouns 'they' and 'them' refer to the inhabitants of Europe and, in the third and fourth sentences, to the inhabitants of Great Britain. Great Britain and its inhabitants remain consistently in the third person ('can they justify the deeds', 'they who ought to be ... the most learned', and 'they should carry on a traffic of the most barbarous cruelty').

To summarize: for Cugoano, 'we' includes African slaves and abolitionists, and 'they' includes the inhabitants of Europe and Britain. By close attention to the pronouns used by Cugoano, we can conclude that his textual persona incorporates both 'slave' and 'abolitionist', but precludes, or indeed is defined in opposition to, 'European' and 'Briton'. Cugoano therefore does not identify himself as a Briton. His choice of the third person plural in writing about Britain reveals Cugoano's fundamental dissociation from Britain, which in these passages is identified far more powerfully with the slave trade than with the forces of abolition. In 1787, 'black Briton' could therefore be a descriptive term (according to historians – see Gerzina, 1995, p.5 – there were between 15,000 and 20,000 black people in London in 1800), but for the likes of Cugoano, Britain's involvement in slavery made it difficult for him to assume 'British' as a component of his own sense of identity.

What genres of writing does Cugoano employ?

The term 'genre' refers to the type, kind or species of writing, and is a term in literary criticism with a long history. For example, in his *On the Art of Poetry*, Aristotle distinguishes between the classical Greek genres of comedy, tragedy and epic and provides detailed descriptions of each. As new genres of writing have emerged, so literary critics have differentiated them from earlier ones, and have attempted to list their defining characteristics or 'generic markers'. Genre criticism has also been extended to more recent cultural forms, so that, for example, we now discuss film genre, with the generic markers of the western, the gangster movie, the romantic comedy, and so on, identified and analysed. The slave writings of the period 1770–1830 might themselves be classified as a distinct genre, but on closer inspection, we note that they are rather more complicated texts, and in fact combine a number of existing genres. Cugoano's *Thoughts and Sentiments* is a case in point, as in extract 1 alone we can identify three distinct genres: the political tract, the autobiography, and the religious sermon. In the balance of *Thoughts and Sentiments*, Cugoano also writes in the genres of philosophical reflection, historical narrative and economic analysis, and we discuss each of these in turn below. In discussing the genres Cugoano employs, we attempt first to define each one, and then to assess how Cugoano obeys (or challenges) the generic markers of each.

The genre of the *political tract* flourished in Britain in the second half of the eighteenth century, as literacy spread and readership increased at a rapid rate. With books still expensive at this stage, political tracts most often appeared in the more affordable form of newspapers, periodicals and pamphlets. The cultural historian Raymond Williams records that after the American Revolution in 1776, the audience for political tracts grew especially quickly, with Dr Richard Price's *Observations on the Nature of Civil Liberty* (1776) selling 60,000 copies, and Tom Paine's *Rights of Man* (1791) selling 50,000 copies within a few weeks. Williams concludes that in this period '[i]t seems clear that the extension of political interest considerably broadened the reading public by collecting a new class of readers, from groups hardly touched by earlier expansion (1971, pp.184–5).

Political tracts varied greatly in content and ideology, but they all shared certain generic markers: a critical diagnosis of British society, an attack on political adversaries, and a blueprint or set of proposals outlining alternative political solutions. In addition, political tracts frequently contained extensive citation of other authorities in support of their argument, and these authorities could include the Bible, reason, and writers of the same political persuasion. Cugoano's *Thoughts and Sentiments* therefore appeared at a propitious moment, and it displays all the qualities of the genre. First, Cugoano ruthlessly exposes the complicity of British political institutions (like the courts in the *Zong* case) in supporting slavery. Second, a substantial proportion of *Thoughts and Sentiments* is taken up with rebutting the arguments of those who defended slavery, including James Tobin, David Hume and Gordon Turnbull. Third, Cugoano concludes with detailed proposals (see Anthology I, extract 4, pp.157–60) as to what practical steps should be taken in order to abolish the slave trade and emancipate all slaves. Finally, Cugoano quotes liberally from the Scriptures to support his case against slavery, appeals to reason to justify his abolitionist arguments, and cites (not always with acknowledgement) the views of fellow critics of slavery such as James Ramsay, Thomas Clarkson, Anthony Benezet and Patrick Gordon.

A second genre that Cugoano utilizes is the emerging eighteenth-century genre of *autobiography*. The literary historian Felicity Nussbaum notes that '[i]n mid eighteenth-century England, autobiographical writing gives groups of marginalized people – not only Dissenters, but women, criminals, and the labouring and middling classes – a voice and a story to tell, eventually making their lives a consumable product in an increasingly consumerist society' (1989, p.86). To this list of new autobiographies, we might add those of slaves like Cugoano and Equiano. One of the most common of the new forms of autobiography was the spiritual autobiography, which followed a rigid sequence: from abject and sinful beginnings to a moment of crisis that precipitates self-lacerating introspection, repentance and conversion to Christianity, and finally, to a state of grace in God. Slave autobiographies in the period loosely followed this sequence, but diverged in at least two ways. First, the supposed original condition of sin for a slave was often the condition of freedom in Africa that preceded capture, a condition that did not quite match the spiritual autobiography's requirement of abject sinfulness. A second factor that distinguished slave autobiographies from the other new forms of autobiography in the eighteenth century was the specific pressures imposed by abolitionist campaigning. The critic Helen Thomas explains that 'like all forms of autobiography, these "confessional" [slave] testimonies existed both as unrestrained, personal utterances and as highly self-conscious literary performances [that] were consciously aimed at public consumption and intrinsically shaped by editorial intervention' (2000, p.176). In balancing the slave narrator's 'unrestrained, personal utterances' and the abolitionists' desire to satisfy 'public consumption', the latter consideration enjoyed priority. In the words of another critic, the aim of the abolitionists with regard to slave autobiographies was 'to explain slavery to an ignorant audience, not to chart an individual life' (Skora, 1988, p.109), and details of events in the slave's life that contradicted this imperative were excluded.

EXERCISE To what extent do the autobiographical passages (Anthology I, extract 1, pp.132–7) in Cugoano's *Thoughts and Sentiments* satisfy the generic requirements of the spiritual autobiography?

DISCUSSION These passages follow the standard sequence of the spiritual autobiography only very loosely, in part because Cugoano's African origins, while certainly not Christian, were also not unambiguously sinful:

> I was born in the city of Agimaque, on the coast of Fantyn; my father was a companion to the chief in that part of the country of Fantee, and when the old king died I was left in his house with his family; soon after I was sent for by his nephew, Ambro Accasa, who succeeded the old king in the chiefdom of that part of Fantee known by the name of Agimaque and Assinee.
>
> (p.132)

Cugoano describes his African childhood before capture as one of 'peace and tranquillity' (p.132), and he provides attractive images of an idyllic Africa where people and nature flourish in harmony, with children 'going into the woods to gather fruit and catch birds' (p.132). He then describes his own capture and the suffering of his African compatriots: 'This made me cry bitterly, but I was soon conducted to a prison, for three days, where I heard the groans and cries of many, and saw some of my fellow-captives' (p.134). Cugoano's status as both victim and witness of the horrors of slavery is emphasized here, as it serves directly the agenda of the abolitionist cause. Cugoano proceeds to describe his transition from child of Africa to West Indian plantation slave:

> Brought from a state of innocence and freedom, and, in a barbarous and cruel manner, conveyed to a state of horror and slavery: this abandoned situation may be easier conceived than described. From the time that I was kid-napped and conducted to a factory, and from thence in the brutish, base, but fashionable way of traffic, consigned to Grenada, the grievous thoughts which I then felt, still pant in my heart; though my fears and tears have long since subsided.
>
> (p.135)

The passage captures with painful accuracy how the trauma of enslavement continues to echo as a defining moment in Cugoano's personal history. However, he is swift to emphasize that his own agonies were but part of a much larger history of exploitation, with thousands more enslaved Africans 'suffering in all the extreme bitterness of grief and woe, that no language can describe' (p.135).

The crucial moment of Cugoano's conversion to Christianity is recorded in vague and general terms. Indeed, his gratitude to God reads more as compensation for loss of his homeland than as an unequivocal act of redemption:

> although I have been brought away from my native country ... thanks be to God for his good providence towards me.
>
> (p.136)

However, once a convert, Cugoano certainly does not stint in praising the Lord:

> But, above all, what have I obtained from the Lord God of Hosts, the God of the Christians! in that divine revelation of the only true God, and the Saviour of men, what a treasure of wisdom and blessings are involved?
>
> (p.136)

When he reaches Britain, Cugoano expresses a strong desire to educate himself, and applies himself 'to learn reading and writing, which soon became my recreation, pleasure, and delight' (p.136). For Cugoano, however, literacy is not simply an end in itself; rather it is a means to strengthen his own contribution to the struggle against slavery:

> Since, I have endeavoured to improve my mind in reading, and have sought to get all the intelligence I could, in my situation of life, towards the state of my brethren and countrymen in

> complexion, and of the miserable situation of those who are barbarously sold into captivity, and unlawfully held in slavery.
>
> (p.136)

With the acquisition of literacy, Cugoano himself becomes an abolitionist campaigner. Throughout these passages, therefore, Cugoano negotiates awkwardly the somewhat contradictory demands of the enslavement narrative and the spiritual autobiography. The spiritual autobiography is a journey from the darkness of unbelief into the light of salvation, whereas Cugoano's enslavement narrative was a journey from 'innocence and freedom' to 'horror and 'slavery' – from light into darkness, if you like.

The third genre prominent in *Thoughts and Sentiments* is that of the *religious sermon*. Religious sermons in late eighteenth-century Britain did not only circulate in churches; like political tracts, they were frequently published as pamphlets, and they enjoyed a wide readership. The generic markers of religious sermons included: frequent citation of the Scriptures; a desire to recruit converts to their particular version of Christianity; threats of damnation should the Word of the Lord be ignored; promises of salvation should God's Word be heeded; and theological debate with competing Christian doctrines. *Thoughts and Sentiments* displays many of these generic markers: Cugoano quotes liberally from the Scriptures; God's Word is interpreted as opposed to slavery, and those who uphold slavery are threatened appropriately; and Cugoano attacks not only Catholic doctrine but also Protestant theology, which accommodates slavery. To elaborate: in his very first sentence, Cugoano describes slavery as 'the great shame and disgrace of all Christian nations' (extract 1, p.129), and in the second paragraph, he quotes for the first of many times (not always accurately) from the Bible:

> [Opponents of slavery] have the warrant of that which is divine: *Open thy mouth, judge righteously, plead the cause of the poor and needy; for the liberal deviseth liberal things, and by liberal things shall stand.* And they can say with the pious Job, *Did not I weep for him that was in trouble; was not my soul grieved for the poor?*
>
> (p.130; italics in original)

These quotations come from the Old Testament, and endorse Cugoano's project of speaking out on behalf of the poor and suffering. In the spirit of the Old Testament prophets, Cugoano 'judges righteously' the beneficiaries of slavery, and his 'soul grieves for the poor' slaves. The fervour of Cugoano's 'righteous judgement' prompts Vincent Carretta, a recent editor of Cugoano, to argue that *Thoughts and Sentiments* should be categorized as a jeremiad, a particular sub-genre of religious sermon 'named after the Old Testament prophet Jeremiah, who denounced the sins of the Hebrew community and warned of divine retribution should the evil behavior continue' (1999, p.xxii).

A fourth genre that Cugoano explores occasionally in *Thoughts and Sentiments* is that of *philosophy*. Philosophy as a genre in the eighteenth century was rather different from the abstract, theoretical academic discipline it has become today. Although eighteenth-century philosophers certainly did not shrink from abstract reflection on the 'Big Philosophical Questions', they also wrote at great length on what we today think of as separate academic disciplines: history, economics, politics, anthropology and aesthetics. To give but one example, Immanuel Kant, one of the most famous Enlightenment philosophers, devoted the largest period of his career to the teaching of anthropology and cultural geography, and wrote five long essays and two books in these areas (Eze, 1997, pp.2–3). The philosophical writings of the eighteenth century therefore often engaged in detail in areas of direct interest to Cugoano, and although there is no direct evidence that Cugoano read philosophers like Montesquieu, Hutcheson and Raynal, it is certainly the case that he repeated the substance of their ideas. Cugoano endorses Montesquieu's insistence that all men are born equal; Hutcheson's belief in the individual liberty of all men; and Raynal's defence of natural justice and reason. Furthermore, Cugoano steadfastly proclaims Enlightened reason as a sure guide in all matters, second only in authority to the true Christian faith. Of course, not all Enlightenment philosophers opposed slavery, and Cugoano's response to them was uncompromising.

EXERCISE What did Cugoano make of the arguments of Enlightenment philosophers who condoned slavery? Read the passage below, in which Cugoano responds to Hume's view of Africans, in order to formulate your answer. Cugoano quotes (without mentioning him by name) Hume's view that:

> Some pretend that the Africans, in general, are a set of poor, ignorant, dispersed, unsociable people; and that they think it no crime to sell one another, and even their own wives and children; therefore they bring them away to a situation where many of them may arrive to a better state than ever they could obtain in their own native country.
>
> (Extract 1, p.141)

He responds to this view as follows:

> This specious pretence is without any shadow of justice and truth, and, if the argument was even true, it could afford no just and warrantable matter for any society of men to hold slaves. But the argument is false; there can be no ignorance, dispersion, or unsociableness so found among them, which can be made better

> by bringing them away to a state of a degree equal to that of a cow or a horse.
>
> (p.141)

DISCUSSION Where Cugoano encountered instances of Enlightenment philosophy that denied his cherished ideals of equality and human rights – as in the case of Hume's notorious footnote to his essay 'Of national character' – he was swift to dismiss them in the strongest terms. It was a view widely held – and endorsed by Hume – that Africans were a 'poor, ignorant, dispersed, unsociable people' as long as they remained in Africa, and that to transport them *anywhere* else would unquestionably improve their lot. For Cugoano, such views are 'without any shadow of justice and truth', as they ultimately justify treating Africans in a way 'equal to that of a cow or a horse'. On account of Hume's elevated reputation, his intervention in slavery debates provided a prestigious, and therefore powerful, justification for the slave-owners in their resistance to abolition, and Cugoano is therefore especially emphatic in refuting Hume's contribution.

Does the existence of such divergent views on slavery and race in Enlightenment philosophy between, for example, Raynal and Hume mean that we should discard – as Cugoano does with Hume – all Enlightenment philosophy as incoherent, or even fatally contaminated by an intrinsic racism? The historian Robin Blackburn, writing about the 1780s, acknowledges the problem and suggests:

> In different ways abolitionism, democratic politics and Enlightenment philosophy all contained within them the potential to develop a secular doctrine of universal human rights. But this impetus could be checked and confused, as it was in both the United States and Britain during the last decade of the eighteenth century.
>
> (1988, p.155)

Cugoano's response to Enlightenment philosophy was accordingly a strategic one, as he embraced the tendencies within it that promoted 'a secular doctrine of universal human rights', but he was ruthless in rejecting those tendencies that accommodated or justified the suffering of African slaves.

In extracts 1 and 3, we can therefore identify elements of four distinct genres – political tract, autobiography, religious sermon and philosophy. Cugoano combines these different genres in order to give the most effective possible expression to his loathing of slavery. Before we move on to consider how Cugoano engages with Enlightenment thought, I want to draw your attention briefly to two further genres that he employs in *Thoughts and Sentiments*, namely history and economics. Although both emerge as self-contained intellectual disciplines only in the nineteenth century, Cugoano provides in his text powerful historical and economic arguments against slavery that deserve to be considered in their own terms.

As regards his use of *history*, Cugoano writes a version that is in sympathy not with the famous European explorers but rather with the Native Americans and Africans on the receiving end of colonialism. He observes that '[h]istory affords us many examples ... of many crying under the heavy load of subjection and oppression, seeking for deliverance' (quoted in Carretta, 1999, p.60). Cugoano finds examples of oppressed groups 'seeking for the deliverance' in the Bible, and also in the histories of colonialism in the Americas and in Africa. Writing first of the Americas, Cugoano describes the excesses of the Spanish colonial adventurers Hernán Cortés (1485–1547) and Francisco Pizarro (1475–1541), and concludes:

> The history of those dreadfully perfidious methods of forming settlements, and acquiring riches and territory, would make humanity tremble, and even recoil, at the enjoyment of such acquisitions and become reverted into rage and indignation at such horrible injustice and barbarous cruelty.
>
> (Extract 2, p.145)

Cugoano's history of the European penetration of Africa is not as extensive as his history of the Americas, but his conclusions are identical. His sympathies are entirely with the enslaved Africans, and he describes the European slave traders as 'robbers, plunderers, destroyers and enslavers of men' (p.146), and as the ultimate betrayers of Christian virtue.

In his engagement with *economics*, Cugoano rejects the view put forward by figures such as Edward Long that Britain's economic survival depends upon the maintenance of slavery. Cugoano argues first that imperial expansion through slavery has had damaging consequences for Britain's domestic economy:

> however wide [the British] have extended their territories abroad, they have sunk into a world of debt at home, which must ever remain an impending burden upon the inhabitants.
>
> (Extract 2, p.148)

Second, he argues – as Adam Smith had done – that free labour is much more economical than slave labour:

> It is certain, that the produce of the labour of slaves, together with all the advantages of the West-India traffic, bring in an immense revenue to government; but let that amount be what it will, there might be as much or more expected from the labour

> of an equal increase of free people, and without the implication of any guilt attending it ... [T]he free and voluntary labour of many, would soon yield to any government, many greater advantages than any thing that slavery can produce.
>
> (Extract 3, p.156)

For Cugoano, it does not follow that because free African labour is superior to slave labour, Africa should therefore return to its pre-colonial state; rather he concludes that Africa should be integrated more thoroughly into the economy of Britain.

How does Cugoano engage with Enlightenment thought?

It is important to register the publishing context into which Cugoano's *Thoughts and Sentiments* appeared in 1787. In the eighteenth century, Britain led Europe with respect to the emergence of an independent press. With the establishment of the journal *Craftsman* in 1726, followed soon after by *The Gentleman's Magazine*, 'the press was for the first time established as a genuinely critical organ of a public engaged in a critical public debate: as the fourth estate' (Habermas, 1992, p.60). By the final third of the century, the number of newspapers, periodicals, ballads and pamphlets in Britain had increased, providing a forum for public debate and constituting a substantial check on the exercise of political power. After the French Revolution, 'the public's involvement in the critical debate of political issues had become organized to such an extent that in the role of a permanent critical commentator it had definitively broken the exclusiveness of Parliament' (Habermas, 1992, p.66). The critical framework for political debate in the press was provided by what the philosopher Jurgen Habermas, repeating Kant's words, describes as 'the public use of reason' (1992, p.28). What Habermas means by this phrase is the enlightened, critical exchange of ideas through the medium of an independent press, with reason installed as the ultimate arbiter for all disputes. Political commentators as opposed as Paine and Burke appealed to the authority of reason to bolster their arguments; what we now need to consider is the extent to which Cugoano did likewise.

EXERCISE Read through the following short quotations from *Thoughts and Sentiments* and say why you think Cugoano refers to 'reason' and 'enlightenment' with such frequency:

1 '... what is required, is evidently the incumbent duty of all men of enlightened understanding, and of every man that has any claim or affinity to the name of Christian, that the base treatment which the African Slaves undergo, ought to be abolished' (Anthology I, extract 1, p.130).

2 'But what the light of nature, and the dictates of reason, when rightly considered, teach, is, that no man ought to enslave another; and some, who have been rightly guided thereby, have made noble defences for the universal natural rights and privileges of all men. But in this case [of slavery], when the learned take neither revelation nor reason for their guide, they fall into as great, and worse errors, than the unlearned' (quoted in Carretta, 1999, p.28).

3 '... the pretences that some men make use of for holding of slaves, must be evidently the grossest perversion of reason, as well as an inconsistent and diabolical use of the sacred writings' (quoted in Carretta, 1999, p.29).

4 '... there is nothing in nature, reason, and scripture can be found, in any manner or way, to warrant the enslaving of black people more than others' (quoted in Carretta, 1999, p.45).

5 '... even those who are elevated to high rank of power and affluence ... can shut their eyes at this enormous evil of the slavery and commerce of the human species; and, contrary to all the boasted accomplishments, and fine virtues of the civilized and enlightened nations, they can sit still and let the torrent of robbery, slavery, and oppression roll on' (quoted in Carretta, 1999, p.49).

6 'In all these places [in West Africa] it is their grand business to traffic in the human species; and dreadful and shocking as it is to think, it has even been established by royal authority, and is still supported and carried on under a Christian government; and this must evidently appear thereby, that the learned, the civilized, and even the enlightened nations are become as truly barbarous and brutish as the unlearned' (quoted in Carretta, 1999, p.73).

7 'For it is evident that no custom established among men [slavery] was ever more impious; since it is contrary to reason, justice, nature, the principles of law and government, and the whole doctrine, in short, of natural religion, and the revealed voice of God' (quoted in Carretta, 1999, p. 80).

8 'And as Great-Britain has been remarkable for ages past, for encouraging arts and sciences, and may now be put in competition with any nation in the known world, if they would take compassion on the inhabitants of the coast of Guinea, and to make use of such means as would be needful to enlighten their minds in the knowledge of Christianity, their virtue, in this respect, would have its own reward' (Anthology I, extract 4, p.159).

9 '... the many Anti-christian errors which are gone abroad into the world, and all the popish superstition and nonsense, and the various assimilations unto it, with the false philosophy which abounds among Christians, seems to threaten with an universal deluge; but God hath promised to fill the world with a knowledge of himself,

> and he hath set up his bow, in the rational heavens, as well as in the clouds, as a token that he will stop the proud ways of error and delusion' (Anthology I, extract 4, pp.165–6).

DISCUSSION Cugoano refers to 'reason' and 'enlightenment' with such frequency because the terms carry great rhetorical weight. Defenders of slavery routinely insisted that it was *they* who had reason on their side, so Cugoano quite simply had to show conclusively that it was in fact *his* ideas that accorded with reason, and further that they were the more enlightened. It is interesting to note that when he invokes reason, Cugoano invariably *also* cites as authority for his opinion any combination of: 'the laws of nature' – see quotations 2, 4 and 7; 'the Word of God' – see quotations 2, 3, 4, 7 and 9; and 'justice' and 'the principles of law and government' – see quotation 7. The coupling of reason and Christian doctrine is especially pronounced in *Thoughts and Sentiments*, and is precisely captured in Cugoano's phrase 'rational heavens' in quotation 9, which he declares to be the appropriate antidote to the combination of 'popish superstition and nonsense' and 'false philosophy'. Cugoano's references to 'enlightenment' serve a similar function, as he uses the adjective 'enlightened' to denote a humane code of conduct unequivocally opposed to slavery. He accordingly berates individuals and nations who claim to be enlightened while at the same time deriving benefit from slavery – see, for example, quotations 1, 5 and 6. For Cugoano, true enlightenment can only be achieved when nations such as Britain turn their backs on slavery, and engage instead with Africa compassionately in a spirit of Christian brotherhood (see quotation 8).

EXERCISE To conclude this unit, now read extract 4 (Anthology I, pp.157–68). Again, try to identify Cugoano's textual persona, his use of genre, and his engagement with Enlightenment thought.

DISCUSSION We have already noted that Cugoano's textual persona is a composite or hybrid made up of a number of different identities: 'African innocent', 'West Indian slave', 'Enlightenment intellectual', 'non-Catholic Christian', and 'abolitionist campaigner'. This hybrid identity is the product of the economic, political, cultural and religious forces of the age, with each of the three corners of the slave triangle – Africa, West Indies, Britain – partly defining it. In *Thoughts and Sentiments*, different parts of Cugoano's identity are to the fore in different sections of the text, but crucially he never relinquishes his earlier forms of identification (African, slave) when he moves to Britain. Rather, the earlier identities are retained, and subsumed in what ultimately becomes his primary form of identification, namely 'Christian'. On the final page, Cugoano explains his sense of how Christianity can incorporate without cancelling out prior forms of identification: 'And Christianity does not require that we should be deprived of our own personal name, or the name of our ancestors; but it may very fitly add another name unto us, Christian, or one anointed' (p.167). Cugoano's conclusion here generalizes his own experience of Christian conversion, and his own personal African name – as opposed to his Christian name John Stuart – is displayed on the cover of *Thoughts and Sentiments.*

In the closing pages of *Thoughts and Sentiments*, the two dominant genres are those of the religious sermon and the political tract. We have just noted how religious concerns prevail at the conclusion of *Thoughts and Sentiments*, with Cugoano emphasizing his Christian identity and proclaiming the Word of God; what remains is for us to identify the elements of the genre of the political tract. We noted earlier that one of the generic markers of the latter was the inclusion of some form of political blueprint or set of proposals, and in this respect Cugoano does not disappoint. Cugoano has three preliminary proposals: one, that days of mourning and fasting be declared to mark the horrors of slavery; two, that slavery itself (not just the slave trade) be immediately abolished; and three, that military means be deployed in West Africa to enforce the termination of slavery. In addition, Cugoano also supports (with qualifications) the specific project of repatriating Africans in Britain and the USA to Sierra Leone, and more generally promotes the integration of British and African economies. He argues that should Britain abolish slavery in Africa, 'they might have settlements and many kingdoms united in a friendly alliance with themselves' (p.159). This means in effect that Britain should in fact colonize Africa more comprehensively, but on the basis of partnership rather than enslavement, and that the transition from slavery to a partnership based on free labour should be managed cautiously, with slaves educated in Christianity and good working habits. Cugoano is so confident about these proposals that he claims his alternative plan will bring Britain 'ten times its share in all the profits that slavery can produce' (p.160).

There are a couple of moments in extract 4 where Cugoano challenges in indirect ways certain widely held assumptions about the European Enlightenment. The first is in his second reference to Hume. Cugoano quotes the pro-slavery views of Gordon Turnbull and connects them to '*Hume*, or to his friend *Tobin*. The poor negroes in the West-Indies, have suffered enough by such religion as the philosophers of the North produce' (p.166). Reason and abolition were inextricably tied in Cugoano's arguments, whereas certain other 'philosophers of the North' like Hume condoned slavery. For Cugoano, any sympathy for slavery fundamentally betrayed the authentic liberating impulse of Enlightenment reason. The second moment of interest in extract 4 is also a challenge to the unquestioning elevation of Europe above Africa. In an aside, Cugoano registers his continuing loyalty to the memory of his African childhood, insisting that '[w]e want many rules of civilization, in Africa; but, in many respects, we may boast of some more essential liberties than any of the civilized nations in Europe enjoy' (p.161). This contrasts with the more negative observations we encountered in Park's *Travels*, and it is worth noting that historians continue to debate the precise nature of pre-colonial West African societies along the lines established by these late eighteenth-century writers. Although Cugoano does not use the words 'reason' or 'enlightenment' here, 'civilization' and 'liberties' carry a similar positive charge, and he subversively suggests that Africa is not by definition inferior to Europe in these terms.

---

4 Conclusion

In this unit we have first of all examined the arguments for and against slavery in the period 1770–1807. Second, we have deployed two important critical concepts: the idea of a 'textual persona', a construction distinct from the historical figure of the author; and the critical term 'genre', a type or kind of writing. Third, we have looked closely at how Cugoano has drawn upon key Enlightenment ideas such as reason, and deployed them to serve his anti-slavery arguments. In Unit 15, we continue our enquiry and look at the period 1807–33, exploring the history of slavery at that time, extending our application of critical resources to two symptomatic slave narratives of the age of revolution, and finally comparing late eighteenth- and early nineteenth-century slave narratives.

References

Baird, J.D. and Ryskamp, C. (eds) (1980–95) *The Poems of William Cowper*, 3 vols, Oxford, Clarendon Press.

Blackburn, R. (1988) *The Overthrow of Colonial Slavery 1776–1848*, London, Verso.

Boswell, J. (1933) *Boswell's Life of Johnson*, intro. C.B. Tinker, 2 vols, New York, Oxford University Press (first published 1791).

Carretta, V. (ed.) (1999) Quobna Ottobah Cugoano: *Thoughts and Sentiments on the Evil of Slavery*, Harmondsworth, Penguin.

Davis, D.B. (1975) *The Problem of Slavery in the Age of Revolution 1770–1823*, London and Ithaca, Cornell University Press.

Drescher, S. (1999) *From Slavery to Freedom: Comparative Studies in the Rise and Fall of Atlantic Slavery*, New York, New York University Press.

Dyson, R.W. (ed.) (1998) Augustine: *The City of God against the Pagans*, Cambridge, Cambridge University Press.

Eze, E.C. (1997) *Race and Enlightenment: A Reader*, Cambridge, Mass., and Oxford, Blackwell.

Flew, A. (ed.) (1988) David Hume: *An Enquiry Concerning Human Understanding*, La Salle, Open Court (first published 1748).

Gerzina, G.H. (1995) *Black London: Life before Emancipation*, New Brunswick, Rutgers University Press.

Habermas, J. (1992) *The Structural Transformation of the Public Sphere*, trans. T. Burger, Cambridge, Polity Press (first published 1962).

James, C.L.R. (1989) *The Black Jacobins: Toussaint L'Ouverture and the San Domingo Revolution*, 2nd edn, New York, Vintage.

Long, E. (1970) *History of Jamaica, Volumes I and II*, ed. G. Metcalf, London, Frank Cass (first published 1774).

Martin, S.I. (1999) *Britain's Slave Trade*, London, Macmillan.

Nussbaum, F.A. (1989) *The Autobiographical Subject: Gender and Ideology in Eighteenth-Century England*, Baltimore, Johns Hopkins University Press.

Sandiford, K.A. (1988) *Measuring the Moment: Strategies of Protest in Eighteenth-Century Afro-English Writing*, London and Toronto, Associated University Press.

Segal, R. (1995) *The Black Diaspora*, London, Faber.

Skora, J. (1988) 'Is the slave narrative a species of autobiography?' in J. Olney (ed.) *Studies in Autobiography*, New York, Oxford University Press.

Smith, A. (1986) *The Wealth of Nations, Books I–III*, ed. A. Skinner, Harmondsworth, Penguin (first published 1776).

Thomas, H. (2000) *Romanticism and Slave Narratives: Transatlantic Testimonies*, Cambridge, Cambridge University Press.

Williams, R. (1971) *The Long Revolution*, Harmondsworth, Penguin.

Unit 15
Slave writings (2)

Prepared for the course team by David Johnson

Contents

Study components

Weeks of study	*Supplementary material*	*Audio-visual*	*Anthologies and set books*
1	Illustrations Book	–	Anthology I

Objectives

After reading Unit 15 you should:

- be able to discuss the history of Britain's role in Atlantic slavery in the period 1807–34;
- appreciate the textual strategies of 'persona' and 'genre' employed in Robert Wedderburn and Mary Prince's slave writings;
- understand the place of Enlightenment and Romantic thought in the writings of Wedderburn and Prince.

Aims

The first aim of Unit 15 is to place Robert Wedderburn's *The Horrors of Slavery* (1824) and *The History of Mary Prince* (1831) in the historical context of the period from the abolition of the slave trade in 1807 to the emancipation of slaves in 1834. The second aim is to consider the range of literary, linguistic and rhetorical qualities of the slave narratives, including most notably the textual persona(e) assumed, and the different genres of writing employed in expressing their opposition to slavery. The third aim is to consider how slave narratives of the early nineteenth century utilize, extend and criticize the ideas of the Enlightenment and Romanticism, and our final aim is to identify the differences between the slave narratives of the late eighteenth century and those of the early nineteenth century.

1 Introduction

When the British Parliament abolished the slave trade in 1807, there were already 600,000 slaves in the British West Indies, and the hope of abolitionists was that with the end of the trade their living conditions would improve significantly. These hopes were dashed, as all evidence from the West Indies indicated that for slaves on the sugar plantations, conditions were worse than ever. From campaigning against the slave trade, the focus therefore changed to the full emancipation of all slaves. With pressure exerted on slavery both by the slaves themselves and by the abolitionists, the reformed British Parliament voted in 1833 to free all slaves under the age of six on 1 August 1834, and all adult slaves, who first had to serve a six-year apprenticeship, on 31 July 1838. These successful campaigns frame both Robert Wedderburn's writings and *The History of Mary Prince*, but before we look in detail at their work, we need to ask: what were the historical factors that influenced slave writings in the post-abolition period? Take brief notes of the discussion that follows.

2 Slavery in the age of revolution

Written in the 1780s, Cugoano's *Thoughts and Sentiments on the Evil of Slavery* preceded the major revolutions of the late eighteenth century, most obviously the French Revolution of 1789, but also the large-scale slave uprisings in Santo Domingo from 1791 to 1804. Despite its anger, Cugoano's work therefore appeals for the most part to rational solutions, enlightened Christian sentiment, and the exercise of reason in public affairs. In the writings of Wedderburn, and to a lesser degree Prince, there are also appeals to reason and Christian forbearance, but there is also the consciousness that revolutionary change is both possible and desirable. Wedderburn and Prince's sensibilities are not unusual for the period; indeed, historians looking back at their age have frequently characterized it not so much as an age of Enlightenment as the age of revolution. A recent interpretation of this period as one defined by revolution is that of historians Peter Linebaugh and Marcus Rediker, who argue that workers from 'the commons, the plantation, the ship, and the factory' (2000, p.327) transformed the social landscape at the end of the eighteenth century:

> In 1760–1835, the [workers of all races] launched the age of revolution in the Atlantic, beginning with Tacky's Revolt in Jamaica and continuing in a series of uprisings throughout the hemisphere. The new revolts created breakthroughs in human praxis – the Rights of Mankind, the strike, the higher-law doctrine – that would eventually help to abolish impressment and

> plantation slavery. They helped more immediately to produce the American Revolution, which ended in reaction as the Founding Fathers used race, nation, and citizenship to discipline, divide, and exclude the very sailors and slaves who had initiated and propelled the revolutionary movement. The liberty tree, however, sprouted branches elsewhere in the 1790s – in Haiti, France, Ireland and England.
>
> (2000, p.329)

Instead of seeing the political achievements of 1760–1835 – democratic governance, equality before the law, and human rights – as the work of enlightened rulers and rational intellectuals, Linebaugh and Rediker give the main credit for these achievements to the slaves, workers, sailors and farm workers engaged in revolutionary struggles. Both Wedderburn and Prince's lives were intimately implicated in these struggles, and we need now to expand briefly upon the key moments of slave resistance in this period.

The bloody struggle in Santo Domingo drew to a close in 1804, with the French finally driven out with losses of 60,000 lives, and Dessalines declaring an independent republic in 1805. In the years immediately following the liberation of Haiti, slave resistance in the West Indies was contained, with the next major uprising of Bussa's Rebellion in the British colony of Barbados only in 1816. The rebel slaves destroyed plantations and set buildings alight, but only one white and one black civilian were killed; reprisals were severe, with 50 rebels killed in fighting, a further 214 executed, and 144 deported. The next uprising was in 1823 along the Demerara River in Guyana, where about 2,000 rebel slaves with some help from sympathetic missionaries presented demands for better working conditions, including more time to work their own land. Again, the response of the planters was uncompromising, and in the repression that followed 250 slaves lost their lives, with victims strung up on gibbets in front of the affected plantations as a warning to surviving slaves. The third major slave uprising took place in Jamaica in 1831, and its scale was unprecedented in the British West Indies, with between 20,000 and 30,000 slaves and a small number of sympathetic Baptist and Methodist missionaries involved. Known subsequently as the Baptist War, this uprising too was marked for the disproportionate scale of the plantation owners' reprisals. The slaves killed 14 whites and destroyed over £1m. worth of property; 200 rebel slaves were killed in the fighting, 312 were executed afterwards, and the white colonists burnt down nine Baptist and six Methodist chapels. Although public opinion in Britain routinely flinched at stories of slave violence, news of the planters burning churches and persecuting missionaries and black Christians was a quite different matter, and these stories were turned to immense propaganda advantage by the abolitionists.

In addition, it is important to register that in the first decades of the nineteenth century, and particularly in the years 1812–22, there were a number of radical political challenges to the British state that aspired to emulate the revolutionary victories in France and Santo Domingo. The historian George Rudé provides the following summary of the popular uprisings in Britain during this period:

> The years of the Regency were among the most disturbed and riotous in England's recent history ... In May 1812, the Prime Minister himself, Spencer Perceval, was assassinated in the lobby of the House of Commons. The same year there were food riots and a recrudescence of *taxation populaire* [popular seizures of goods and property] in places as widely dispersed as Falmouth, Bristol, Sheffield, Nottingham, Bolton, and Carlisle; and Londoners rioted against the Corn Law of 1815. There were the Spa Fields riots and agricultural disturbances the following year. It was a period of minor rebellions and risings of the poor: such as the march of the so-called 'Blanketeers' from Manchester, the Pentridge 'revolution', and the Huddersfield 'rising' of 1817; and two years later, the yeomanry cut down a great reform meeting in the massacre of 'Peterloo' at Manchester. As sensational as any of these episodes, while they lasted, were the Luddite riots in the midlands and northern counties.
>
> (1995, p.71)

At times, leaders of these uprisings gestured to a common cause with the West Indian slaves, but for the most part they railed against the indigenous institutions of both the new capitalist class and the old landowning classes in Britain's ruling oligarchy.

Slave rebellions in the West Indies were, of course, closely monitored by abolitionists in Britain, although their own anti-slavery campaigns in Britain had an independent momentum. The period from 1807 to 1815 was dominated by the war with France, and anti-slavery efforts were limited to trying to end participation in the slave trade by other European powers, and trying to protect plantation slaves by having them registered. It was believed that by registering all slaves in the West Indies it would be possible to measure demographic details about slave conditions, but these efforts were resisted, and it took until 1819 for Parliament to pass a bill – in diluted form – requiring the registration of slaves. From 1815 to 1823, anti-slavery remained relatively peripheral in public debate, and it was only when the Society for the Mitigating and Gradually Abolishing the State of Slavery throughout the British Dominions was established in 1823 that slave emancipation again became a major political issue. Within a year, 220 local branches of the Society had been formed, and 825 petitions had been presented to Parliament. The emphasis in the campaign swiftly changed from gradual to immediate emancipation, with the scale of protest escalating rapidly, and peaking in 1832–3. The abolitionist speaker George Thompson claimed to have addressed 750,000 listeners when he passed through Manchester in 1832, Henry Whiteley's abolitionist pamphlet *Three Months in Jamaica* (1833) sold 200,000 copies within a month, and of the more than 900 anti-slavery petitions submitted to Parliament in 1833, there included one signed by 187,000 English women (Drescher, 1999, p.67). In the 1820s, anti-slavery had been associated with parliamentary reform, and the successful passage of the 1832 Reform Act meant that it was the reformed Parliament – representing an electorate of 6–8 million as opposed to 4–5 million previously – that passed the Abolition of Slavery Bill in August 1833. The slave-owners received £20 million in compensation from the British tax payer (40 per cent of the budget) to make good their economic losses suffered as a result of the emancipation of the slaves.

As regards the economics of British West Indian slavery in the first third of the nineteenth century, there is evidence that profit levels were substantially down in comparison to the previous century. Furthermore, as India increasingly provided raw materials such as cotton and tea for British industries and markets more cheaply, so the importance of the West Indies within the economy of the British empire declined. There is no doubt that slavery continued to be profitable for the West Indian slave-owning class, but as ideas of free labour and free markets gradually took hold – and, crucially, proved to be more profitable – so the political campaigns against slavery became irresistible. Pragmatic statesmen like Lord Palmerston recognized as much when in 1842 he looked back at the passing of slavery with the following thoughts:

> Let no man imagine that those treaties for the suppression of the slave trade are valuable only as being calculated to promote the great interests of humanity, and as tending to rid mankind of a foul and detestable crime. Such indeed was their great object and their chief merit. But in this case as in many others, virtue carries its own reward; and if the nations of the world could extirpate this abominable traffic, and if the vast population of Africa could by that means be left free to betake themselves to peaceful and innocent trade, the greatest commercial benefit would accrue not to England only, but to every civilized nation which engages in maritime commerce. These slave trade treaties therefore are indirectly treaties for the encouragement of commerce.
>
> (Quoted in Walvin, 1992, p.309)

Cugoano's ideas on free labour and free trade borrowed from Adam Smith – a minority position in 1787 – are repeated here 55 years later as the respectable opinions of an establishment politician.

As regards the intellectual context in the decades after the French Revolution and Santo Domingo uprising, the proponents of slavery and abolition repeated substantially the same arguments. The main development in pro-slavery thought in this period was an increased appeal to science as the basis for explaining racial difference, with Charles White's *An Account of the Regular Gradation in Man* (1799) the

most influential work in this tradition. According to White, Africans were a distinct and inferior species, and not only were his ideas quoted in the years to follow by the British pro-slavery lobby, but they also influenced European theories of race. In pro-abolition thought, the Enlightenment arguments were repeated with greater conviction, and philosophical justifications for slave emancipation were elaborated. The following passage in the novelist and political philosopher William Godwin's *Enquiry Concerning Political Justice* (1793) captures the post-Revolution attitude to slavery nicely. Godwin first paraphrases the pro-slavery position, and then sets out his own views:

> 'The slaves in the West Indies,' they said, 'are contented with their situation, they are not conscious of the evils against which you exclaim; why then should you endeavour to alter their condition?' The true answer to this question, even granting them this fact, would be: 'It is not very material to a man of a liberal and enlarged mind whether they are contented or no. Are they contented? I am not contented for them. I see in them beings of certain capacities, equal to certain pursuits and enjoyments. It is of no consequence in the question that they do not see this, that they do not know their own interests and happiness ... Abridged as they are of independence and enjoyment, they have neither the apprehension nor spirit of men. I cannot bear to see human nature thus degraded. It is my duty, if I can, to make them a thousand times happier than they are, or have any conception of being.'
>
> (1985, pp.392–3)

Note that Godwin does not necessarily accept that slaves are contented, but argues that *even if they were*, he as someone of 'liberal and enlarged mind' felt a basic impulse of compassion that was repelled by the degradation of human nature caused by slavery. The existence of slavery imposed a duty on figures like Godwin to ameliorate their condition, subject to the qualification 'if I can'.

3 Robert Wedderburn

Robert Wedderburn (1762–1835) was born in Jamaica, the son of James Wedderburn, a wealthy sugar plantation owner and doctor, and Rosanna, an African-born slave. When Rosanna was five months pregnant with Robert, James Wedderburn sold her and their unborn child, and a series of subsequent sales separated Robert from both his slave-owning father and slave mother. Robert was baptized in the Church of England, and received a rudimentary mission education that ended when he was five years old. In the absence of his mother, he was brought up by his maternal grandmother, 'Talkee Amy', a well-known Kingston figure with a reputation for casting spells and magic. His vulnerability on the impoverished margins of free society in Jamaica drove him to join the Royal Navy at the age of 16, and he first arrived in London in 1778. Historical records of Wedderburn's experiences in London in the 1780s and 1790s are sketchy, but there is indirect evidence that they included participation in the 'anti-Popery' Gordon riots of 1780 and the Nore Mutiny of 1797 during a second spell in the Navy. In between, he learned the trade of tailor, but failed to gain admission to the tailors' guild and therefore earned only a precarious living, which he supplemented by petty crime. In October 1786, Wedderburn was converted to Evangelical Methodism, and in 1802 wrote a short pamphlet entitled *Truth Self-Supported; or a Refutation of Certain Doctrinal Errors Generally Adopted in the Christian Church*, which described his conversion. Wedderburn duly added preaching to his list of accomplishments, and was registered as a Dissenting minister when in 1813 he joined the circle of the agrarian radical Thomas Spence. Spence's political vision was for a revolutionary redistribution of land, and the combination of his prophetic fervour, programme of enlightened economic reform, and utopian ideal of community attracted Wedderburn strongly. Fusing his own versions of Evangelical, Enlightenment and Spencean thought, Wedderburn in 1817 wrote articles for the six issues of his journal *Axe Laid to the Root, being an Address to the Planters and Negroes of the Island of Jamaica*. In 1819, Wedderburn established his own chapel in Soho, and drew substantial congregations with his charismatic and unconventional style of preaching. Wedderburn's prominence in the political debates of the period is attested by the cartoon reproduced in the Illustrations Book (see Plate 15.1) which depicts him arguing in a pub with Robert Owen, who is the subject of Units 18–19. (You might find it useful to return and reassess this cartoon after you have studied Robert Owen.) Wedderburn was closely involved in the political intrigues against the government of the day, narrowly missing both the Peterloo Massacre in 1819 and the thwarted Cato Street Conspiracy in 1820. He was nonetheless convicted of blasphemy in 1821, and jailed for two years in Dorchester prison. William Wilberforce visited him there, and advised him to further the abolitionist cause by penning his autobiography, advice that Wedderburn followed, with the result that *The Horrors of Slavery; exemplified in the Life and History of Rev. Robert Wedderburn* appeared in 1824. On his release from prison, Wedderburn returned to preaching but with limited success, and the final decade of his life was punctuated with further difficulties, including two more years in prison from 1829 to 1831 for running a brothel. He died in poverty at the age of 72.

It is useful to contrast Wedderburn's life history briefly with that of Cugoano. The two men's lives have much in common: experience of slavery in the West Indies, the benefit of white patronage in London, the experience of Evangelical conversion, and the self-conscious use of autobiography as an expression of abolitionist sentiment. However, the differences between them are at least as striking. Whereas Cugoano had been born and captured in Africa, had been sold into slavery, and had survived the notorious middle passage, Wedderburn's experience of slavery was confined to the West Indies. Second, in contrast to Cugoano's writings, which focus principally on the abolition of the slave trade with emancipation a distant dream, Wedderburn's most substantial writings come after the abolition of the slave trade in 1807, and focus on the struggle for emancipation. Wedderburn also differs from Cugoano in that he attacks with equal zeal the exploitation of West Indian slaves and the 'wage slaves' of Britain's Industrial Revolution. A further difference between the two men is that whereas Cugoano represents himself as an exemplar of black self-improvement, Wedderburn represents himself as an outcast and victim. However, perhaps the most important difference relates to Wedderburn's relative failure to integrate in 'respectable' London society; he was never befriended as Cugoano was by the middle-class abolitionists, and his political extremism and life on the fringes of the criminal underworld excluded him from the privileged circles inhabited by Cugoano. For Wedderburn's editor Iain McCalman, '[i]t is this unrespectability or roughness which distinguishes Wedderburn so decisively from his predecessors [like Cugoano]' (Wedderburn, 1991, p.5).

A brief description of the four extracts from Wedderburn's writings reproduced in Anthology I is necessary. Extracts 6 and 8 are required reading, and extracts 5 and 7 are optional extra reading. In the discussion to follow, I refer principally to passages in the required reading, but will also mention brief passages from extracts 5 and 7. To sum up the content of these extracts: extract 5 is from Wedderburn's 1802 pamphlet describing his conversion to Evangelical Methodism, *Truth Self-Supported*; extract 6 is from articles Wedderburn wrote in 1817 for *The Axe Laid to the Root*; extract 7 is from his unsuccessful defence to the court against the charges of blasphemy in 1820. This defence was in fact **ghost-written** by the 'Reverend Erasmus Perkins', the nom de plume of Wedderburn's friend George Cannon, whom McCalman describes as a 'suave and devious Spencean' (Wedderburn, 1991, p.28). Extract 8 is from Wedderburn's *The Horrors of Slavery*, which also includes an angry exchange of letters in *Bell's Life in London* magazine between Wedderburn and his half-brother, Andrew Colvile. Wedderburn's spelling is if anything even more eccentric than Cugoano's, but once again I have retained his original spelling in my quotations from his writings.

EXERCISE Now read extracts 6 and 8 (Anthology I, pp.170–84 and pp.191–202). As you read, bear the following questions in mind:

1 What textual persona does Wedderburn assume?

2 What genres does Wedderburn employ in his writings?

3 How does Wedderburn engage with Enlightenment thought?

We shall discuss in detail each of these questions in turn.

What textual persona does Wedderburn assume?

In extract 6, the articles written in 1817 for his magazine *The Axe Laid to the Root,* Wedderburn emphasizes his West Indian origins, and claims to speak in the name of God, justice, humanity and reason. He sets out his credentials in the opening paragraph with considerable energy:

> Be it known to the world, that, I Robert Wedderburn, son of James Wedderburn, esq. of Inveresk, near Musselborough, by Rosannah his slave, whom he sold to James Charles Shalto Douglas, esq. in the parish of St. Mary, in the island of Jamaica, while pregnant with the said Wedderburn, who was not held as a slave, (a provision made in the agreement, that the child when born should be free.) This Wedderburn, doth charge all potentates, governors, and governments of every description with felony, who does wickedly violate the sacred rights of man – by force of arms, or otherwise, seizing the persons of men and dragging them from their native country, and selling their stolen persons and generations. – Wedderburn demands, in the name of God, in the name of natural justice, and in the name of humanity, that all slaves be set free; for innocent individuals are entitled to the protection of civil society; and that all stealers, receivers, and oppressors in this base practice be forgiven, as the crime commenced in the days of ignorance, and is now exposed in the enlightened age of reason.
>
> (pp.170–1)

Note in the first instance Wedderburn's shift from first person in the opening line ('I, Robert Wedderburn') to third person ('This Wedderburn') in the second sentence in order to represent himself. The textual persona disclosed by the first person 'I, Robert Wedderburn' relates to personal and family biographical details, and it is significant that there is no finite verb in the first sentence. The first-person Wedderburn is thus presented as passive, the product of a brutal family history contaminated by slavery. By contrast, the authorial identity disclosed by the third person 'This Wedderburn' relates to public and political commitments, and is presented as a man of action – in the second sentence he 'charges all potentates', and in the third sentence 'demands ... that all slaves be set free'. This third-person Wedderburn also speaks as a man who gives voice not only to Christian righteousness, but also to the values of 'natural justice', 'humanity' and 'the enlightened age of reason'. The result is an authorial identity that combines being both victim of his own cruel historical circumstances ('I, Robert Wedderburn'), and defiant agent of his own political destiny ('This Wedderburn').

EXERCISE Now reread the autobiographical sections of extract 8, *The Horrors of Slavery* (Anthology I, pp.192–7) and identify the textual persona(e) assumed by Wedderburn.

DISCUSSION Wedderburn describes himself in the Dedication to Wilberforce as '[a]n oppressed, insulted, and degraded African' (p.191), and starts his autobiography by recounting his family history. On his father's side, he goes back to his grandfather, a staunch Jacobite who was executed for high treason. His father James Wedderburn restored the wealth of the family by hard work, first as a doctor and then as a sugar plantation owner. According to Wedderburn, while his father was poor, 'he was chaste as any Scotchman, whose poverty made him virtuous; but the moment he became rich, he gave loose to his carnal appetites, and indulged himself without moderation, but as parsimonious as ever' (p.193). Of his father's many sins, Wedderburn emphasizes in particular his violence and sexual cruelty towards women slaves, describing him as a 'bantam cock upon his own dunghill' (p.194). Wedderburn describes his father's devious and brutal treatment of his slave mother, and in an important passage explains both his mother's and his own rebellious spirit as products of his father's cruelty:

> Hath not a slave feelings? If you starve them, will they not die? If you wrong them, will they not revenge? Insulted on one hand, and degraded on the other, was it likely that my poor mother could practise the Christian virtue of humility, when her Christian master provoked her to wrath? She shortly afterwards became again pregnant [with Wedderburn]; and I have not the least doubt but that from her rebellious and violent temper during that period, that I have inherited the same disposition – the same desire to see justice overtake the oppressors of my countrymen – and the same determination to lose no stone unturned, to accomplish so desirable an object.
>
> (p.195)

In the opening questions of this passage, Wedderburn paraphrases Shylock's famous speech from Shakespeare's *The Merchant of Venice*:

> I am a Jew. Hath not a Jew eyes? ... If you prick us do we not bleed? If you tickle us do we not laugh? If you poison us do we not die? And if you wrong us shall we not revenge?
>
> (*The Merchant of Venice*, Act III, Scene I, ll.49–56)

The allusion is appropriate because in the same way that Shylock insists that Christians and Jews share a common humanity, Wedderburn insists here that the white plantation owners and the black slaves share a common humanity. Furthermore, just as Shylock's rhetorical question establishes that Christian and Jew alike react to wrongs perpetrated with a desire for revenge, so Wedderburn sees the slave's desire for revenge as a natural human response to wrongs suffered. Wedderburn's intense identification with his mother, as well as with his slave grandmother, means that he consciously takes on their identity as 'rebellious and violent', an identity he sees not as in any way innate, but as produced by the brutality of slave masters.

Although *The Horrors of Slavery* reads to some extent as Wedderburn's personal vendetta against his slave-owning father, it is significant that he translates his own and his mother's personal experiences of suffering under slavery into a political commitment on behalf of all slaves. He makes this clear in the angry exchange of letters with his half-brother Andrew Colvile published in *Bell's Life in London* magazine, where he describes his origins as follows:

> One of the conditions of the sale [of my mother by James Wedderburn] was, that her offspring, your humble servant [Robert Wedderburn], was to be free, from its birth, and I thank my GOD, that through a long life of hardship and adversity, I have ever been free both in mind and body: and have always raised my voice in behalf of my enslaved countrymen!
>
> (p.200)

In this exchange with Colvile, Wedderburn is at pains to stress his poverty. He clearly identifies himself as one of London's impoverished working class when he explains why he asked his wealthy relatives for money: 'I was at that time, Mr. Editor, in extreme distress; the quartern loaf was then 1s. 10d., I was out of work, and my wife was lying in, which I think was some excuse for applying to an *affectionate brother*, who refused to relieve me' (p.201).

Finally, in discussing Wedderburn's textual persona, I want to note briefly the shift in Wedderburn's persona in his defence against the charge of blasphemy in 1820 ghost-written by George Cannon (extract 7). The 'Wedderburn' constructed by Cannon in this defence is a mix of exaggerated humility and high learning. On the one hand, 'Wedderburn' declares:

> However humble I may be as a member of society, and whatever efforts may be made to degrade me and render me contemptible in the eyes of the world, I have nevertheless the pride, and the

> ambition, to flatter myself, that even my simple exertions will one day or other be of no mean importance to the cause I am embarked in, which is that of *Religious Liberty* and the *Universal Right of Conscience.*
>
> (pp.185–6; italics in original)

Towards the end of his defence, he once again emphasizes this idea that his humble origins and appearance belie a formidable ability to tell the truth: 'If I am a low, vulgar man, and incapable of delivering my sentiments in an elegant and polished manner, am I to be condemned, when I find two pages in the Bible most palpably contradicting each other, for asserting that one of them must be A LIE? (p.190). On the other hand, 'Wedderburn' here quotes extensively from learned authorities, including Voltaire, Helvetius, Machiavelli and Shaftesbury, in order to defend himself against the charge of blasphemy. This second urbane textual persona in the defence is therefore quite different from the one in *The Axe Laid to the Root* and *The Horrors of Slavery.* McCalman speculates that had Wedderburn used 'his own plain and moving words' (Wedderburn, 1991, p.28) instead of allowing Cannon's circumlocutory style to speak through him, he might well have received a more lenient sentence.

To conclude: as in the case of Cugoano, Wedderburn combines a number of different personae in his writings. He writes as a Christian convert and independent preacher; as a victim and product of the sexual violence endemic in plantation slavery; as a defiant agent of his own personal history; as a man of enlightened reason, and (in Cannon's ghost-written form) a man of learning; as a 'rebellious and violent' free black speaking on behalf of all slaves; and finally, as a member of London's impoverished working class. Again, as with Cugoano, Wedderburn's hybrid identity is the product of the political, religious and economic forces of his age, with the experiences of exclusion and poverty in the West Indies and Britain defining his identity. Different aspects of his identity are to the fore in different sections of his writings, and although there are occasional moments when the textual persona he assumes threatens to fragment into incoherence, Wedderburn ultimately holds together the different aspects of his identity. If for Cugoano the textual persona of 'Christian' contains all his other personae, for Wedderburn it is more difficult to ascribe one persona such ascendancy.

What genres does Wedderburn employ in his writings?

The most prominent genre that Wedderburn employs in his writings to express his loathing of slavery and all those who benefit from it is that of the *religious sermon.* The radical message of Wedderburn's sermons, however, means that the dividing line between religious sermon and political tract is difficult to draw. In *Truth Self-Supported*, he describes his life-changing encounter with Evangelical Methodism, but he also makes it clear that for him Methodism fails to provide answers to many difficult questions. The perceived weaknesses in Methodist doctrine are addressed for Wedderburn in the ideas of Spence, and more particularly in Thomas Evans's *Christian Policy, the Salvation of the Empire* (1816), which stressed the communism of the early Christians and the betrayals of the institution of the Church. In the fourth issue of *The Axe Laid to the Root*, Wedderburn in an open letter to Miss Elizabeth Campbell, a sympathetic plantation owner he knew in Jamaica, paraphrases Evans's argument as follows:

> The Christians of old, attempted this happy mode of living in fellowship or brotherhood, but, after the death of Christ and the apostles, the national priests persuaded their emperor to establish the Christian religion, and they also embraced, in hypocrisy, the Christian faith. They took possession of the Church property and called it theirs, which remains in their hands to this day; but they have taken care to hedge it about with laws which punish with death all those who dare attempt to take it away.
>
> (Extract 6, p.183)

It was for expressing such views both in his pamphlets and from the pulpit that Wedderburn was charged with blasphemy. That he refused to recant these views under threat of prison is clear from the defence ghosted by Cannon, which simply repeats the criticisms of the Church in more florid terms. Cannon/Wedderburn describes his (Wedderburn's) campaign against established religion as an attempt 'to divest the simple Deistical and Republican system of Jesus, of those gaudy appendages, those trumpery additions, with which craft and ignorance combined, have conspired to corrupt its native purity, its original simplicity' (extract 7, p.190).

Wedderburn added at least two of his own personal inflections to Evans's doctrine, laying emphasis firstly to what he saw as the common deception of West Indian slaves and British 'wage slaves' at the hands of the Established Church. Second, Wedderburn clung to a belief in the power of a vengeful Old Testament God, and fused this belief with a residual faith in the voodoo and obeah powers of slaves like his charismatic grandmother Talkee Amy. In the *Horrors of Slavery*, for example, he describes the workings of God's punishment in the case of his 70-year-old grandmother being flogged by a cruel master on the basis of a wrongful accusation by another woman slave. After the flogging:

> ... my grandmother had full satisfaction soon afterwards. The words of our blessed Lord and Saviour Jesus Christ were fulfilled in this instance: 'Do good to them that despitefully use you, and in so doing you shall heap coals of fire upon their heads.' This

> woman had an only child, which died soon after this affair took place (plainly a judgment of God); and the mother was forced to come and beg pardon of my grandmother for the injury she had done her, and solicit my grandmother to assist her in the burial of her child.
>
> (Extract 8, p.196)

Wedderburn's interpretation of God's judgement in this case reassures him that the perpetrators of slavery as a class will not be spared by their public declarations of Christian faith; God, for Wedderburn, is firmly on the side of the poor on both shores of the Atlantic.

The second genre Wedderburn employs is the *political tract*, and he draws heavily upon traditions of radical political pamphleteering associated both with figures like Paine and Spence and with abolitionist writers like Cugoano and Equiano.

EXERCISE Reread the second issue of Wedderburn's *The Axe Laid to the Root* (extract 6, pp.177–80) and summarize Wedderburn's analysis of political history, indicating the relation between his religious, economic and political ideas.

DISCUSSION Wedderburn extends his attack on the established versions of Christianity and the owners of the land to the political institutions and forms of the British state. Addressing 'the slaves of Jamaica' (p.177), he declares the official discourse of British liberty and constitutional governance to be a hypocritical pack of lies:

> I would have you know, with all the proud boasting of Europeans they are yet ignorant of what political liberty is: the Britons boast of the perfection of their free government, and excellent constitution, and yet they are constantly finding fault with their rulers. You would hardly think it possible that tens of thousands of Englishmen, would give their votes to elect a Member, for a cheap dinner, and a day's drunkenness, others for a few pounds, some for promises of future rewards, and yet take a solemn oath that they gave their vote freely, and the person they voted for is the man of their choice. Many of them know, at the same time, that they are telling lies.
>
> (p.177)

Wedderburn here echoes the arguments of radicals of the time like William Cobbett who were campaigning for electoral reform, and in particular for an expanded franchise and an end to wealthy individuals being able to effectively buy seats for themselves in Parliament. Wedderburn's critical analysis of the British political system includes a brief history that resembles his histories of religion and economics in that he identifies an origin free of inequality succeeded by the cynical corruption of the founding ideals:

> The government of England was founded on principles of liberty, and it is said, its constitution is the work of a wise and brave people, who, considering that all power was derived from them, and was to be subservient to their happiness. After they had formed this constitution, and recovered, by their exertion their liberty, they had not sense to keep it, they placed it into the hands of those they called their three States, then their freedom ceased that is to say, they chose three masters. These three, when they agree, may dispose of their lives and properties. Britons, where is your liberty now? Why, it is in the hands of your governors, you have made them omnipotent, they can do any thing; they can make bastards lawful; ... they can make right wrong, or wrong right; ... and, at the same time, they make it right that hundreds of thousands of Africans may be stolen, and sold, like cattle, in the market; in truth, they can do, what is impossible for God to do.
>
> (pp.177–8)

Wedderburn's message to the 'slaves of Jamaica' therefore is that British claims to be 'defenders of liberty' should be treated with suspicion, and that Jamaican slaves should reject British forms of government in favour of a more democratic dispensation. Wedderburn's blueprint for a post-emancipation Jamaican political system includes: universal franchise; one representative for every 2,000 citizens; annual elections for representatives; no white representatives and no representatives who earned more than £500 per year; abolition of the death penalty and all forms of torture; and compulsory military service for men and women.

The third genre employed by Wedderburn is that of *autobiography.* However, the conventions of the spiritual autobiography – from state of abject sinfulness to moment of crisis and introspection, to repentance and conversion to Christianity, and finally to state of grace in Christian living – fail to provide an adequate structure for Wedderburn. In his earliest attempt at autobiography, *Truth Self-Supported* (1802), (extract 5, pp.168–70), Wedderburn tries to fit his own personal history into the Christian conversion narratives popularized and encouraged by religious leaders such as John Wesley. Like Cugoano, Wedderburn describes how, through the life-changing experience of conversion, he passed from a state of sin and ignorance to a state of grace. Describing himself as a 'Diamond in the rough', Wedderburn appeals to his readers to accept his story because of his 'unpolished ability to send [the following essential truths] forth into the world, with their deserved splendor' (p.168). Writing of himself in the third person, Wedderburn deals only briefly with his origins in the West Indies, not mentioning his proximity to slavery.

Instead, he emphasizes his dissolute life on arriving in England, where he lived 'amongst a set of abandoned reprobates; he there became a profligate, and so continued for the space of seven years; Conscience frequently smiteing him, and telling him, that the way he pursued was the road to everlasting ruin' (pp.168–9). In the next paragraph, he describes his conversion, when 'the author stopped to hear a preacher of Mr Westley's connection' (p.169). The effect of the preacher's words on Wedderburn is dramatic:

> The words that [the preacher] spoke, struck his mind with strong conviction of the awful state he was in, both by nature and practice; he noticed, that the minister asserted with confidence, that he would pledge his own soul, that every man, conscious of the enormity of sin, and willing to turn from the evil of his ways, and accept of the mercy offered in the Gospel, the Lord would abundantly pardon; and he [Wedderburn] was enabled, by the Holy Spirit, to accept with joy, the offered Grace.
>
> (p.169)

Up to this point, Wedderburn's spiritual autobiography matches precisely those of thousands of other eighteenth-century conversion narratives. However, having embraced Christ and therefore 'considering himself ... under Grace' (p.169), Wedderburn examines the various competing doctrines and develops his own unique interpretation of Christianity. Still writing about himself in the third person, Wedderburn confidently claims that since he is 'wiser than his teachers, he shall now undertake to instruct them' (p.169).

The autobiographical passages in *The Axe Laid to the Root* and *The Horrors of Slavery* are much the same as those in *Truth Self-Supported*, as Wedderburn emphasizes his godless ways and the intensity of his conversion experience, but fails dismally to achieve the final stage of grateful and pious obedience. Instead, he questions details of doctrine and sets himself up as an independent preacher. In *The Horrors of Slavery*, Wedderburn does satisfy two basic requirements of the spiritual autobiography in that he provides the kinds of brutal details about the degrading impact of slavery on his life that the abolitionist required, and he also emphasizes his own spiritual impoverishment before converting to Christianity. However, at the same time he subverts the conventions of the genre in at least two ways. The first way is quite subtle: in the opening paragraphs, Wedderburn's description of his lineage recalls how a slave auctioneer would describe a slave up for sale. Auctioneers would describe slaves dispassionately, outlining their ancestry and holding them as objects of merchandise for potential buyers to scrutinize. (You will read a description of a slave auction in the extracts from Mary Prince's autobiography.) By adopting a similar style to describe his father and grandfather, Wedderburn thus inverts the conventional rituals of power in the slave economy. The second way in which Wedderburn confounds Wilberforce's requirements is much more obvious. Wedderburn declares with great passion an unrepentant commitment to his subversive political beliefs: 'though I was immured for two years in his Majesty's gaol at Dorchester, for daring to express my sentiments as a free man, I am still the same in mind as I was before, and imprisonment has but confirmed me that I was right' (extract 8, p.192). However, if Wedderburn failed to satisfy Wilberforce, it was also the case that from Wedderburn's perspective the form of the Evangelical spiritual autobiography failed him because it simply did not allow him to express the ideas and feelings that drove him. As a result, he sought different and less constraining genres – political tract, sermon, economics – in order to give expression to his thoughts on slavery *and* other forms of oppression.

A fourth genre Wedderburn employs (arguably a 'sub-genre' at this time) is that of *economic tract*. Closely tied to his religious and political beliefs, Wedderburn places considerable independent emphasis on the economics of slavery. It is clear from Wedderburn's writings that he rejects the trading charters and protectionism associated with mercantilism, but crucially he also rejects the free trade capitalism of Adam Smith embraced by Cugoano. For Cugoano, the coupling of 'free labour' and 'free trade' in the modernizing discourse of Smith's economic theory was persuasive, but for Wedderburn Smith's ideas (in the crude form he encountered them) amounted to simply another variety of economic exploitation. What Wedderburn favours is a third alternative, namely an economic dispensation based on the common ownership of land. The influence of Spence on Wedderburn is especially strong in this context, as Wedderburn's polemical defence of Spence in the first issue of *The Axe Laid to the Root* makes clear:

> The Spenceans presume that the earth cannot be justly the private property of individuals, because it was never manufactured by man; therefore whoever first sold it, sold that which was not his own, and of course there cannot be a title deed produced consistent with natural and universal justice. Secondly, that it is inconsistent with justice, that a few should have the power to till or not to till the earth, thereby holding the existence of the whole population in their hands ... To have a parliament, and every man to vote, is just and right; a nation without it, may be charged with ignorance and cowardice: but without an equal share in the soil, no government can be pure, let its name or form be what it may.
>
> (Extract 6, pp.173–4)

As in the case of religion and politics, so too here in his economic thought Wedderburn proposes an original state of 'purity' that is corrupted. He argues that land originally held in common has by deception come to be held by the few, and only a return to a form of society that resembles that original state of nature can guarantee a just economic order. It is also striking that Wedderburn sees political democracy ('every man to vote') without economic equality ('without an equal share in the soil') still to be an 'impure' form of government. The implication is that for Wedderburn a redistribution of wealth remains a prerequisite for society to be organized in a manner 'consistent with natural and universal justice'.

How does Wedderburn engage with Enlightenment thought?

Although Wedderburn does not use the terms 'reason' or 'enlightenment' with the same frequency as Cugoano, I have identified four instances in the extracts in Anthology I. These are reproduced in the exercise that follows.

EXERCISE What ideas and arguments does Wedderburn associate with 'reason' and 'enlightenment' in the passages below?

1 'Wedderburn demands, in the name of God, in the name of natural justice, and in the name of humanity, that all slaves be set free; for innocent individuals are entitled to the protection of civil society; and that all stealers, receivers, and oppressors in this base practice be forgiven, as the crime commenced in the days of ignorance, and is now exposed in the enlightened age of reason' (extract 6, pp.170–1).

2 'Lissen to [the clergy of every description] as far as your reason dictates of a future state, but never suffer them to interfere in your worldly affairs; for they are cunning, and therefore are more capable of vice than you are' (extract 6, p.172).

3 'It appears to me very necessary, for it is only by rational contention that truth is to be attained, It is not right to take for granted that the Spenceans are fools, and mad traitors:– it is their opinion they are wise, loyal, and in their senses, and they alone, respecting landed property' (extract 6, p.173).

4 'Reason informs, and admonishes us, that true philosophers, and men of virtue, have in every age loved and honored the simple Truth, and have turned aside from following the ancients, whenever their opinions have been found erroneous and bad; and that the inquisitive searcher after truth should prefer it to his life, and should not be deterred by the fear of death, or the threats of torture, from speaking and acting according to justice' (extract 7, p.187).

DISCUSSION Wedderburn's reference to the 'enlightened age of reason' in quotation 1 is in a similar spirit to Cugoano's use of Enlightenment terms in that it links the exercise of reason with both abolition and a spirit of forgiveness with regard to the beneficiaries of slavery. However, in the next three quotations, Wedderburn associates the exercise of reason with rather different political conclusions. In quotation 2, he argues that far from confirming the teachings of the Christian Church, reason should be employed as a means of protection against the cunning and vice of the clergy. In quotation 3, in awkward syntax, Wedderburn argues that 'rational contention' proves the truth of Spencean communism and in particular the advantages of the collective ownership of land. Quotation 4 – written by Cannon on behalf of Wedderburn – insists that reason must be independent in its pursuit of truth and justice, and cannot be subordinated to the authority of the ancients. The association of reason and these revolutionary impulses suggests that for Wedderburn the kinds of cautious and rational alternatives to slavery contained in Cugoano's proposals (Anthology I, extract 4, pp.157–60) were simply no longer convincing. Further, with the examples of revolutionary transformations in France and in Santo Domingo, swift and radical social transformation seemed *possible*, and Wedderburn and his fellow Spenceans were therefore more confident in anticipating and imagining revolutions in their own society.

We have located Wedderburn in his historical context, applied the critical concepts of textual persona and genre to his writings, and considered how he engages with Enlightenment ideas. We postpone a detailed comparison of Cugoano and Wedderburn until we have discussed the writings of Mary Prince.

4 Mary Prince

Mary Prince (1788–*c*.1834) was born into domestic slavery in Bermuda. Her first owner Charles Myners sold her to Captain Darrel, who gave her to Captain Williams. Williams some years later in turn hired her out to Mrs Pruden, whose daughter Fanny taught her how to read. On the death of Mrs Williams, Prince was separated from her mother and siblings and sold to Captain I—, who treated her brutally. In 1805, Captain I— sold her on to Mr D—, who took her to work for five years in the salt ponds on Turk's Island. Prince returned with Mr D— to Bermuda in 1810, and was then sold on once again in 1815 to John Wood. Wood took Prince to Antigua, and while in Antigua she was converted by Moravian Christians, and also married a freed slave Daniel James in 1826. In 1828, the Woods took her to England, and while there she fled to the Anti-Slavery Society in London and claimed the freedom English law guaranteed slaves while in England. Faced with the choice of remaining a free woman in England or returning as Wood's slave to her husband in Antigua, she chose the former and was employed as a domestic servant by Thomas Pringle, the secretary of the Anti-Slavery Society. Prince dictated her *History* to Susannah Strickland, a friend of the Pringles, and it went through three editions in the first year of its publication in 1831. The authenticity of the *History* was questioned by pro-slavery spokesman James McQueen in *Blackwoods Magazine*. Pringle successfully sued the owner of *Blackwoods* for libel in 1833, but subsequently lost a libel case brought against him by Prince's erstwhile owner Wood because he could not afford to bring witnesses from the West Indies to corroborate her story. Prince appeared in court for both cases, but her subsequent fate is unknown, and scholars have assumed that the absence of any subsequent records of her means that ill-health and near-blindness led to her death.

Before considering the text of Prince's *History*, it is important to highlight briefly certain aspects of her particular historical context. The first aspect to note is that although she was not a plantation slave, conditions in Bermuda were notoriously harsh, especially on the salt ponds of Turk's Island. Furthermore, the ending of the slave trade in 1807, rather than ameliorating conditions for slaves, in fact made them in many instances far worse. The historian Robin Blackburn points out that the years following the Napoleonic Wars – the period of Prince's enslavement – 'witnessed an intensification of slave exploitation as planters and managers strove to increase output from a static or declining work force' (1988, p.428). In other words, with no new slaves arriving from Africa, the declining numbers of slaves already in the West Indies were forced to work even harder. The timing of Prince's arrival in London at the end of the 1820s was also significant, as it coincided with an upsurge in anti-slavery activism. Between 1826 and 1832, 3,500 anti-slavery petitions were presented to the House of Lords alone, and the plantation owners and their supporters were growing increasingly shrill and desperate as they faced the prospect of slave labour being outlawed. The following review of Prince's *History* from the *Bermuda Royal Gazette* of 22 November 1831 is of direct interest. I have quoted from it at length because it not only captures the controversy generated by the publication of Prince's own particular story, but also conveys a sense of the general panic felt by the slave-owners in the years immediately preceding emancipation:

> Mr Wood, a highly respected merchant of Antigua, many years ago, in Bermuda, purchased for 67 pounds sterling, a slave named Mary Prince who earnestly entreated him to buy her and relieve her from the miserable situation in which she states herself to have been. After living in Mr Wood's family for 13 years, during which time he paid her ten guineas a year, on Mr Wood preparing to come to England, she begged so hard to go with him and her mistress, Mr Wood was induced to permit her, on her earnest entreaty that change of climate would benefit her health, and as an encouragement to good behaviour, promised that she should be free on her return to Antigua. In England, her behaviour became unbearable; she refused to work – declared that the roast beef and veal was 'horseflesh' – that 'she would not

> eat cold meat, not being accustomed to it in Antigua'; and after a variety of similar conduct was told by her master that she must either return to Antigua, or as she was free in England, she must leave his house, as he could not keep the peace of his family undisturbed. She at length left his house, taking with her several trunks of clothes and about 40 guineas in money, which she had saved in Mr Wood's service. The Anti-Slavery Society lent a not unwilling ear to the statement of this woman, and the result is the pamphlet before us, published under the editorship of the vilest description ... We cannot omit stating that Mr and Mrs Wood who are thus calumniated by the hired advocate of the Anti-Slavery Society (who sees nothing but purity in a prostitute because she knew when to utter the name of the Deity, to turn up the whites of her eyes, and make a perfect mockery of religion), are described by the most respectable magistrates and members of council in Antigua as standing as high as human beings can stand. We take our leave of this disgusting conduct, which goes far to compromise a society, which numbers many eminent and worthy individuals among its members, by warning the public to receive with doubt and distrust, statements from a quarter so jaundiced in a great public question, which equally concerns the welfare of masters and slaves.
>
> (Quoted in Ferguson, 1993, pp.37–8)

This review in its self-righteous anger expresses the weight of pro-slavery opinion that Prince was trying to dislodge by relating her *History*. Although the *Bermuda Gazette*'s version of Prince's relationship with the Woods differs wildly from Prince's version in her *History*, the reviewer's claim that 'the most respectable magistrates and members of council in Antigua' see the Woods' reputation 'as standing as high as human beings can stand' is more convincing. In writing her *History*, Prince was therefore taking on formidable adversaries.

What textual persona does Prince assume?

As in the cases of Cugoano and Wedderburn, so too in Prince's case there are historical questions about the extent to which white collaborators intervened and modified their words. Recall that scholars have suggested that Cugoano was assisted in *Thoughts and Sentiments* by his friend Equiano and possibly by a third collaborator, and that Wedderburn on occasions was aided – or possibly even sabotaged – by George Cannon. Prince's voice too was mediated by a white interlocutor, Susannah Strickland, and the circumstances of the production of the *History* are set out by Pringle in his preface to the book:

> The narrative was taken down from Mary's own lips by a lady [Strickland] who happened to be at the time residing in my family

> as a visitor. It was written out fully, with all the narrator's repetitions and prolixities, and afterwards pruned into its present shape; retaining, as far as was practicable, Mary's exact expressions and peculiar phraseology. No fact of importance has been omitted, and not a single circumstance or sentiment has been added. It is essentially her own, without any material alteration farther than was requisite to exclude redundancies and gross grammatical errors, so as to render it clearly intelligible.
>
> (Prince, 2000, p.3)

Modern editors and scholars have generally accepted Pringle's claims that there were no conscious or deliberate attempts by him and Strickland to manipulate Prince's testimony. Paul Edwards and David Dabydeen, for example, conclude that 'Pringle's editorial work appears sensitive to the need to refrain from intrusion and preserve the narrative tone of Mary Prince's life story' (1991, p.157). The possibility of there having been unconscious pressure on Prince to tailor her personal history to suit the needs of her sponsors and expectations of her audience is one we shall return to presently.

EXERCISE Now read *The History of Mary Prince* (Anthology I, extract 9, pp.203–28). As you read, consider (and make notes on) the textual persona Prince assumes. Then return to the unit.

EXERCISE Reread the following passage from extract 9, which describes Prince's sale in the Bermuda slave market to Captain I— after the death of Williams. As you read, consider the textual persona Prince assumes:

> We followed my mother to the market-place, where she placed us in a row against a large house, with our backs to the wall and our arms folded across our breasts ... My heart throbbed with grief and terror so violently, that I pressed my hands quite tightly across my breast, but I could not keep it still, and it continued to leap as though it would burst out of my body. But who cared for that? Did one of the many by-standers, who were looking at us so carelessly, think of the pain that wrung the hearts of the negro woman and her young ones? No, no! They were not all bad, I dare say, but slavery hardens white people's hearts towards the blacks; and many of them were not slow to make their remarks upon us aloud, without regard to our grief – though their light words fell like cayenne on the fresh wounds of our hearts. Oh those white people have small hearts who can only feel for themselves.
>
> At length the vendue master [auctioneer], who was to offer us for sale like sheep or cattle, arrived, and asked my mother which

> was the eldest. She said nothing, but pointed to me. He took me by the hand, and led me out into the middle of the street, and, turning me slowly round, exposed me to the view of those who attended the vendue. I was soon surrounded by strange men, who examined and handled me in the same manner that a butcher would a calf or a lamb he was about to purchase, and who talked about my shape and size in like words – as if I could no more understand their meaning than the dumb beasts. I was then put up to sale. The bidding commenced at a few pounds, and gradually rose to fifty-seven, when I was knocked down to the highest bidder, and the people who stood by said that I had fetched a great sum for so young a slave.
>
> (pp.206–7)

DISCUSSION Prince conveys the painful humiliation of her sale by two vivid comparisons. The callous words of the white bystanders fall 'like cayenne on the fresh wounds of our hearts', and her treatment at the hands of the potential buyers is likened to that of a butcher considering 'a calf or a lamb he was about to purchase'. Her sense of humiliation is confirmed by her exclusion from the commercial discourse regulating her sale. Reduced to an object of property, she has no access to the dialogue between auctioneer and buyers that is to determine her fate; the white men converse with each other 'as if I could no more understand their meaning than the dumb beasts'. The interrupted shift in pronouns in this passage is also revealing. Starting out for the slave market with her mother and siblings, Prince writes of herself and her sisters in the first person plural – 'we followed my mother'. Next, she is isolated from her family, and continues the story in the first person singular – 'he took me by the hand ... [and] I was soon surrounded'. At the next stage, the overwhelming pressure exerted by the ritual of the sale is to crush the humanity of the author by defining her not as a person capable of generating first-person narratives, but as a mute object of property akin to 'a calf or a lamb'. However, although Prince acquiesces in the sale – she has no choice, of course – in the longer term she successfully resists this pressure to reduce her to property by refusing to fall silent and by producing her own history.

A second aspect of Prince's textual persona emphasized in her *History* is her status as a *woman* slave. As Wedderburn's writings indicate, the sexual abuse of women slaves was commonplace in the West Indies, and the abolition movement responded to protest the forms of oppression specific to them (see Figure 15.1). Evidence of sexual abuse is provided in oblique terms in Prince's *History* because it was important not to offend the sensibilities of English readers. However, there are still a number of passages where the sexual exploitation of slave women is

Figure 15.1 Detail from a nineteenth-century abolition banner, reproduced by courtesy of Anti-Slavery International, London.

clearly set out. The most damning passage is Prince's description of being forced to bath Mr D— during the time they had returned to live in Bermuda:

> He had an ugly fashion of stripping himself quite naked, and ordering me then to wash him in a tub of water. This was worse to me than all the licks [floggings]. Sometimes when he called me to wash him I could not come, my eyes were so full of shame. He would then come to beat me. One time I had plates and knives in my hand, and I dropped both plates and knives, and some of the plates were broken. He struck me so severely for this, that at last I defended myself, for I thought it was high time to do so. I then told him I would not live longer with him, for he was a very indecent man – very spiteful, and too indecent; with no shame for his servants, no shame for his own flesh.
>
> (p.216)

The horror of this experience is conveyed less by Prince's actual words as 'pruned' by Strickland and Pringle than by what she has left unexpressed. That the experience was 'worse to me than all the licks' hints at terrible abuse, as does the repetition of the words 'indecent' and 'shame', and the awkward syntax of the last sentence quoted above. Prince's identity as a woman slave is also registered by her frequent asides about the destruction of the family under slavery. Certain male slave narratives, notably that of Equiano, also make much of the slaves' loss of family and kin, but Prince's *History* repeats with particular poignancy the slave mother's experience of the loss of family. To quote but one of many examples, Prince during her unhappy time with Captain I— reflects, 'I then took courage and said that I could stand the floggings no longer; that I was weary of my life, and therefore I had run away to my mother; but mothers could only weep and mourn over their children, they could not save them from cruel masters – from the whip, the rope, and the cow-skin' (p.211).

The pattern here of first describing her own particular experiences as a slave – 'I could stand the floggings no longer' – and then generalizing from them to speak for all slaves – 'mothers could only weep and mourn' – is sustained throughout the *History*. The severity of slave treatment depicted in a series of etchings by William Blake continued with little change in Prince's lifetime (see Figure 15.2). This consistent emphasis on the fact that her experience as a slave is typical rather than in any way exceptional is the third aspect of Prince's textual persona as spokesperson for all slaves. In other words, the first person 'I' of Prince's narrative speaks not only for the experiences of one woman slave from the West Indies but for all women slaves. There are many examples: after describing how Mr D— had beaten her 'till my body was raw with gashes', Prince notes '[y]et there was nothing very remarkable in this; for it might serve as a sample of the common usage of the slaves on that horrible island' (p.213). A couple of pages on, Prince describes how Mr D—'s son had killed an old slave woman, and comments '[i]n telling my own sorrows, I cannot pass by those of my fellow-slaves – for when I think of my own griefs, I remember theirs' (p.215). Prince expresses her sense of responsibility as spokesperson for all slaves emphatically in her closing appeal:

> All slaves want to be free – to be free is very sweet. I will say the truth to English people who may read this history that my good friend, Miss S—, is now writing down for me. I have been a slave myself – I know what slaves feel – I can tell by myself what other slaves feel, and by what they have told me. The man that says slaves be quite happy in slavery – that they don't want to be free – that man is either ignorant or a lying person. I never heard a slave say so.
>
> (pp.227–8)

Insisting upon the authenticity of her experience as a slave and upon her unassailable connection with other slaves, Prince angrily disputes the complacent attitudes towards slavery that she encounters in England. The view that 'slaves be quite happy in slavery' is rejected on the basis of

Figure 15.2 William Blake, The Execution of the Breaking on the Rack, *1800, from* Narrative of a Five Years' Expedition against the Revolted Negroes of Surinam *by John Gabriel Stedman, London, 1806. Photo: by permission of the British Library, London (shelfmark 145 f.16).*

Prince's own experience as a slave *and* on the basis of what she knows other slaves feel.

The fourth component of Prince's textual persona is that of being a Christian. Prince's conversion to Christianity came at a relatively late stage in her life, several years into her period with the Woods in Antigua. She describes attending a Methodist prayer meeting, where the confession of a black slave-driver made a powerful impression on her, causing her to reflect on her own sins: 'I felt sorry for my sins also. I cried the whole night, but I was too much ashamed to speak' (p.220). The meeting prompted her to join the Moravian Church, where she was welcomed and taught to read, and had her new-found sense of personal sin reinforced: 'I never knew rightly that I had much sin till I went there. When I found out that I was a great sinner, I was very sorely grieved, and very much frightened. I used to pray God to pardon my sins for Christ's sake' (p.220). Soon after her conversion, Prince married Daniel James, and two years later in 1828 went to England with the Woods, where she claimed her freedom. Her own agency in these dramatic events, however, is understated, as she credits God as the architect of her fate. The most significant passage reflecting her faith in God is where she reflects upon whether to stay in England as a free woman or return to her husband in Antigua as a slave:

> Mr Mortimer [a clergyman friend of Pringle] tells me that he cannot open the eyes of my heart, but that I must pray to God to change my heart, and make me to know the truth, and the truth will make me free.
>
> I still live in the hope that God will find a way to give me my liberty, and give me back to my husband. I endeavour to keep down my fretting, and to leave all to Him, for he knows what is good for me better than I know myself. Yet, I must confess, I find it a hard and heavy task to do so.
>
> (p.227)

The encouraging Christian message that Mortimer tries to offer to Prince as consolation makes only a partial impression on her state of mind as she wrestles with her impossible choice. Furthermore, Prince struggles to suppress her life-long habits of defiant self-reliance and to place all trust in God.

The final aspect of Prince's textual persona is achieved in England, namely that of a free servant. She describes how she felt disorientated at the prospect of being free in England: 'I knew that I was free in England, but I did not know where to go, or how to get my living; and therefore, I did not like to leave the house' (p.224). However, once she had left the Woods, she cherished her freedom, grateful for the opportunity to do paid work. Prince expresses her discomfort at living on the abolitionists' charity: 'I did not like to be idle. I would rather work for my living than get it for nothing' (p.226). She then generalizes from her own experience of doing paid work in England to speak on behalf of all slaves in this respect: '[Servants in England] have their liberty. That's just what *we* want. We don't mind hard work, if we had proper treatment, and proper wages like English servants, and proper time given in the week to keep us from breaking the Sabbath' (p.228; italics in original).

To conclude: as with the textual personae of Cugoano and Wedderburn, Prince's textual persona is a hybrid made up of 'slave', 'woman', 'slave spokesperson', 'Christian', and finally 'free servant'. The tensions generated by these different personae are finally contained by the requirements prescribed in the narrative of Christian abolitionist spiritual biography, and in particular by the definition of what it means to be a Christian convert. At times, Prince's difficult life experiences strain against this narrative and persona – recall her confession that she finds trusting God in choosing between her English liberty and her West Indies husband 'a hard and heavy task to do'. Nonetheless, the ultimate impression remains one of a coherent textual persona, of a narrator dedicated to seeing her journey to freedom repeated by all slaves.

What genres of autobiography does Prince employ?

In the sections on Cugoano and Wedderburn, we turned at this point to discuss the variety of different genres – religious sermon, political tract, philosophy, economics and history – that they employed in expressing their opposition to slavery. In the case of Prince's *History*, there is no equivalent ranging across different genres as Prince confines herself to the genre of autobiography. Accordingly, we focus in more detail on the formal requirements of autobiography and pose the following questions:

1 What were the generic markers of slave autobiographies in the early nineteenth century?

2 What qualities does Prince's *History* share with these different sub-genres of slave autobiography?

As regards question 1, the first point to emphasize about autobiography as a genre is that it held a particularly strong attraction for black writers in Britain in the late eighteenth and early nineteenth centuries. Recall that the eighteenth-century writings of Sancho, Equiano and Cugoano were the first publications ever by black writers in England, and that Prince's *History* was the first published autobiography by a black woman. Edwards and Dabydeen explain the appeal of autobiography to these early black writers as follows: 'The need to tell the experienced truth from the point of view of the black man or woman explains why early black writing has to be autobiographical rather than cast in the mould of novels, poems and plays, conveying the felt immediacy and authenticity, of actual lived experience' (1991, p.157). There were exceptions to this general rule, notably the poetry of Phillis Wheatley, but certainly for Prince the form of autobiography accommodates, and indeed encourages, 'immediate and authentic' descriptions of 'actual lived experience'.

Within the general category of slave autobiography, there are several distinct sub-categories: the eighteenth-century British slave narrative; the early nineteenth-century US slave narrative; the early nineteenth-century escaped-woman-slave narrative; and the hoax slave narrative. We need to define each of these sub-categories in more detail. The eighteenth-century British slave narratives, like those of Sancho, Cugoano and Equiano, are characteristically by an African-born narrator who 'dwells on events chronologically, their aim to instruct readers and encourage humanitarian concerns' (Ferguson, 1993, p.22). The early nineteenth-century US slave narrative typically contains 'the fugitive slave, the direct assault on slavery as an institution, and concrete examples of abuse' (Ferguson, 1993, p.24). The early nineteenth-century escaped-woman-slave narratives were reported in the *Anti-Slavery Reporter*, and they provided 'details of the legal dispute, authenticating apparatus by eyewitnesses, details of trial testimony, numerous and hideous goings-on and occasional resistance, and some account of abolitionist activity' (Ferguson, 1993, p.25). The fourth sub-category of slave narrative, the hoax, is parasitic on the first three, but warrants mention because of its prominence in the late eighteenth and early nineteenth centuries. According to Helen Thomas, some hoax slave narratives such as *Authentic Narrative of the Late Fortunate Escape of R.W. Loane* (1805) and George Vason's *Authentic Narrative of Four Years' Residence at Tongataboo* (1810) 'reveal a semi-pornographic and quasi-anthropological agenda under the guise of the "confessional" captivity genre' (2000, p.179). Other hoax narratives, such as *Joanna, or the Female Slave: A West Indian Tale* (1824) even had their slave narrators speaking out *against* emancipation. While exploiting public interest in slavery, the proliferation of these hoax slave narratives also inevitably fuelled debates over the authenticity of works like Prince's *History*. What runs through all these sub-categories is a prominent strand of Christian redemption, with liberation from slavery either preceded or accompanied by conversion to Christianity.

EXERCISE Bearing in mind the requirements and expectations of slave autobiography, assess the extent to which Prince's *History* (a) conforms and (b) deviates from the requirements of slave autobiography.

DISCUSSION (a) It is clear that Prince's *History* conforms to many of the requirements of slave autobiography. Like the eighteenth-century British slave narrative, the *History* provides a chronological account of her life, accompanied by exhortations to her readers to display humanitarian sentiments towards slaves. Like the early nineteenth-century US slave narratives, the *History* includes abundant descriptions of abuse, a tale of a fugitive slave escaping, as well as a passionate attack on the institution of slavery. As in the cases of escaped women slaves reported in the *Anti-Slavery Reporter*, Prince's autobiography provides – particularly in the final pages – details of abolitionist activities and the legal hurdles involved in attaining freedom from slavery. Finally, Prince's *History* conforms substantially to the structure of the Christian conversion, starting in a state of ignorance and sin, experiencing a moment of conversion followed by repentance with the Moravians in Antigua, and finally attaining a state of Christian acceptance after her liberation in England.

(b) To discover the extent to which Prince's *History* deviates from the requirements of slave autobiography, we need to search in the text for moments of resistance to the expectations of the genre. The obvious place to start such a search is with the relation between Prince and her white patrons Strickland and Pringle, who actively translated the fragmented details of her life story into the form of a slave autobiography. The dominant view of Strickland and Pringle's role in facilitating Prince's *History* has been a generous one, with the two white editors cast as neutral agents in enabling Prince to speak. Certain critics in recent years, however, have been more critical, with Clare Midgley, for example, arguing that Strickland and Pringle wanted to cast Prince exclusively as a victim and oversee her transition from rebellious slave to obedient servant. According to Midgley, 'black agency in undermining slavery is devalued, and under the auspices of the Anti-Slavery Society, freedom is gained as a gift of white philanthropists who leave class relations undisturbed' (1992, p.90). While this might seem an overly harsh judgement of Strickland and Pringle, it is nonetheless the case that Pringle's Preface and Notes emphasize Prince's conversion and rescue, but never amplify her unusually vigorous defiance of her slave masters. Recall that Prince had five slave masters (Myners, Darrel/Williams, Captain I—, Mr D—, and the Woods) at a time when domestic slaves commonly remained with the same master throughout their lives, and that several of her masters had sold her because she refused to capitulate to cruel treatment. Add to this the numerous occasions she tried to escape and her efforts in Antigua at raising money to buy her freedom, and there is in fact substantial textual evidence of Prince behaving less as passive victim waiting for an abolitionist benefactor than as active agent determining her own fate. Finally, recall Prince's ambivalent acceptance of God's will in coming to terms with the choice confronting her between her husband and her liberty – 'I endeavour to keep down my fretting, and to leave all to Him' (p.227). This ambivalence means that Prince never quite satisfies entirely the final requirement of slave autobiography, namely an unquestioning acceptance of God's will; trusting all to God remains for Prince a 'hard and heavy task'.

How does Prince engage with the ideas of the Enlightenment and Romanticism?

In the sections on Cugoano and Wedderburn, we turned at this stage of our discussion to examine how they engaged with the ideas of the Enlightenment and Romanticism, and discovered that both writers had indeed assembled their arguments against slavery with extensive reliance on appeals to 'reason' and 'enlightenment'. As regards the values of the Enlightenment, Prince is quite different from Cugoano and Wedderburn, as her narrative is written entirely in personal terms, and she makes no explicit appeal to Enlightenment ideals and principles. Slavery in Prince's narrative is never presented as contrary to reason; rather it is described as against human feeling. In this respect, *The History of Mary Prince* therefore shares with many other texts of Romanticism (including the later hymns discussed in Unit 10) a central concern with expressions of sentiment, emotion and individual suffering. The form of Prince's *History* – Pringle's brief explanatory preface followed by Prince's detailed personal account – suggests further that for abolitionists, expressions of physical and emotional pain such as those in Prince's autobiography carried greater rhetorical weight than reasoned argument, and that they accorded with the changed mood of the time.

Now that we have discussed Wedderburn and Prince in some detail, we are in a position to address the fourth aim of this unit by answering the question: what are the differences between the slave writings of the late eighteenth and the early nineteenth centuries?

The most obvious difference, and one we have discussed already, lies in the very diverse personal biographies and very different contexts of these three writers. The most relevant details for Cugoano are his birth and childhood in Africa, his experience of the middle passage, and the fact that he wrote *Thoughts and Sentiments* during the Enlightenment, before both abolition and the French and Santo Domingo Revolutions. For Wedderburn, the most significant details are his birth and youth as a free mulatto in the West Indies and his lengthy involvement in radical politics in London in the post-abolition, post-revolutionary years of the early nineteenth century. For Prince, the most significant details are her life as a domestic slave in the West Indies, mostly in the post-abolition years, and her brief but intense involvement in the campaign for emancipation in London in the years 1828–33. Their very different life experiences inevitably mark their respective writings profoundly.

The second difference relates to the textual persona(e) assumed by the eighteenth-century Cugoano and the nineteenth-century Wedderburn and Prince. A key element of Cugoano's identity is that he represents himself as an 'Enlightenment intellectual', and he expresses the confident belief that through the public exercise of reason solutions to religious, political and economic problems inherited from a superstitious past can be solved. Although Wedderburn claims to embody Enlightenment rationality when paraphrasing Spence's economic theories, for the rest neither he nor Prince represent themselves particularly as either voices for, or beneficiaries of, the Enlightenment. Wedderburn's textual persona rests much more substantially on his claims to be a radical or even revolutionary thinker, and Prince's fuses her origins as a woman slave with her subsequent liberation and conversion to Christianity.

The third difference relates to the genres utilized by Cugoano, Wedderburn and Prince in order to articulate their opposition to slavery. Both Cugoano and Wedderburn express their opposition to slavery in a combination of genres – religious sermon, political tract, autobiography, economics, philosophy and history – whereas Prince is confined to the genre of autobiography. How they use the genre of autobiography also differs in interesting ways. All three write under the patronage of white Christian abolitionists, and their autobiographical writings therefore bear strong similarities. All three strain also against the formal requirements of the slave autobiography, with Cugoano and Wedderburn going well beyond autobiography to other available discourses to attack slavery, and Prince subverting the form in more subtle ways. The main difference between the eighteenth- and nineteenth-century slave autobiographies is that whereas Cugoano presents his life story as testimony to the African capacity for self-improvement, both Wedderburn and Prince represent themselves as more profoundly damaged by slavery, as victims and as resilient survivors of slavery.

The final difference between Cugoano and Wedderburn and Prince lies in their respective efforts to engage with Enlightenment ideals. Cugoano expresses a constant belief in the progressive and modernizing promises of the Enlightenment. Hence his faith in the economic theories of Adam Smith, and his hope that Africa might be colonized *more* comprehensively by Britain so as to function in time as an equal trading partner. Hence too his anger with Hume for betraying in his racist views what Cugoano takes to be the fundamentally humane values of the Enlightenment. Wedderburn, despite on occasions invoking the authority of reason, articulates a variety of post-revolutionary reactions against the Enlightenment and rejects both mercantilist and free trade theories of economics in favour of Spence's ideas for land redistribution. As Prince is confined to the writing of autobiography, she does not explicitly engage with the public vocabulary of Enlightenment, but does give expression to the Romantic valorization of feeling.

References

Blackburn, R. (1988) *The Overthrow of Colonial Slavery 1776–1848*, London, Verso.

Drescher, S. (1999) *From Slavery to Freedom: Comparative Studies in the Rise and Fall of Atlantic Slavery*, New York, New York University Press.

Edwards, P. and Dabydeen, D. (1991) *Black Writers in Britain 1760–1890*, Edinburgh, Edinburgh University Press.

Ferguson, M. (1993) Introduction to *The History of Mary Prince, a West Indian Slave, Related by Herself*, ed. M. Ferguson, Ann Arbor, University of Michigan Press.

Godwin, W. (1985) *Enquiry Concerning Political Justice*, ed. I. Kramnick, Harmondsworth, Penguin (first published 1793).

Linebaugh, P. and Rediker, M. (2000) *The Many-Headed Hydra: Sailors, Slaves, Commoners, and the Hidden History of the Revolutionary Atlantic*, Boston, Beacon Press.

Midgley, C. (1992) *Women against Slavery: The British Campaigns 1780–1870*, London and New York, Routledge.

Prince, M. (2000) *The History of Mary Prince, a West Indian Slave*, ed. S. Salih, Harmondsworth, Penguin, (first published 1831).

Rudé, G. (1995) *The Crowd in History*, London, Serif.

Shakespeare, W. (1997) *The Merchant of Venice* in *The Norton Shakespeare*, ed. S. Greenblatt *et al.* New York and London, W.W. Norton and Co.

Thomas, H. (2000) *Romanticism and Slave Narratives: Transatlantic Testimonies*, Cambridge, Cambridge University Press.

Walvin, J. (1992) *Black Ivory: A History of British Slavery*, London, HarperCollins.

Wedderburn, R. (1991) *'The Horrors of Slavery' and Other Writings*, ed. I. McCalman, Edinburgh, Edinburgh University Press.

Further reading

For useful discussions of slave writings, see:

Edwards, P. and Dabydeen, D. (1991) *Black Writers in Britain 1760–1890*, Edinburgh, Edinburgh University Press.

Gates, H.L. (1988) *The Signifying Monkey: A Theory of African-American Literary Criticism*, New York, Oxford University Press.

Kitson, P. and Lee, D. (eds) (1999) *Slavery, Abolition and Emancipation: Writings in the British Romantic Period*, 8 vols, London, Pickering and Chatto.

Sandiford, K.A. (1988) *Measuring the Moment: Strategies of Protest in Eighteenth-Century Afro-English Writing*, London and Toronto, Associated University Press.

Thomas, H. (2000) *Romanticism and Slave Narratives: Transatlantic Testimonies*, Cambridge, Cambridge University Press.

On slavery in general in the period 1770–1840, see:

Blackburn, R. (1988) *The Overthrow of Colonial Slavery 1776–1848*, London, Verso.

Davis, D.B. (1975) *The Problem of Slavery in the Age of Revolution 1770–1823*, London and Ithaca, Cornell University Press.

Drescher, S. (1999) *From Slavery to Freedom: Comparative Studies in the Rise and Fall of Atlantic Slavery*, New York, New York University Press.

Linebaugh, P. and Rediker, M. (2000) *The Many-Headed Hydra: Sailors, Slaves, Commoners, and the Hidden History of the Revolutionary Atlantic*, London, Verso.

Walvin, J. (1992) *Black Ivory: A History of British Slavery*, London, HarperCollins.

Conclusion to Block 3

Prepared for the course team by David Johnson

The extraordinary reach of the ideas of the Enlightenment and Romanticism is demonstrated in the work of the writers in this block. Newton, Cowper and Wilberforce both reproduce and transform the religious discourse of Evangelical Christianity in ways that bear the clear influence of Enlightenment and Romantic ideas. The tendency of the earlier hymns to celebrate God's reason gives way in later writings to an increasing emphasis on sentiment and personal feelings. What is also crucial about their work is that it circulated well beyond the literate elite, and provided a vocabulary and sense of meaning to increasing numbers of Britain's labouring classes. Park's writings embody many of the values and aspirations of Enlightenment reason, particularly in their emphasis upon scientific observation and deduction. His West African journeys provide us with an insight into an Enlightenment intellectual testing his world-view against a challenging and quite alien environment. Like the Christian writers in Units 10–11, Park too reached a wide audience, and enhanced substantially the prestige of scientific travel and exploration. Finally, the slave writers demonstrate that the ideas of the Enlightenment and Romanticism could be effectively appropriated by those from beyond Europe in order to criticize certain forms of European tyranny, notably slavery, but also (in Wedderburn's case) the exploitation of Britain's poor. What these writers collectively show is that the meanings of key terms and values of the Enlightenment and Romanticism such as 'reason' and 'sentiment' were contested, and that a wide variety of thinkers used them creatively in order to argue their respective positions. In Block 4, we move on to consider representations of the Lake District and Robert Owen, and discover yet further different expressions of Enlightenment and Romantic thought.

Glossary

Introduction

Chattel slavery: the form of slavery associated with Ancient Greece and Rome. Chattel slaves had the status of property, and could be bought and sold by their owners, who had power of life and death over them. They were acquired by military conquest, comprised many different ethnicities, and were employed in a variety of economic roles.

Discourse: the term used to describe actual language usage within society. 'Discourse' refers to the vocabulary, terminology, idioms, linguistic conventions that people use in a particular social or ideological context: for example, in the context of talking about religion, science and slavery.

Slave triangle: the term used to describe the route travelled in the New World or Atlantic slave trade that thrived from the sixteenth to the nineteenth centuries. Traders took manufactured goods from Europe to West Africa, where the goods were exchanged for captured slaves, and the slaves were then transported to the Americas. In the Americas slaves were exchanged for tropical agricultural produce, notably sugar, coffee and tobacco. To complete the triangle the tropical produce was delivered to Europe where it was sold on to European merchants and, ultimately, to European consumers.

Unit 10

Atonement: the Christian theological doctrine that through sacrificing himself on the Cross, Jesus Christ reconciled humankind to God by taking upon himself the just divine penalty for our sinfulness.

Calvinist: someone who subscribes to the theological belief system associated with John Calvin (1509–64), which is characterized particularly by the idea that some are predestined to salvation and others to damnation.

Dissenters: the followers and descendants of those who refused to conform to the Church of England in 1662, following the restoration of Charles II.

Methodism: the movement of itinerant preaching and religious societies founded by John Wesley, George Whitefield and others. Methodists initially saw themselves as operating within the Church of England, but by the end of the eighteenth century they had in effect become a separate denomination.

Pietist movement: a religious trend originating in later seventeenth-century Germany emphasizing personal experience of God and anticipating some of the characteristics of the eighteenth-century Evangelical movement.

Puritanism: the more austere and radical Protestant tendency in late sixteenth- and seventeenth-century English Christianity.

Revival: a phase of intense collective religious experience and conversion, usually stimulated by Evangelical preachers such as Wesley or Whitefield.

Unit 11

Baptist: Baptists, distinctive by their insistence on adult baptism, were one of the main groups of Protestant Dissenters whose forbears left the Church of England in the seventeenth century.

Congregationalist: Congregationalists, distinctive by their stress on the autonomy of the local congregation, were one of the main groups of Protestant Dissenters whose forbears left the Church of England in the seventeenth century.

Unitarian: Unitarians were Dissenters who professed a strongly Enlightened and rational view of religion, tending to discount the supernatural and to emphasize the unity of God rather than the divinity of Jesus Christ.

Units 12–13

Ascribed status: the status or social honour accorded a person by virtue of the place to which he/she was born in a social hierarchy.

Great Chain of Being: the idea that nature formed a continuous, unchanging ladder in which each species occupied a preordained rung and differed from the species above and below it in minute ways.

Solipsism: the philosophical thesis that a person cannot be certain about the existence of the world outside herself; the only proposition of which she can be absolutely sure is that she herself exists.

Unit 14

Free labour/Free trade: the economic system associated with Adam Smith that precluded entirely any intervention in the market by the state or the sovereign.

Genre: this refers to the type, kind or species of writing. For example, Aristotle distinguished the genres of comedy, tragedy and epic in classical Greek literature, and modern film critics distinguish film genres such as the musical, western and romantic comedy.

Mercantilism: the economic system based on the state or the sovereign granting charters or trade monopolies to individual traders, thus protecting them from competition.

Middle passage: the forced journey of slaves from Africa to the Americas.

Textual persona: the first person or 'I' of a text. The textual persona can be an obvious literary construct – such as Cowper writing in the textual persona of a slave in 'The Negro's complaint' – or can be much closer to the historical figure of the author of a text, such as Cugoano in *Thoughts and Sentiments on the Evil of Slavery*. The textual persona is constructed in the text and, by close reading, we discern the characteristics of the textual persona.

Unit 15

Ghost-writer: a common practice of the period, where the ghost-writer writes on behalf of another writer providing a 'literary polish' beyond the abilities of the latter. George Cannon ghost-writing on behalf of Robert Wedderburn in his defence against blasphemy is an example.

Index

Page numbers in *italics* refer to illustrations.